Many Come, Few Are Chosen

My Life as a United States Marine

Semper Fi!
Robert D. Harris
10 Nov 2019

Second Edition

Copyright © 2017

Table of Contents

...a tribute...a dedication...to a friend, a leader, a Marine

Colonel Marion Cranford Dalby,
USMC Retired
1922-2008...

In one's life, you meet many men and women...most of them are friendly, modestly intelligent, interesting and a pleasure to have as an acquaintance or a friend. If you are extremely fortunate, you will meet one or two individuals who will truly, positively affect your career...cause you to lift and reset your goals and objectives ...and literally change your life. As one grows older and has essentially "completed the career game", one often looks back over the years and wonders what your life would have been like, if you had not met such an influential individual... for awhile you think about "what might have been" ...then you suddenly stop...your mind "smiles" and you feel that "rosy glow" as it warms your thoughts...for more than a few moments you savor the memories and then say to yourself..."wasn't that a wonderful experience". I don't know what my life would have been like if I had not met Cranford Dalby, but I am so pleased that I did. So now you know why I dedicate this modest story to the most outstanding Marine I met during my twenty some years in the Corps.

He was a man, take him for all is all
I shall not look upon his like again

William Shakespeare

Prologue

Not too many years ago, during a nationally televised debate, a candidate for the Vice Presidency began his remarks by asking, "Who am I"? and "Why am I here"? His candidacy was doomed to failure long before he opened his mouth, but his questions were quite valid in retrospect.

In effect, a couple years ago, I essentially asked myself the same questions, but in relation to what my descendants would want to know about me during my years on this earth.

I have long been a Civil War "Buff" of sorts, and I have enjoyed finding a personal account of some soldier from those days and learning what he and his buddies were doing on an ordinary day. In one published diary of a "Johnny Reb" from Mississippi, he told of the daily experiences, most quite mundane, but I found it extremely interesting and enjoyed the "deja vue" feeling of reliving his life vicariously through his simple scribbling.

One would expect an Eisenhower or a MacArthur to write their memoirs...it's essentially mandatory! Those men and women who have served in high places and who have participated in momentous undertakings must record their life and experiences for posterity. However, no one expects a person with some rather modest accomplishments, in comparison with those of the world's leaders, to tell the stories of his or her life. Who would be interested in reading about a rather ordinary man or woman?

I made the decision to undertake this task (...and it has been a task...pleasurable, but still a task!) because I hoped that some one in our family, perhaps many years from now, would be curious as to what happened in the lives of their Great-Grandparents...just as I was interested in the life of a poor soldier, totally unrelated some 150 years ago.

I must say that through it all, my dear wife Marie has endured much grief and anxiety. While she understands my passion for completing the effort, she has challenged me for devoting so many hours to the undertaking and consequently failing to spend time with her and generally neglecting many of my husbandly duties. Now that the work of the last ten or so months is reaching a conclusion, I expect she, too, will be relieved and pleased with the end product.

Today as I reach my 86th birthday, I hope that those who read these humble writings will learn that we experienced all of the human emotions...the periods of great joy and of great remorse and the normal ups and downs of everyday living.

We have met some wonderful people along the way and each of them contributed to our happiness and enjoyment...and an occasional moment of despair...in a multitude of ways. Consequently, you will read of some of these people throughout the stories. Their names are of little importance to you or to the story, but I included them in recognition of the important part they played in shaping our lives

Therefore, I want to remind the reader of these recollections of days gone by that life is really a "people business". The people in your family, in your workplace and those you find to be your friends and acquaintances are very important. Earl Nightingale, the noted motivational speaker, said you should remember to treat the next person you meet as if he or she is the most important person in the world.

We wish you success in your "people" business, your life. May you experience all the joy and happiness and success you earn and deserve. Remember, as others have said, life is not a dress rehearsal.

Introduction You Can't Tell A Player Without A Program

Some parts of this book of memoirs, the "sea stories", do not necessarily follow a chronological line. So, it may help you, the reader, to have a simple biographical sketch of my life to put the various stories in some sort of a perspective.

If you were to ask Marie, my wife, whom I love dearly, she would attest to the fact that I am a "talker". I admit it! I love to talk with people about our life experiences. Yes, I know there have been numerous occasions when I have "talked the ear off" some innocent friend or stranger, and told them much more than they really wanted to know. It seems that I am never able to recognize the moment when I should "shut up". I always feel this pressing need to provide some extra bit of information. Marie believes that she can recognize this moment when I should "shut up". I don't know how reliable she is in this regard because she frequently indicates that it is time to stop talking before I have even begun! Maybe it's because she has heard most of my stories many, many times over the sixty-some years we have been together?

I cannot count the times I have felt that nudge or the kick on my leg, the signal to "cool it". I generally find the interruption annoying and go back to my story telling with renewed vigor. Perhaps I am such a "talker" because I don't have any fear about talking to someone. I enjoy talking to some complete stranger while shopping. I can't ever remember when I was ever afraid to get up in front of a group of people and talk!

The only time I ever remember having this "stage fright" feeling was when at about the age of eleven, my parents set me up to play the accordion at some adult gathering. I knew I was not a very good accordionist.

The fact became obvious when I stumbled through "Over the Waves" and "Under the Double Eagle" or "La Something or Other". Definitely, I was not ready for "prime time"

I believe anyone will do better when talking to an individual or a group when you "know what you are talking about" or at least have an educated opinion on the subject. Those who know me well, or not very well, soon recognize I have an opinion on almost any subject. I will admit, some of my opinions are not always well founded in facts, but, in those instances, they probably represent my values and strong feelings about honesty, loyalty and faithfulness.

So, as you read through the "sea stories" to follow, you may have difficulty envisioning when in the last century these events occurred, hopefully the following chronological outline will be of some help.

A Thumbnail Review of My Life

Robert George Harris was born September 6, 1923 in a house on Olcott Avenue in East Chicago, IN. The second son of William George Harris and Myrtle Adelle Dunck. My brother, William Chester was born on April 10, 1921 and died of pneumonia on January 30, 1922 at the age of 10 months.

1924-1928. First Residence of memory was a small two-bedroom house on Hickory Street, Hammond, IN. I did not attend Kindergarten.

1929-1932. Second Residence was a newly built house on Marshall Avenue, Hessville, IN. My mother's sister Olive and her husband Bill Haman built a matching house next door. At age 6, I attended Marshall School where I completed grades 1 through 4.

1932-1937. Third Residence, a small two-bedroom upstairs apartment at the corner of Page Street and Industrial Avenue, Flint, MI. Later we moved downstairs in same house to larger apartment. Attended Dort Elementary School, Grades 5 and 6 and Whittier Junior High School, grades 7 and 8. Began High School in Fenton, MI. 1937-1938. Lived in a cottage on Dart's Landing, Lake Fenton, (then Long Lake), Fenton, MI.

1938-1941. Parents purchased house at 14337 Swanee Beach (Long Lake), Fenton MI. Attended Fenton High School, Fenton, MI for Grades 9 through 12. Graduated in June 1941.

1941-1943   Student at Michigan State College, East Lansing, MI. Completed freshman and sophomore years before being ordered to active duty in USMC. Resided at rooming house, 302 M.A.C. Avenue, East Lansing, MI during freshman year and Sigma Alpha Epsilon fraternity house on 131 Boque Street, East Lansing, MI during sophomore year.

1943-1944.   Marine Private, Marine V-12 Unit, University of Michigan, Ann Arbor, MI. Completed four semesters of study before being transferred. Resided in Chicago House, West Quadrangle, a University of Michigan Residence Hall. Married Marie Durant on June 24, 1944. Marie lived with her parents at 110 ½ S. Leroy Street, Fenton, MI.

October 1944-January 1945.   Completed Marine "Boot Camp" at Parris Island, South Carolina. Promoted to Private First Class upon completion. Marie resided with her parents at 110 ½ S. Leroy Street, Fenton, MI until she joined me in Fredericksburg, VA in June 1945.

January 1945-February 1945 .Completed Officer Candidates Applicant's program at Camp Lejeune, NC before being transferred to MCS Quantico, VA.

14 February 1945-6 June 1945. Served as member of the 7th Platoon Leaders Class, MCS, Quantico, VA. Commissioned a 2nd Lieutenant, USMCR on June 6, 1945. On April 28, 1945, Marie and I became parents when our son Robert James was born at the Woman's Hospital in Flint, MI. I received the news in Quantico in a telegram from my father. Flew home immediately after graduation and saw our son for the first time!

June 1945-3 October 1945.   Completed Officer's Field Artillery School, Quantico, VA. Resided in one room with shared bath on Charles Street, Fredericksburg, VA with Marie and infant son,

Robert. Later moved to a two-room apartment on Winchester Street near the Kenmore Mansion in Fredericksburg.

7-10 October 1945.   Reported to Camp Lejeune, NC and was re-assigned to duty at Naval Ammunition Depot (Goose Creek), SC.

14 October 1945-12 March 1946.   Marine Barracks duty at NAD, Charleston, SC.   Marie and Bobby joined me and we lived in town house apartment on the depot.

11 April 1946-April 18 1946.   Transferred for purposes of separation from service to Marine Separation Center, U.S. Naval Training Station, Great Lakes, IL. Released to inactive duty on April 18, 1946. Moved to parent's home at 14337 Swanee Beach, Fenton, MI. Marie, Bobby and I lived with my parents for about two months.   I was employed at AC Spark Plug Co., as Plant Layout Engineer, Works Engineering Department on Dort Highway in Flint, MI.

June 1946-11 December 1946.   Lived with Jean and Cam Loucks, (Marie's sister and brother-in-law) at 4315 West Jefferson Avenue, Ecorse, MI.   I was employed by the J. B. Webb Engineering Company in Detroit, MI as a draftsman.   Also living in the house were three young people, Diane and Lynda Loucks and Bobby. Applied for a regular commission in the USMC and was accepted.

15 December 1946-March 1948.   Returned to active duty in USMC as a regular officer with rank of 2nd Lieutenant.   Assigned to "B" Battery, 10th Marines, 2nd Marine Division, Camp Lejeune, NC. Resided with Marie and Bobby in a row-type apartment at Holly Ridge, NC.   Our daughter, Patricia Marie was born on March 27, 1948 at the US Naval Hospital, Camp Lejeune, NC.

March 1948-August 1948.   Continued to serve in the 10th Marines. Moved from Holly Ridge to a two-bedroom house in Midway Park, NC, a government housing community just outside the main gates of Camp Lejeune, NC

August 1948-6 November 1948.   Continued to serve in 10th Marines. Moved into Government Quarters on base.   Occupied a three-bedroom house for about three months until transferred. . Promoted to 1st Lieutenant as of 12 September 1948.

23 November 1948-August 1949. Was a student in the Guided Missile Systems Officer Course (MOS 1181), U.S. Army Air Defense School, Fort Bliss, TX. Graduated in August 1949. Resided in The Jacqueline Apartments in Ysleta, TX with Marie, Bobby and Patty.

September 1949-July 1951. Served in the Marine Guided Missile Unit, Naval Air Missile Test Center, Point Mugu, CA. I was one of the group of twelve Marines who developed the Marine Air Support Radar System, AN/MPQ-14. Resided at 223 McMillan Avenue, Oxnard, CA with Marie, Bobby and Patty.

August 1951-August 1952. Served with the 1st Marine Air Support Radar Team operating with 1st Marine Division, Korea during the Korean War. Marie, Bobby and Patty continued to reside at 223 McMillan Avenue, Oxnard, CA.

September 1952-January 1953. Served with Marine Air Control Squadron at Marine Corps Air Station, El Toro, CA setting up unit for the training of Marines in the operation of the MPQ-14 system. Promoted to Captain as of 25 June 1952. Resided at 2108 S. Rosewood Avenue, Santa Ana, CA with Marie, Bobby and Patty.

January 1953-June 1953. Served as a Battery Commander, 3rd Battalion, 12th Marines, 3rd Marine Division at Camp Pendleton, CA. Resided at 612 Monterey Drive, Oceanside, CA with Marie, Bobby and Patty.

June 1953-October 1953. Served as "G" Battery Commander, 3rd Battalion, 12th Marines, 3rd Marine Division at Camp Fuji, Japan. Marie, Bobby and Patty returned to home at 223 McMillan Avenue, Oxnard, CA.

October 1953-20 June 1955. Served as Schools Platoon Commander, Marine Barracks, U.S. Naval Training Station, Great Lakes, IL Resided at 23 Admiral Drive, Forrestal Village, North Chicago, IL with Marie, Bobby and Patty.

20 July 1955- 26 June 1958. Was a student at the U.S. Naval Postgraduate School, Monterey, CA. Resided at 1055 Rosita Road, Del Rey Oaks, CA with Marie, Bobby and Patty. Promoted to Major in 1956. Graduated in Absentia from Michigan State University in 1956 with B.A. (Mathematics). Graduated from USNPGS with M.S. Electrical Engineering on 12 June 1958

4 August 1958- June 1961. Served as Head, Engineering Branch and later as Chief of the Missile Science Division, U.S. Air Defense School, Fort Bliss, Texas. Division conducted the Guided Missile Staff (Systems) Officer course. Resided a 5219 Marcellus Avenue, El Paso, TX with Marie, Bobby and Patty.

July 1961-4 September 1962. Served with 12th Marines, 3rd Marine Division in Okinawa as S-3, 1st Battalion and as Regimental S-.4 Lived in quarters at Camp Hague and Camp Sukiran. Marie, Bob and Pat resided in rented house at 14441 Appletree Lane, Fenton, MI. Bob and Pat attended Fenton Schools.

9 October 1962-June 1964. Served as Artillery Officer, Marine Corps Equipment Board, Marine Corps Development Center, Quantico, VA. Resided at "Cinder City" B.O.Q. at Quantico, VA while Marie, Bob and Pat continued to live at 14441 Appletree Lane. After Bob completed his senior year and graduated from Fenton High School in 1963. Marie and Pat joined me in Quantico where we lived in Quarters 390-B. Promoted to Lieutenant Colonel on 1 June 1964

July 1964-30 September 1965. Served as Assistant to the Director, Remote Area Conflict (Project AGILE), Advanced Research Projects Agency (ARPA), Department of Defense, Pentagon, Washington, D.C. Resided with Marie and Pat at 7717 Webber, Annandale, VA. Bob was student at Michigan State University residing at Wonders Hall, MSU, East Lansing, MI. Pat attended Annandale High School. Retired from USMC effective October 1, 1965 as Lieutenant Colonel in order to accept W.K. Kellogg Fellowship at Michigan State University to pursue PhD in Community College Leadership Program.

September 1965-June 1966. Began doctoral program at Michigan State University. Resided at 620 Snyder Road, East Lansing with Marie, Bob and Pat. My Grandmother Clara Johnson died at the home of my parents in Fenton, MI on October 30, 1965.

June 1966-August 1968. Daughter Patricia graduated from East Lansing High School, June 1966 and began studies at MSU. Purchased residence at 1054 Grand River Avenue, East Lansing, MI. Continued to study in PhD program. Appointed an Instructor on MSU faculty, working as researcher in Office of Institutional Research. Received PhD in June 1968. Bob received B.A. in December 1967, married Jean Boyko on January 13, 1968, and reported for active duty as 2nd Lieutenant, USMCR to Quantico, VA. Pat married Daniel J. Badaluco in June 13, 1968. Marie's father, Harry Durant, died during heart operation, at Henry Ford Hospital on July 6, 1967.

July 1968-July 1975 Appointed as founding President of Johnson County Community College, Overland Park, KS. Marie and I purchased a home at 9848 Cedar Street, Overland Park, KS.

July 1975-July 1977 Served as President of Middlesex County College, Edison, NJ. We lived in residence on campus at 104 Hof Road, Edison, NJ.

July 1977- July 1980 Served as President of McHenry County College, Crystal Lake, IL. We purchased a home at 4715 Burman Drive, Crystal Lake, IL

January 1980- June 1987. Purchased at home at 10101 White Lake Road, Tyrone Township, Fenton, MI. Worked as a representative for J.M. Jayson Co. of Buffalo, New York. Wholesaled investment products in Real Estate and Energy to Security Brokers in Michigan and Ohio. In 1983, son Bob resigned from FBI and joined me in the securities business. Established Harris Financial Group with Bob as co-owner. Was a charter member of the Fenton Rotary Club Previously a Rotarian in Overland Park, KS; Edison, NJ; and Crystal Lake, IL.

My parents died during this period. My father, Bill Harris, died at Cresmont Convalescent Home on October 2, 1982 after a two- year illness. On January 22, 1986, my mother, Myrtle, died at the Flint Osteopathic Hospital. No matter how old you are, you cannot prepare for the death of your parents. When it happens, it hurts!

June 1987-June 2000. Continued wholesaling securities. In 1990 formed home mortgage company, American Mortgage Management Corporation (AMMCOR). Harris Financial continued as financial planning and Investment Company. After my mother died, we remodeled my parent's home on Lake Fenton, and moved into the lake house. Bob's wife, "Duffy" died at her home of a cardiac arrest on August 6, 1988 at the age of 41. On November 5, 1990, we lost Marie's mother, "Nell" Durant. She lived to celebrate and enjoy her 90th birthday, when relatives and friends from Canada and all over joined her for the day.

June 2000-August 2003 Retired from active participation in Harris Financial Corporation, since retiring from business, my major activity has been related to work for the Rotary and the Fenton High School Alumni Association. Served as President of the Fenton Rotary Club for the year 1999-2000. Was honored by selection to the Fenton High School Hall of Fame in 2003.

2003 =2013. Enjoyed "retirement", spending winters in Florida and enjoying life on the lake in the Michigan summers. Became an avid writer of books about the Village of Fenton, the Marine Corps and the Fenton Rotary Club

2013- present. Tragically, my wife Marie suffered kidney failure and died on May 13, 2013 We had been married 69 years at the time of her death. Since her passing, I have continued writing and I spend my winter months in California at the home of my daughter Patricia.

Several pages of our "Photo Album" are to be found interspersed within the book. The Photos in these "Album" pages are not necessarily associated with the subject matter in the adjacent text.

Part I Many Come, Few Are Chosen

For almost twenty-five years of my life the U. S. Marine Corps demanded and received my primary attention. It was a service I gave willingly and with great pride. As a young man, I was given opportunities to learn, the responsibilities of leadership and the privilege to serve with the most dedicated and loyal of all Americans. I honor the Marines, past and present, whose dedication and blood, sweat and tears created and continue to maintain such a worthy brotherhood. Not everyone can be a U.S. Marine. It is said that many come, but few are chosen. Not everyone is willing to make the necessary commitment. However, once you do accept the obligation and become a Marine, you are a Marine for life. One of the "chosen" was our son, Robert James Harris, pictured below as a newly commissioned Second Lieutenant in December 1967.

Often one fails to recognize the fact that not only the one who wears the uniform becomes the Marine, but his family also accepts responsibility and many of the same challenges. During my service, there were frequent separations required by duty overseas or lengthy maneuvers, or temporary assignments away from home for days or weeks. During these times, my family was left at home or in some strange location while I was away performing the task assigned. Frequent changes of station resulted in many "moving days", changing of schools and making new friends. Marie and I actually moved into 21 houses between 1945 and 1965. This does not include the number of motels and guesthouses we occupied while waiting for more permanent quarters. Our son Bob was fortunate to only attend two high schools...the first two years in El Paso, Texas and his last two years in Fenton, Michigan. Our daughter Pat did each of her high school years in a different school: Fenton, Michigan; Quantico, Virginia; Annandale, Virginia and East Lansing, Michigan. It's a fact, the wife and children of Marines are required to make sacrifices comparable to those of the uniformed Marine.

It was a wonderful ride; I wouldn't have wanted to miss it! To the men and women of the Corps and their families...Semper Fidelis!

Captain Robert G. Harris
At Marine Barracks, USNTC,
Great Lakes, Illinois. 1953

1st Lieutenant Robert J. Harris
at Camp Lejeune, North Carolina
1971

Chapter 1   Join The Marines
And See…

Did you ever arrive someplace and wonder how you got there? To this day I don't remember why I joined the Marines! I never knew anyone who was in the Marines, I played "soldier" when I was a small boy, my father had served in the Army, and none of my relatives were ever in the Marine Corps. How did it happen that when the "joining up" time arrived, I chose the Marine Corps? All of my high school buddies and college friends seemed to be heading for the Air Corps. But here it was, the first and original "Pearl Harbor" day, and I was thinking about joining the Marines.

Upon returning to my rooming house in East Lansing on the evening of December 7, 1941, I found my house-mates quite excited and glued to the radio for more reports on the attack. Everyone was talking about what they would or should do in response to this attack on our country. There was talk about going to the nearest recruiting station early the next day and do the right thing! I can't recall whether I was in a group that went to the Lansing Post Office on Monday or not. If I wasn't in the group, I feel as if I were there, because I know that the Recruiters at the Post Office were swamped with young men anxious to join the Armed Services as soon as possible. In one way or the other, I learned the college men in the crowd who were interested in joining the Marine Corps were advised to go back to the campus and wait for the arrival of an officer procurement team. It seemed the Marine Corps was recruiting college students for an Officer Candidate program and the recruiters were scheduled to arrive at Michigan State College in the very near future.

The Marine "team" arrived at MSC in early March 1942 in the person of a Second Lieutenant William L. Bachelor. "Bill" Bachelor was a graduate of MSC and had been a football "hero" at Michigan State in the late 1930s. I recall seeing Lieutenant Bachelor for the first time in a room at the Union Building. He looked just great in his undress Blue uniform with the leather Sam Browne belt. Of course, at the time I didn't know the uniform was designated as the "Undress Blues" or that the cordovan leather belt with the strap over the right shoulder was known as a "Sam Browne" belt. That knowledge was to come later. At the first meeting, the officer program was presented and even though I had turned 18 years of age six months earlier, there was requirements to have my parents sign one of the papers before I could sign up. This meant I had to go home to Fenton, have my parents sign the papers and return them to Lieutenant Bachelor the next day.

I can't specifically recall this trip back to Fenton, but it was probably like many others I made before and after that day…I "hitch-hiked". My normal hitchhike route was east on Grand River Boulevard to Brighton and north from Brighton to Fenton. One must remember there were no "expressways" in 1941. Even Grand River, which ran all the way from Lansing to Detroit, was, for the most part, no more than a two-lane paved road. US 23 from Brighton to Fenton was just a two-lane paved road which ran up and down the hills, curving left and right as it made it's way north. Compared to the traffic on these routes today, the number of cars on the roads in those days was quite light. Those individuals driving the roads in 1941 were more willing to offer a ride to a young fellow standing along the side of the road with his thumb upraised, especially if he had a small suitcase with large green and white "S" on its side. Catching a ride was not difficult even when there were just a few cars on the roads.

I suspect it was still quite cold in March and standing for long periods along the road was not too enjoyable. I know in 1941, I did not own a good topcoat or overcoat. All I had was the shell of a light khaki cloth raincoat. I can attest to the fact that it was not made to keep one warm. I used to "freeze" wearing that coat on many of the trips, but it was the only outer garment I owned at that time.

I made the round trip to Fenton, and returned the signed papers to Lieutenant Bachelor the next day. The result was that on March 9, 1942, I was enlisted as a Private in the Marine Corps Reserve Class IIIb. Class IIIb Marines were the reservists who were "officer candidates". Under this program, I was to stay in school, continue my studies and await the call to active duty. They did, however, require the Marine Class IIIb reservists to enroll in some correspondence courses from the Marine Corps Schools. It was in connection with doing the correspondence study homework, that I met a John C. Wickham, a fellow student at MSC. We would get together and do the correspondence requirements. He was a "rich kid" from Birmingham or Bloomfield Hills in the Detroit area and he had attended military schools as a youngster. In spite of our different backgrounds, we got along very well and I rather liked the fellow. But as it turned out, I really didn't know him very well!

The wait for the "call to active duty" seemed like it would never come. It wasn't until sometime in the spring of 1943 that the "IIIb Reservists" at MSC learned that as of July 1, 1943 we would be activated and assigned to the "V-12" program at the University of Michigan. The Navy and the Marine Corps had established a program for the preparation of their officer candidates which they designated "V-12". They had selected a number of colleges and universities throughout the nation at which they placed a V-12 Unit. The University of Michigan, Notre Dame, Alma, Purdue, University of Minnesota are just a few of the schools selected to have V-12 Units.

At the University of Michigan, the Navy and Marines took over the West Quadrangle, a university residence hall complex. West Quad was located directly "behind" the Michigan Union building. It was made up of many "houses". There were about 2000 sailors and 200 Marines assigned to the U of M V-12 unit. The Marines occupied Chicago and Lloyd Houses. A Captain Joseph Hoffman commanded the Marine Detachment, Navy V-12 Unit. He was assisted by a Marine Gunner (a Warrant Officer) named Croyle. W.W. Croyle was short, gruff and a real "son-of–a-bitch". He was just what Captain Hoffman and all of us needed at that time. Captain Hoffman was mild soft-spoken gentlemen, in his forties, a reservist who was "too old to fight" but available and capable of administering a unit of 200 Marine "novices". I would guess he was an insurance man or a banker in civilian life, using the common "stereotypes" for those occupations. There was a Platoon Sergeant Sheppard, who was the Unit's First Sergeant. There were three or four other enlisted non-commissioned officers. I can recall a red-faced, chubby Sergeant Rubin and a Corporal Robert Atkins. Finding Corporal Atkins in Ann Arbor came as a complete surprise. Corporal Robert Atkins, who I knew as "Junie" Atkins, had been at Fenton High School when I attended the school. Even though he was a couple years ahead of me at Fenton High School, we knew each other well. Needless to say, I was very pleasantly surprised to see him in Ann Arbor. We both avoided being conspicuously "friendly". I didn't know it at the time, but having "Junie" as one of my NCOs would significantly influence my future wedding arrangements, but that's another story!

It was on July 1, 1943 when I arrived in Ann Arbor, along with a couple hundred other Marines, and reported for active duty. One of the first things those in charge did was to ask the assembled "crowd" if anyone had had any prior military service or training, such as military schools. Of course, my "friend" John Wickham stepped forward and he was summarily appointed a "cadet" officer. We then were herded into something resembling a military formation and the "cadet" officers "took" charge. John Wickham was placed in charge of my group. It wasn't long before we got to know the "real" John Wickham. In no time most of us were calling him "Wick" or something that sounded something like that!

If we were to fast-forward to 1948 for a moment, we would find 1st Lieutenant Harris and his wife living in Quarters at Camp Lejeune directly across the street from the Quarters of 1st Lieutenant John C. Wickham and his wife. The Wickhams were big entertainers. It seemed like most of their guests were Majors and a few Colonels. Their guest list never included any of their neighbors, even their "old friends" the Harrises. John had once told me his goal was to become the Commandant of the Marine Corps. He was really working at it, but I am pleased to report he didn't make it!

We were all issued uniform clothing and we followed a military regimen throughout the summer months, prior to the beginning of classes in the fall. The parking lot on the north end of the West Quad became our "grinder" and we spent several hours each day that summer learning close order drill, the position of a soldier, saluting, proper wearing of the uniform and more or less how to look and act like a Marine. We didn't have weapons, so the close order drill was not under arms. While the marching was quite beneficial, we did very little marching once the school year began. Each V-12 student, Navy or Marine, went as individuals to their classes, maintained their own class schedules, were allowed to participate in student activities, including intercollegiate sports. Other than having to return to the West Quad for muster and "lock-up" each evening, the V-12ers "college" days continued very much as if they were civilian students.

Soon after we reported, we all lined up to receive our college registration assignments. The two main categories, as far as the Marine Corps was concerned, were "Liberal Arts" and "Engineering". All "Liberal Arts" Marines were scheduled to complete two semesters and then be sent on to Officer training. On the other hand, the "Engineering" Marines were to go to school for four semesters before they were to move on to Officer training

When my turn arrived, I was standing in front of Sergeant Rubin and he handed me my assignment and said, "Engineering". At that I said to Sergeant Rubin, "Sir, there must be a mistake, I am not an Engineer". He looked at the papers and then at me and said. "You're a math major, aren't you?" I replied, "Yes sir". Then he said, "That's Engineering to us". And so I began my days at the U of M as an Engineer.

We were free to arrange our own class schedules, select our own classes, etc. As an Engineering student, I would need to take some engineering courses, such as Engineering Physics, Mechanical Drawing, and other advanced Mathematics (which I intended to take anyway.)   Before leaving Michigan State, I had consulted with my advisor, Dr. Paul L. Dressel, about what courses I should take at the U of M, which would be in line with my degree objectives. He had made some suggestions, and told me to visit with a Professor Bateman at U of M. He considered the Professor to be an excellent person and distinguished in Mathematical Statistics, which was my field of interest. Consequently, I visited with Professor Bateman and explained the apparent conflict in being assigned to the College of Engineering and my desire to pursue a course of study in Statistics. Together we worked out a program that would satisfy the College of Engineering and allow me to follow a program in Statistics.

When I enrolled at Michigan State as a new freshman, I originally wanted to enroll in Engineering. But I didn't! The truth is I "chickened-out". Even though I had very good grades in high school, especially in Mathematics, I didn't take chemistry and I didn't particularly like the Physics course I had experienced at FHS. So, at the last minute, I enrolled in Business Administration. It was a couple of terms later before I finally decided on Mathematics (Statistics) as a major.

My original room assignment was on the second floor of the building and I shared the room with Edwin C. Hamann of Mio,

Michigan and Sydney Hanks of Marysville, Michigan. "Ned" Hamann was a serious engineering student who was transferred from Michigan State and we became close friends. "Ned" was to be the Best Man at our wedding, however he suffered an appendicitis attack a few days before the day of the wedding and I had to find a substitute. But, that's another story. "Ned" finished up his engineering degree in three semesters and moved on in the program. I next saw him on the night I arrived in Camp Lejeune, many months later. He was activated during the Korean conflict and we were able to reconnect at Camp Pendleton. The last time we visited with Ned and his wife in Schererville, Indiana in about 1979. During our visit, "Ned" received an urgent call from the Standard Oil Refinery in Whiting, Indiana where he was a senior engineer. It seems that a huge underground water line had ruptured. I remember asking him how he expected to find the location of the break and he replied "No problem, just look for the lake!"

Sid Hanks was another kind of fellow. He was the son of the Superintendent of Schools in Marysville at that time. Sid was a "whiner" and in my opinion,

he didn't have the "right stuff" to become an officer. On one occasion, we all received a series of "shots". The shots were put in both arms. That night, Sid who slept in the upper bunk above "Ned" moaned all night, laying on his stomach with both of his "wounded" arms hanging from each side. It wasn't a surprise when Sid was removed from the program. I don't remember what the reason for his dismissal was, but it was probably best for him and the Marine Corps. During my time in training at Quantico, we had an exercise with some landing craft in the Potomac River. The day of our exercise, we were moved to the docks of Quantico by bus and then assigned to the different landing craft moored there. I was very surprised to find PFC Sidney Hanks as one of the crewman on the landing craft I had boarded. We had a short reunion and Sid seemed to have matured and was right with the world.

The West Quadrangle gates were "chained" each evening at 6 P.M. A muster was taken then and after the muster, anyone who wanted to leave the Quadrangle for any good reason could do so by checking out and leaving through the only unlocked gateway. That gateway was designated as the "Quarter Deck". There was always an "Officer of the Deck" available on the "Quarter Deck". The permanent staff officers assigned to the V-12 Unit took their turns serving as the Officer of the Deck The duty list included our Gunner W.W. Croyle, USMC.

At 10 PM, there was a second and final muster for the day. Each floor (deck) in each of the houses had an individual designated as the "Mate of the Deck". It was his duty to take the muster of the people on his deck (a "floor" for civilians!) and report his findings to the Officer of the Deck. Those individuals who were reported as absent for the musters were listed as "Missing Muster" and unless they had a good explanation, they were placed "On Report" and were subject to disciplinary action. So, you see, if one wanted to avoid trouble, one would not want to be reported as "missing" a muster. There were certainly a lot of deals worked, where someone would be absent and his "Mate of the Deck" would report him as "present". The Mate of the Deck was in big trouble, however, if he was caught "Reporting a False Muster". Reporting a False Muster was a courts-martial offense

There were all kinds of stories about some Mate of the Deck who was helping his buddy and turned in a false muster (reporting his friend as "present"} and then his buddy would be picked up by the Military Police in downtown Detroit about the same time the muster report was being delivered to the Officer of the Deck. Several budding careers as Naval or Marine officers were "nipped" by such incidents.

It wasn't long before both sailors and Marines had found ways of getting extra "liberty" by escaping West Quad and enjoying an evening on the town. Many went as far as Detroit for the night, arriving back in Ann Arbor just in time to make the morning muster, get cleaned up and go to class. One way to "escape" was to arrange for your "Mate of the Deck" to mark you as present at both the evening muster and the late night muster. However, as I have mentioned, the "Mate of the Deck" was taking a huge risk by covering for a friend.

One popular way of "escaping" was to wait until the evening muster was taken, and under the cover of darkness, go out through one of the windows of a first floor room. The corner room on the first floor of Chicago House was the Marine's favorite avenue of escape. Immediately after going out the window of that corner room, you were sheltered by some very large shrubbery. Once outside, hidden in the bushes, you could pick your time to leave, and when the "coast was clear", cross the road and disappear into the "forbidden" city. The reverse procedure was used to reenter the residence hall. I have often wondered how and why, the occupants of that room allowed this to happen. They must have had a very difficult time studying or sleeping in that room with all the traffic going and coming all night.

One of the two occupants of that room was Gerald Ter Horst. Jerry Ter Horst later became a journalist of repute with the Detroit News. But he is, probably, better remembered as the Press Secretary for President Gerald Ford. His notoriety was enhanced when he resigned as Press Secretary because he was in disagreement with one of the President's positions.

About once a week, I would take off for Fenton for an unauthorized overnight stay. It worked really well for months. I would hitchhike out of Ann Arbor in the afternoon, stay all night in Fenton and then take an early bus from Fenton to Ann Arbor. The bus arrived about 5 AM at the Union Building. I would leave the bus, go into the Union and read the morning paper. When the gates of the West Quadrangle were unchained at 6 AM, I would stroll from the Union directly through the gates to my room in Chicago house. It just worked out perfectly until one day!

I was the" Mate" of my deck. As such, I would make out the muster report and, since I had an Assistant, I would give him the report for delivery to the Quarter Deck. On those occasions when I planned to travel to Fenton, I would sign the reports early in the afternoon and he would deliver the muster report to the Quarter Deck at the scheduled times. On this particular day, I had left the signed reports with my assistant as usual. I had left for Fenton that afternoon and I would not return until slightly after 6 AM, the time of the morning muster.

When I came back that particular morning, my assistant was noticeably disturbed. Then he told me what had happened during my absence. When he took the early evening report to the Quarter Deck, he found Gunner Croyle on duty. The Gunner told him to tell Private Harris to report to him on the Quarter Deck. When the time for the late evening muster arrived, my assistant knew it was not possible for him to turn in a muster, signed by me, and having me "Present". He had to make his own report having me marked "Absent". He turned in the muster report and told the Gunner he was unable to contact me with his previous instructions. He tried to lighten the situation by telling him he had heard from others that I was in another part of the

Quadrangle studying with some sailors and he expected I would show up momentarily. As you may surmise, I was quite unprepared for this revolting development! However, I decided to face the music and deliver the 6 AM report to the Gunner myself. When I reported to the Gunner he was not very talkative, stern face and all, and he said I was being placed on report and I would have to explain my conduct to the Captain.

The next morning, I was on the docket for the Captain's Mast. I was charged with: (1) Being absent from Muster and (2) Reporting a False Muster. Now of the two, the second offense was, by far, the most serious. It was a Courts-Martial offense. If I was found guilty of "Reporting a False Muster", I was certain I would be dropped from the program and be on my way to San Diego. Those who had been "washed out" before were gone to San Diego Recruit Depot ("boot camp") on the next day and some had already been out to the Pacific battles. I thought my "college" days and my dreams of becoming a Marine Corps Officer were about to be suddenly derailed.

The Gunner and the First Sergeant, Platoon Sergeant Sheppard, were standing in the outer office as I passed through it into the Captain's office. I came to attention in front of the Captain, who was sitting behind his desk, and barked out, "Private Harris, reporting as ordered, Sir". The Captain, who had a heavy mustache and wore glasses, picked up the charge sheet and started reading the charges. He read the first charge, "Being absent from a Muster". He put down the sheet and began to lecture me on the sins of missing a muster. He spoke in a calm, fatherly kind of voice. He obviously was interested in convincing me that I should never miss a muster again. I was convinced, but he kept on talking about the evils of being absent. Finally, he ended the lecture and prescribed the remedy, my punishment for committing this horrendous offense, he said "Private Harris, I am restricting you to barracks for two weeks" I said "Yes Sir", did an about face and marched out of the office. Once I was in the outer office and another offender had entered the Captain's office, the Gunner asked me "What did you get?" I replied "Two weeks restriction, Sir" The look on the Gunner's face was one of complete disbelief; he threw his cap down on the desk and said something like "God Damn". I left the office, obviously greatly relieved and grateful for another chance, which I took two weeks later!

I am of the opinion that Captain Hoffman never even read the second charge. I believe he picked up on the first charge and was carried away with lecturing me on the seriousness of missing a muster. He "sentenced" me after the lecture, before he read the second charge. If the more serious charge had been the first on the list, who knows what would have been the outcome. I believe it would have made a significant difference in my life and the life of many of my friends and family. But, that's another story!

Marie Durant, and I had a favorite place for taking pictures in the rear of the (then) new Community Center. These pictures were taken while I was a Private in the USMC V-12 Unit at the University of Michigan. 1943

Most certainly, the most significant event in my life occurred on June 24, 1944. Marie Durant and I became "man and wife". With my scheduled transfer from Ann Arbor pending, Marie and I talked of being married before my departure. We were in love and had been since my second year in high school. I was nearly twenty-one years of age and Marie was only six months younger than me. It was "marrying time"! However, there were several serious complications we had to consider.

When I joined the Marine Corps officer program, which evolved into the V-12 program, one of the provisions of the program was that you would remain unmarried until completion of the program...i.e. receiving your commission as a Second Lieutenant. Already, several of the Marines in our V-12 unit had been dismissed from the program once it was discovered they were married. Further, one of my Non-Commissioned officers, Corporal Junie Atkins was from our town, Fenton Michigan. Atkins' family lived in this small town and we were certain that if we were married in Fenton, a small town, everyone in town would know of the marriage…including the Atkins family! Once Corporal Atkins learned of the marriage, he would be duty bound to report the fact to his commanding officer. If he withheld the information from the Marines, he would be knowingly abetting disobedience. We didn't want to put our friend in this situation. However, if we were to be married somewhere away from Fenton, would the "news" get back to Fenton and would the Atkins family learn of the marriage?

Many years later, in the 1980s, I visited with Junie Atkins at one of our high school reunions, and Marie and I had an opportunity to ask him if he learned of our marriage back in 1944. We were pleased to learn that he had not heard anything about it!

The rector at my Episcopal church in Fenton, Reverend W. Thomas Smith, had recently been transferred to a church in Highland Park, Michigan, a suburb of Detroit. I had a ten-day leave in late June that would allow time for a marriage and a short honeymoon. So, we decided to "go for it" and risk the consequences and be married in the Emmanuel Episcopal Church in Highland Park.

Our wedding went off "without a hitch" after I was able to replace my best man, Edwin "Ned" Hamann, with another Marine friend, Bob Henderson of Grosse Point, Michigan. Unfortunately, Ned was operated on for appendicitis two days before our wedding date. Bob Henderson took a "blood" oath not to reveal anything about our wedding.

About a week before the wedding, Marie and I met with Reverend Smith. He wanted to talk to us about marriage, and counsel us on what marriage was all about. During our discussion, he brought up the fact that there was a war going on and that I was in the Marine Corps. He asked us if we had considered the possibility that I could be killed or maimed in this war and leave Marie and our children fatherless. Both Marie and I responded, almost in unison, we had considered that, and "we were not going to have any children until after the war was over". Ten months after our marriage, on April 28, 1945, Robert James Harris was born. You might say he was born prematurely, since the war didn't end until August 6, 1945

The "Happy Couple"...June 24, 1944

Marie had taken a job in a local machine tool company in Fenton, and became a "Rosie the Riveter" type during the war. While I was being paid $50 month as a Private in the Marine Corps, Marie was earning $50 a week operating a Milling Machine. When we went to purchase our wedding license, I was "short on cash", so Marie came forth with the cash to pay the license fee! Some women were liberated long before "women's lib" became popular?

Chapter 2   Boot Camp Delayed
Is Not
Boot Camp Denied

For some reason the Marine Corps did it "ass backwards", or so it seemed. The Marine Corps decided to have the officer candidates in the V-12 program undergo the basic military training after they completed the academic phase of the program. So, after being on active duty 16 months, I left the Michigan V-12 program for "boot camp" at the Marine Corps Recruit Depot, Parris Island, SC.

The Michigan V-12 contingent boarded the train at the Ann Arbor Depot sometime after dark on the Halloween evening 1944. Marie and my parents were at the station to see us off, along with a hundred or so of our Marine buddies. It was a celebratory event for most of the Marines; finally we were on our way toward commissioning and doing our part in the Great War. At the same time, it was a sad time for some of us as we said good-bye to our loved ones. I was able to spend most of the time with Marie and my parents during the loading period, since some of my friends carried my sea bag aboard the train. In fact, most of the Marines who were staying behind came aboard the train and helped the departing ones get their gear aboard. Some of them got carried away with the festivities and didn't get off the train in time and went all the way to Detroit before they could disembark

The train was made up of several "cattle cars" with bunks three high. Since it was Halloween, many of my comrades became quite exuberant and some were running through the train with sheets over their heads. I suspect some of them had brought more than their sea bags aboard the train! Our train went through Cleveland and Pittsburgh on its way to Washington, D.C. At each stop we picked up more groups of V-12 Marines from the various colleges along the way. We were allowed off the train at each of the stations including the Union Station in the nation's Capitol city. I managed to mail a postcard from each stop and a week later; my loved ones learned belatedly where we had stopped along the way. When we left Washington heading south, we had quite a long train. Other troop trains had come to Washington and a larger train was made up there for the trip south.

It was after dark when we arrived in Port Royal, SC. As we disembarked we were led to an area where many buses were waiting to take us to Recruit Depot, Parris Island, more commonly referred to as just "P.I.". It wasn't long before we were crossing a bridge and passing through a gate area manned by Marine sentries. This was the very first time I had ever been on a military reservation.

We were soon unloading from the buses and rapidly forming into platoons. I was soon to learn I was a member of Platoon #566 and that my Drill Instructor was Platoon Sergeant Halden. He was assisted by Corporal Piotrowski and Private First Class Turner. The details of what happened that evening or even the next day have faded in memory. For the next eight weeks, the memory is generally one of close order drill, mess calls, weapons instruction, inspections, scrubbing and cleaning the barracks, washing and cleaning clothing and equipment, fire watches, and general "hurry up" and "rushing" in every activity. The breaks in activity for sleep, occasional trips to the Triangle PX and outdoor movies were the welcome respites from almost constant physical and mental exercises.

This is the shortest my hair has ever been! But they gave me no choice...and it cost a $1 too! This photo was taken in first week of November 1944 behind the recruit barracks at Parris Island, South Carolina.

We were housed in a two story wood barracks on the "main side" of the base. Each barracks was in the shape of an "H". Each wing accommodated one recruit platoon on each "floor".. Consequently, there were four platoons in each barracks. Platoon #566 was assigned one of the lower squad bays. The parade ground, also called the "grinder", was directly accessible through the front exit door to our squad bay. The exit at the opposite end of the squad bay led to some "laundry racks". In a way when we weren't drilling on the "grinder" we were probably out back doing our laundry or scrubbing on our web gear.

While we were with the V-12 Unit we practiced "close order drill", i.e. marching while in "close" formation. However, here at Parris Island we trained in close order drill "under arms", and the arms were the M-1 rifles. We learned the various movements performed at attention or on the march. Our DI (Drill Instructor), as are all DIs, was very demanding. When your hand hit the rifle during these movements he wanted to hear the pop of flesh against wood and metal. After months as a schoolboy, our hands were not used to such a pounding, especially when it went on for hour after hour and day after day. In the first week, of all of my body parts that ached, my hands were probably the most painful. There was the tale about the recruits who would put their hands against a hot stove in order to toughen them up. I don't think any of us thought that was acceptable. It just took time before we could handle the blows and little or no pain remained.

At the command, "Inspection, Arms!" you would come to the position where the rifle was directly in front of you and in an angled position. The Inspecting Officer would approach, turn and face you and reach out and grasp the rifle. There was tendency for the rifleman to hold on to the rifle as the inspector seized it. This was a "No. No". For those who wouldn't let go of the rifle, the Inspector could grab and move the rifle in such a manner that the lower part of the rifle, the butt, would strike the rifleman in the crotch. If the "boot" didn't learn to release the rifle and smartly move his arms back to his sides, after being "corrected" in this manner, he could end up singing tenor for the rest of his life.

While marching with the rifle, you would hold the butt end of the rifle across the palm of your hand. For those who were just beginning to learn the drill, there was the tendency to fail to close their thumb down on the rifle stock. The thumb would be sticking up like a short twig and it then could become the recipient of a blow from the DIs swagger stick. The DIs carried these short batons, called "swagger sticks", with which they would accentuate their message when making corrections. Again, if you had your thumb whacked a couple times, you became aware it was supposed to be flat against the stock and not sticking up in the air.

From what I have described you might assume that corporal punishment was commonplace. However, that was not the case in our platoon, or most of the V-12 platoons. In the early days of training at P.I. it was the "verbal abuse" we experienced. It seemed that none of the DIs could give orders in a normal tone of voice. Orders were always "shouted".

Each of us took our turn, some more than others, in getting "dressed down" or otherwise publicly berated. It was the norm for the first week or so, but after a while it began to be a rare occurrence. I think our DIs realized our platoon, like the other V-12 platoons, were a lot more intelligent than the average recruit platoon. Granted, we didn't know a thing about weapons or drilling under arms, but we were all quick learners and we responded to their instructions differently from the other "boots".

There was a regular "boot" platoon occupying the barracks next to ours. During our time on the "grinder" we could observe this platoon and other platoons going through their drills. On one occasion, I witnessed their DI completely lose his "cool" with one of the recruits who just couldn't keep his rifle at the proper angle while marching. This DI came up behind him and hit him with his fist right behind the left ear. The "boot" staggered a bit, went to his knees and then up again and never broke step. I would hope he learned how to carry his rifle after that bit of "extra" instruction.

The time we spent at the Rifle Range was a change of pace with less harassment, and for the most part, a pleasant and welcome experience. We hit the rifle range during the coldest period we experienced at Parris Island. The high winds off the Atlantic were cold and constant for days. Firing a rifle in the cold, with rain and high winds played havoc with our target scores. A few days were so bad, they closed the ranges and we had the opportunity to stay in our Quonset huts huddling around the pot-bellied oil-burning stove. However, not all the days were as bad as those described. We had many wonderful cool and sunny days. There were enough of those days for us to learn how to shoot the M-1 rifle, the BAR (Browning automatic rifle) and the carbine

Most of the regular "boots" knew we were college boys and officer candidates. I am positive they thought we were getting "special" treatment because of our status. Occasionally we would have the opportunity to talk with them when we had post "liberty" to visit the PX. There were the occasional sneering remarks akin to "college boys" or something, but there were more stories about their attitude then I ever witnessed in person. There was the one about one of them saying, "You guys aren't so smart, we gotta guy in our platoon who can read and write too"! I doubt if that was really said, but it was repeated over and over again among the V-12ers. We even heard that in one platoon, the DI had to put sand in their shoes before he could get his "boots" to wear them. Do you think that ever happened? It did seem that most of the "boots" we ran into during off times, were from Texas or somewhere in the south. So the idea that they were all off the farm or hillbillies wasn't difficult to sell. There is one example of where I know the regular boots were certain we were getting special treatment.

When we were at the rifle range, the schedule for each meal was very tight. Each platoon was scheduled to arrive at a specific time and they could not enter the mess hall until that time. Most of the platoons would arrive ten to fifteen minutes before their scheduled time and consequently they would have to stand outside the mess hall, in ranks, until their time to enter and eat their meal. As I have already observed, the weather at P.I. while we were at the Rifle Range was very cold and windy. It was not very good weather to stand around waiting to be fed. Our DI was evidently a lot smarter than the others. He had determined the time it took us to form up in our area and march to the mess hall. We always moved out on time and we hit the mess hall exactly on schedule. Consequently, we moved directly into the mess hall and passed by the troops that had been standing in the cold for some time. As we moved past them, we could hear their grumbling and uttering of hostile remarks. They were certain we were receiving special consideration.

The Quonset huts at the Rifle Range were placed in rows, with about ten huts in a row. There must have been about 20 some rows of huts. At the end of the rows of huts were some larger metal buildings that contained the shower and head (toilet) facilities. The urinals consisted of large open sheet metal troughs attached to the side of one wall. Water was continually running through these troughs, so the need to flush after using was not present. The "seating area" for the facility was along the opposite wall. Again there was a continuous flow of water cascading through this trough. Automatic flushing! The seats were fastened to the top of this trough. There was no privacy. You might say that we sat "cheek to cheek". When you were new at the rifle range, you were almost certain to become a victim of what became a ritual. Each group passed it on to the newcomers. It was called "blackening the sights". It began with someone at the upper end of the water flow bundling up a large ball of toilet tissue, setting it on fire and placing it into the stream. As it passed below each individual seated downstream there was the same response repeated over an over again: a loud yelp and sudden leap into the air. The name for the "trick" was taken from the procedure used on the rifle range to improve your "sight picture" when firing the rifle. If you took the small cloth patch used to clean your rifle, put some oil on it and lit it, it would give off a heavy black smoke. If you passed this smoke over the sights on your rifle the metal sights would pick up the black carbon from the smoke and that would improve your "sight picture" when you aimed your rifle at the target.

  Not all was fun and games at the rifle range. Each hut was heated with a small round oil stove that sat directly on the concrete floor. There were eight double-decked bunks in each hut. In a way, I was lucky since my lower bunk bed was directly next to the stove. I was never cold as long as the there was a fire in the stove. However, the heat was very difficult to control. It seemed as if it was either red hot or ice cold. When red hot it was literally "red hot". The metal sides of the stove looked like the horseshoe in the tongs of a blacksmith as it was being removed from the fire. Red hot! Being so close to the heat dried out my skin. I found myself buying Jergens Lotion at the PX just to moisturize my skin. It seemed like the oil can ran out before reveille, so we were always getting out of bed into a cold room. The distance to the head was a good thirty yards down the cement walk. Once you made it into the building with the heads, you often found the building cold and drafty and not much warmer than the hut you left behind. But the shower made up for it all. We always had hot water showers. If we would have had more time, I think some of us would have stayed in there all day. But we were always on a tight schedule. It was a very efficient operation. Not only because it ran on time, but because it was well organized. It really had to be when you think of the hundreds of "knuckleheads" who were shooting a rifle for the first time in their lives.

My fondest memory from the rifle range days occurred one night after "lights out". One of our hut-mates was "Chuck" Benjamin. Chuck had been with me at the Michigan V-12, but I didn't know him very well when we were in Ann Arbor since he lived in Lloyd House and I lived in Chicago House, both in the West Quadrangle. Chuck had a wonderful singing voice, and I often wonder if he ever pursued singing as a professional. This one evening, we were lying in our bunks and we got Chuck to sing "Embraceable You". It was wonderful. Old "blue eyes" couldn't have done it any better!

I also have warm remembrances of lying on the ground behind our barracks at main side, looking up at the stars in the clear night skies. A young fellow name Daniels, an SAE fraternity brother from Denison College in Ohio was usually my star gazing companion. Daniels (for the life of me I cannot remember his first name) knew all about the constellations and he would point them out and tell about their meaning and derivation. He was an exceptionally nice fellow and one of the leaders in our platoon. In fact we had a very unusual thing occur just as we were finishing the last week or so of our training. There must have been a real need for replacements at the time because they began transferring DIs. We first lost PFC Turner and Corporal Piotrowski. Then we lost our number one DI, Platoon Sergeant Halden. Rather than bring another NCO into the platoon, they promoted two of our platoon members to PFC and made them our DIs for the final week. My friend Daniels was one of those selected.

PFC Turner was one strange dude. It seems that PFC Turner had been in the Marine Corps for ions and had been up and down in rank several times. He must have had some problem with alcohol or something like that, but he was always in top condition when he was with the platoon. He was thin, straight and tall. He had served in China and had been a member of the USMC Precision Drill Team at the 1939 Worlds Fair in New York.

Platoon Sergeant Halden was a cigar smoking, rough speaking fellow from Philadelphia, PA. In civilian life he had been a sales representative for Balfour jewelry. Balfour was one of the leading suppliers of class rings and fraternity jewelry. In that capacity he had had lots of experience with college kids. We couldn't have had a better DI at Parris Island. He was demanding and put the right amount of pressure on us at the right time. As we progressed through the training there was less and less of the outrageous shouting and "getting into your face" type of tactics.

The most outrageous act he perpetrated on us occurred in the early days of our stay at P.I. Each of us had a wooden locker box for the storage of our clothing and other items. There was a tray in the box for smaller items: razor, shaving cream, combs, etc. It was also the most likely place to keep your money and other valuables. Each recruit had his own lock to secure his locker box. Sgt. Halden kept harping on the need to secure your gear by locking the lock.

It was expected that when the order came to "Fall Out" everyone would move "on the double" and exit the barracks and get into formation. On such occasions, some of the men would forget to lock their box in the rush to move out. However, there were those that didn't want to take the time to get their keys and open the lock so they would leave the lock closed, but not locked. It appeared as if the lock was secure, but in fact it was open.

On this particular day, we were in the barracks, each of us was doing his own thing, when the DIs appeared and shouted "Fall Out"! Everyone was expected to drop what ever he was doing, dress if necessary and, before leaving, lock his locker box.

We were all in our platoon formation, standing at attention, but the DIs were still in our Squad Bay. Soon we heard a lot of noise coming from the barracks area. It sounded as if they were tearing the place apart. We remained at attention for what seemed a long time before Sergeant Halden came to the front of the formation. He said when he gave the command to "Fall Out" he wanted each of us to move "on the double" and run through our Squad Bay and out the rear exit door and once there we were to fall into formation again.

With the command "Fall Out" we all took off running and ran through the Squad Bay. What we found was that the DIs had checked everyone's locker box to see if it was properly locked. When they found one that was unlocked, they emptied the contents of the locker box into the center of the bay. As 70 men ran through the area, the contents of those unlocked boxes were getting very messed up.

Once we were in formation again in the rear of the barracks, we were ordered to do the run through the barracks again and return to our formation in the front of the barracks. After we had run through the barracks about three or four times, we were dismissed. For those who had failed to lock their boxes, they spent the rest of the day attempting to get their gear back in order. There was a lot of laundry to be done and many items were smashed and irretrievably damaged. Fortunately, I was one of the good guys that day. It was a real lesson for all and needless to say, everyone was careful to keep their locker boxes locked whenever they left the area.

As with any organization, the Marines have had many "characters" during their long history. It isn't often you get to meet or see one of the Corps' legendary characters in person, especially when you are just a "boot". During my stay on Parris Island, the day came when it was our platoon's turn to take our mattresses to be "deloused". We were told that on the next day, we should tear down our "sack" and roll up our mattresses. Our platoon would be shouldering our mattresses and marching to the Post's "delousing" plant that next day. Now that doesn't sound like it would be much fun or very interesting, but wait until you hear the rest of the story! The "delousing" plant was run by Gunnery Sergeant "Lou" Diamond. Who?

Well, during the battle at Guadalcanal in the early days of the war in the Pacific, Gunnery Sergeant "Lou" Diamond was credited with having single handedly destroyed a Japanese destroyer as it cruised by the island. "Lou" Diamond fired a mortar round that went down the stack of the Japanese vessel and caused quite a mess. Everyone in the Marine Corps and many throughout the nation had heard about "Lou" Diamond and we were thrilled with the idea of getting up close to a "legend". The day came and we marched off at "right shoulder mattresses". We got to see the legendary "Lou" Diamond up close. I guess most of us were disappointed. I don't know what we expected, but "Lou" looked like most of the old time Sergeants. He certainly wasn't a "parade ground" Marine, but just a fine looking "old salt".

There was one duty that everyone found especially abhorrent. We had to have someone on guard in the barracks throughout the nighttime hours. It was called the "Fire Watch". There probably was a good reason to have such a sentry, but after a full day of "go, go, go" everyone needed a good nights rest. The duty hours were divided into two hour "watches". The watches started at 2200 (10 PM for civilians) and continued until reveille. I caught the duty on two occasions and both times they were from 0200 to 0400 (2AM to 4AM). What a bummer! You had to be careful not to sleep, even though you were dead tired. You were to patrol the barracks area and be alert to anything unusual, but especially a fire. There was the Sergeant of the Guard who came around and checked on the sentry during each watch. I recall how tired I was during one of my watches. It had been an especially exhausting day of training and I could hardly wake up to assume the duty. During the watch, I went into the head and decided to sit on one of the toilets and rest a few minutes. It must have been only moments later when I fell sound asleep. Luckily, about an hour later, I was awakened by the sound of footsteps coming toward the head. I managed to get myself to my feet just in time to come to attention and report "all is well" to the inspecting NCO. Whew!

Finally, the "boot" training ended. We were all promoted to Private First Class. We were permitted to wear the "Globe and Anchor" on our uniforms. We were Marines! We were to ship out to Camp Lejeune, NC the next day and as a reward all the new Marines were given "Base Liberty". We could go anywhere on the base except into the WR area or the "slop chutes" in the main area of the base. The WR area was where the Women (Marines) Reserves were quartered. One could reason, restricting the ex-boots from that area made sense. Even though we were now members of the Corps, the Marines who made up the permanent station personnel didn't want a hoard of "boots" drinking beer with them. That was a little irritating, but so what, we had some "slop chutes" in the "boot" area that, previously, we had never had an opportunity to visit. The "word" was out that it would behoove all of the ex-boots to strictly adhere to the order and not enter the restricted areas. Our platoon decided to go to the movies together, so at the appropriate time we fell into ranks and marched as a unit to and from the movies. The next day, the "Scuttlebutt" was that other platoons had fellows caught in the WR area or Enlisted Clubs. The MPs had treated them harshly and some were in the hospital recovering from being cracked in the head. We had made the right decision. We were ready for Camp Lejeune! But, that's another story!

Chapter 3 What's An OCA?

Well, we were soon to learn. I never heard of an OCA before, now I *am* one! As our bus drove into the barracks area at Camp Lejeune we soon saw a whole "bunch" of OCA. It was in the early evening of January 3rd 1945, when our buses stopped along the side of one of the area mess halls. It seemed there were Marines, in T-shirts, hanging out of every window. They were cheering or jeering our arrival. I immediately recognized many of those in the windows. There was Elroy Hirsch, Farnum "Gunner" Johnson, Bob Rennebohm and my old friend and "original" Best Man, Edwin C. "Ned" Hamann. It seemed as if all of our greeters were fellows from the Michigan V-12 Unit and they were on mess duty! Later it became obvious why they were cheering. With our arrival, their class moved one step closer to the final phase of the commissioning process. Now we were the new group of "boot" Officer Candidate Applicants, or OCA.

With the exception of Ned Hamann, I didn't get to see any of the others again. Of that group Elroy "Crazy Legs" Hirsch was the most famous. Elroy had been the star running back with the 1942 Wisconsin football team. At Michigan he lettered in four sports. After the war, Elroy Hirsch went on to star with the Los Angeles Rams and was All-Pro for many years. They even made the movie "Crazy Legs" about his football exploits. Later, he was appointed as the Athletic Director at the University of Wisconsin.

Having traveled all day by bus from Parris Island, we were desperately hungry. So, after we removed our gear from the buses and stacked them on the blacktop we moved into the mess hall. We were pleasantly surprised to find the food was being served family style and we were eating off of plates. No more metal trays, but cups and plates. We were now OCA, and maybe there was something to this idea of being "an officer and a gentleman".

After dinner we were directed to our barracks. After we were partially settled in, we had a chance to visit with some of our old friends. Ned Hamann and his group had left Michigan one semester before us. Now, we had caught up with them, so to speak, in about two months.

The OCA organization had been positioned between "Boot" camp and the Officer Candidates School at Quantico, VA less than a year before we arrived. It provided another opportunity for the Marine Corps to screen the applicants for commissioning. It also allowed for better management of the facilities at Quantico. Some OCA classes remained at Lejeune for longer periods than others. Therefore, we really didn't know how long we would be at Lejeune. As it turned out, the first of my group, of which I was a member, left for Quantico on the 14th of February, with only six weeks of OCA time at Lejeune.

It was a real treat to be at Camp Lejeune after Parris Island. The base reminded me of a college campus, albeit a new one without the halls of ivy. The buildings were of red brick with white wood trim and were of the Georgian style of architecture. The term "Camp" generally implies a "temporary" military location. There was nothing "temporary" about Camp Lejeune! The grounds were spacious and well kept. There were wide drives, large theatres and service clubs that would rival any large city.

It wasn't long before we began a rigorous training schedule. It was Reveille at 0530, Classes starting a 0630, Close Order drill, field exercises, more classes, and "Base Liberty" starting at 1030 unless we were held over! Another "rat race"!

This was my first experience with "chits". We had a "chit" for everything. Laundry was sent out to a base laundry (limited to 10 articles a week) and you needed a "chit" to get it back. If you went to one of the area service clubs ("slop chutes"), you bought a "chit" to surrender for a beer. There was a "chit" for this and a "chit" for that. But the 'chit" that gave us the most concern was the one the supervising Officers or NCOs put in your file.

Each of these "overseers" carried a small pad of preprinted forms to be checked if the Officer or NCO noted something "Good" or "Bad" about your behavior or performance. So there were "Good Chits" and "Bad Chits". All of these "chits" were put into your file, along with your tests and other evaluations. When it came time for the decision as to whether you moved on to Quantico, a screening board of officers and NCOs would review your file and make the decision. It behooved you to not accumulate many "bad chits". They used to say, "there are good chits and there are bad chits, but they're mostly bad"! So, it was quite unnerving at times, when you would see one of the command looking in your direction while filling out a "chit".

Everyday, we would have a "Mail Call". All of us would "fall out" in formation in front of our barracks. Soon the Mail Orderly, a Corporal of the permanent staff, would be seen coming out of the barracks dragging several large mailbags behind him. As my story unfolds you will learn that our Corporal was not the brightest bulb on the tree.

Everyone, with no exception, anxiously awaited Mail Call. It was the highlight of the day. So you know any screw-up in our mail delivery was not well received.

Eventually our Corporal would reach the center of the company and order "At Ease" and begin taking bunches of letters from one of the bags. There were about 150 men in our company. We reasoned if he were going to deliver each letter individually it would require an unacceptable amount of time to deliver all the letters. We couldn't understand why he couldn't figure out a more efficient method of distributing the mail.

As this slow process continued, there would be this buzz among the troops as they became increasingly perturbed. Everyone was unhappy, but frustrated as to what could be done about the situation. In a way it was also very funny. There was a lot of snickering and outright laughter as the bumbling Corporal mauled the mail. The Corporals inability to pronounce the addressees name was the circumstance that usually brought down the house,

Day after day, after he mangled one name after another the laughter would get a bit too loud and he would fail to see the humor and he would get mad. He would throw all the mail back into the bags and drag them back to his mailroom in the barracks. I am exaggerating with the example I use when telling this story, but not much.

He would hold a letter in front of his face for several moments, then speak.."Ja...Jo...Jo-Nezz". Everyone was silent wondering what name he was trying to pronounce. Then he would spell the name "J..O..N..E..S". With that the men would howl in laughter. He would become infuriated; put the letters back in the bag and leave.

This went on for about a week, and eventually (so we heard) the Camp Postal Inspector checked his storeroom and found many bags of undelivered mail. With a new Mail Orderly on the job, the problem of poor mail delivery was over...and so were a lot of laughs!

At Lejeune we had the opportunity to handle all of the infantry weapons and we fired these weapons in simulated combat exercises. Additionally, there were many demonstrations of other weapons, which, in some instances, we found very amazing, and always interesting. One such demonstration that sticks in my memory was on the day we traveled out to an area where the Demolition people "played" with the high explosives.

I don't use the word "play" lightly. These people had to be a bit "whacko" from the nonchalant manner with which they handled the explosive material. After we witnessed several "shows" using dynamite, TNT, plastic explosives, bangalore torpedoes, and what have you, they provided us with a "hands on" experience.

There were about 150 OC Applicants in our group. Each of us was handed a ¼ pound block of TNT and a fuse. After we placed the fuse in the block, they put us in single file and we moved down one of the dirt roads in the area. The road was essentially the two tracks made by the wheels of vehicles that used the road. When all of us were positioned along one edge of this narrow road in single file, we were instructed, on command, to light the fuses and toss the block of TNT as far as we could to this one side of the road, then walk, not run, briskly to the other side of the road. So on command, we lit the fuse, hurled the block away from the road as far as possible, turned and walked about 15 feet to the other side of the road. About the time we reached the opposite side of the road, there was this huge explosion behind us. It sounded like a ton of TNT going off at one time. We could feel the rush of air and debris on our backs. The thought occurred to me that this must be as it is in combat, with explosives going off very close to you.

Those fellows I mentioned as part of the "welcoming committee" when we arrived at Camp Lejeune, moved on about a month before my group was transferred to Quantico. I was in the first group of about 60 who were selected to leave Camp Lejeune and start the final phase. We were all "gung ho" to finish up this long journey to the 2nd Lieutenant bars. Up until then, we were starting to believe the saying that V-12 stood for "Victory in 12 Years or Fight". But, that's another story!

Chapter 4   Gold Bars or Bust

Finally, the day had come. We arrived at the Marine Corps Schools, Quantico, Virginia! It was on the 14th of February 1945 when our group finally reached the last rung in the ladder to those "gold bars". We were designated the 7th Platoon Commanders Class (PLC). I became a member of Company "E" commanded by a Captain Does. Captain W. B. Does had seen combat in the Pacific as evidenced by the many rows of ribbons he wore on his uniform blouse. I don't recall ever having a conversation with the Captain, but I wouldn't have been anxious to meet him in those days. Those who had the occasion to visit with the Captain were probably not there by choice. "Keep your nose clean" and stay out of the Captain's office was the general sentiment among the new "Officer Candidates". We now replaced the silver OCA pins on our shirt collars and caps, with silver OC pins.

My Platoon Leader was a 2nd Lieutenant E. R. Scotcher. He had graduated only few months earlier and had been assigned to this OC training job. He had not been overseas. The Lieutenant was one fine officer and individual. His command presence was such that we did what he ordered promptly and ungrudgingly. We considered him to be supportive. If someone had a problem, he could approach the Lieutenant knowing he would help him if it were possible. I had such an occasion as we neared graduation, and I will relate the incident later in this recollection of my days with the 7th PLC at Quantico.

Quantico was a much older Marine installation than Camp Lejeune, but the barracks and other structures were very impressive and in good condition. Our squad bay was located on the second deck (floor) of Barracks "C". About half of the 7th PLC, was in the center squad bay, which was filled with double bunks. I had a lower bunk on the center "aisle" in the sleeping area. Harold Hatch, a fellow from the State of Illinois, occupied the upper bunk. Harold, or "Hal" as we called him, had very ruddy cheeks. I always said he looked as if he had just "plowed the back 40" and he may have in earlier days, because he had some of the characteristics I had always associated with a farmer. He spoke in a cautious manner and was always polite and considerate. We had been placed close to each other ever since Parris Island because of our surnames. Harris and Hatch. Our names were next to each other on the roster and consequently we ended up next to each other in formation, bunking etc. Again, more on Hal Hatch later, because that is another story!

The training at Quantico was about equally divided between classroom studies and fieldwork. Upon arrival we were issued a stack of textbooks, so many that it was difficult to carry them back to the barracks. We went over much of the previous weapons instruction, but in considerably more detail. We were now studying such subjects like Terrain Appreciation, Aerial Photography Interpretation, Infantry Tactics as well as the tactics for employing mortars and machine guns in both the offense and defense. Each of the subjects was weighted as to their considered importance. A grade of 70 was the passing grade. So the product of the grade and the weight yielded points. Accumulating the required point total minimum for the whole course was the goal. You may earn less than the passing grade of 70 in one subject area, but you needed to meet the overall goal. In fact, I received a score of 68 on "81 MM Mortars in the Attack" on April 28th 1945, the day our son Robert was born. I don't know if there is any connection, but I now have no difficulty remembering the date of my one failing grade!

The operations in the field are where the training took a step up. We had been out on various field exercises at Camp Lejeune, but here the training was aimed at developing troop leaders. Each time we were in the field, we were putting the classroom studies on tactics and related areas, into practice. Each of the candidates had an opportunity to operate in the different positions in the Infantry Company, platoon or squad. On one occasion, you may be the Platoon Leader and on another a rifleman in a squad. You were provided many opportunities to make decisions in the various combat type exercises and your performance was noted in the "chits". Oh yes, the "chits" were present at Quantico too! We didn't leave them behind at Lejeune.

One thing one learned is that as an officer you cannot escape responsibility. You are in charge and if someone doesn't follow your orders and "messes" up the operation, you are the one who gets the blame. No excuses. The "buck stops" with you.

Most of us probably dreaded the time when the "role" assignments were announced. Most of us would sigh with relief if we were to serve as a "lowly" rifleman. But eventually, you were assigned a command position with responsibilities. There was no way to avoid being judged as a leader.

In these exercises, blank ammunition was used and the "enemy" troops were Marines from the Training Command at Quantico. Most of the "enemy" had served in the Pacific, which made the "combat" even more realistic. Most of them had experienced the real thing.

I recall the day I was first assigned to command a platoon. The situation was that we were in open terrain, and we were to move into the nearby tree line and search and destroy the enemy. They were expected to be small in number, but dug in. We were warned about snipers in the trees or the enemy hidden in holes, covered by leaves, who would allow your troops to pass over them, then come out of their holes and fire upon you from the rear. I assembled my squad leaders and issued my orders for the attack.

We moved through the open ground without any problem and entered the woods. We had not faced any opposition, when just a few yards from where I was standing, one of the riflemen spotted what he thought was an enemy position. He had noticed something unusual about a tree. Where the tree roots enter the ground, he noticed an opening in one of the "Y" areas. Without hesitation he moved quickly to the tree, pushed the barrel of rifle into the hole and fired. The Umpire for the exercise, immediately blew his whistle, the signal for "stop everything". Not long after a "trap door" near the tree opened and a couple of the "enemy" emerged, each holding his ears. Can you imagine being in a small hole under a tree and having someone fire a blank charge into your confined space? I don't know whether the fellows lost their eardrums with that explosion or not, but I am certain they had a real headache for days to come. We continued the patrol and everything went very well. I received a "good chit", in spite of my trooper's exuberance.

However, on another field problem I was tagged with a "bad" chit where I thought they carried the notion of "responsibility" too far. Our company was in the field firing 30 caliber Heavy Machine Guns in Defense. There was a line of machine gun positions set up along a ridgeline. Each of the guns was responsible to set their line of fire on a given compass direction. It simulated a final line of defense situation where the machine guns interlocked their base lines of fire.

I was given a simple job. My job was to check out one compass for each gun position, deliver these compasses, one compass to each position and at the end of the exercise, pick them up and return them to the weapons storeroom. Now what is simpler than that? I delivered the compasses as ordered and then joined my gun section. We fired for several hours, the sun was setting and it came time to terminate the exercise. When the order to "Secure" was given, everyone began tearing everything down and moving rapidly to the waiting trucks. Everyone was eager to get back to the base. I had not been given any advance warning on the "Secure" so I found myself moving down the line from one position to another picking up the compasses while everyone was in motion. When it was all over I was short one compass. Upon return to base, I moved through the company asking if someone had the missing compass. The replies were all negative. So I had to report that I had "lost" one compass.

The people in charge of the exercise were very upset and I thought they were going to make a Federal case of it. I received a "Very Bad Chit" for my failure to exercise my responsibility to collect all of the compasses. It troubled me for several weeks, since once you received a "bad" chit; it drew more than the usual attention to you. When you are "spotlighted" the chances of getting more chits are increased. And remember there were "good" chits and "bad" chits, but mostly "bad". However, even that would pass, but it sure was worrisome at the time.

Not all my "problems" were that serious. Most of the Marines slept in their "skivvies", their boxer shorts and a "T' shirts. Since a young fellow I had always slept in pajamas, and I didn't intend to change unless absolutely necessary. Our routine in the barracks at Quantico was to shower and shave at night, just before "lights out". My routine was after showering, I would put on my pajamas and parade through the squad bay to my bunk. Every evening as I walked towards my bunk, many of the Marines would "hoot and howl" at me and make threats. I believe I was the only one in the squad bay who wore pajamas. They threatened to take my pajamas and tear them up for rifle rags, etc. It was all in fun and the more they carried on, the more I made of the fact that I was wearing the PJs.

During the section on Demolitions, we studied the characteristics and the best uses of the explosive materials and weapons that would be available to us as infantry officers. One such use was that of "Cratering". I suspect those familiar with strip mining would recognize what we were learning to do. As a class problem we calculated the number of holes, their depth, the distance between holes and the amount of explosives for each hole that was required to "blow" the desired crater. The following day the class went into the field and put our theory into practice. We dug the required number of holes to the calculated depth along this ridgeline. Then we carefully placed the amount of TNT that we had figured was required into each of the holes. The fusing was electrical; so when the system was completely connected we could fire all of the holes with the generator. You would recognize the generator from the movies. It was a box with a plunger. When you pushed down on the plunger it would cause an electric current to be generated that would fire the fused explosives.

After our group had prepared all the charges for the cratering, we moved over a few ridges from the area to be cratered. Finally the time came for the firing. "Fire In The Hole". The plunger was slammed down and in just a moment the whole cratered ridgeline was blown sky high. We all watched the dirt and rocks rising skyward and then they began their return to earth. We began to feel the small particles of dirt striking us and we all moved back away from the falling dirt. The particles seemed to be getting larger and some good-sized pieces of rock began to fall uncomfortably close. Soon it was all over and we issued a sigh of relief. About then, there was the cry for a Corpsman down the line from where I was standing. It seems that one of the falling rocks had struck one of our men.

My friend "Whitey" Adams was standing right next to the fellow who was hit in the head. As "Whitey" later described it to us, a good-sized rock had hit this Marine in the right front of his head, it crushed in his steel helmet and there was blood and bone and tissue showing. By the time the ambulance arrived, we all knew there was little or no hope for his survival. His name was Beers. He was from Missouri and his wife had just recently arrived in Quantico for a visit. On the next day a group of us were walking from the base into the town of Quantico. The railroad station is adjacent to the road leading into the town. We saw his flag draped coffin sitting on a railroad carriage on the station platform. It was a very sad day for all of us.

About a week or so later, it was a sad day for "Whitey" Adams too. No, "Whitey" wasn't killed or injured. Fortunately there was only that one casualty in any group of which I was a member during all of the training we conducted. "Whitey" had been with me at Michigan V-12, through P.I. and the OCA at Camp Lejeune. They convened their first screening board for the 7th PLC and "Whitey" was cut from the program. I wasn't familiar with how well he was doing in the class work or whether he had some bad experiences in the field exercises, but for whatever reason "Whitey" was shipped out of the program. I thought then and I still think "Whitey" would have made one fine officer. Like most of us, we had been ordering Officer's uniforms, and "Whitey" had all of his in hand. With this shortly following Beer's death, it reminded all of us that you could be here one day and gone the next. I never saw "Whitey" again after he left the program.

While at Quantico, we were given weekend "Liberty". With Washington, D.C. only a short bus or train ride away, it was the most popular liberty destination. Groups of PLC Marines would go together and rent a suite in one of the big hotels, such as the Willard, for the weekend. . The stories about the partying, if only half true, were of lots of booze and women. Now, I know what you are thinking, but I honestly never participated. I would spend my weekends in Washington at my cousin Lorraine's apartment in nearby Maryland. Lorraine's husband, Glow Snyder was employed in the Federal Government's agency dealing with the allocation of petroleum. They had a young daughter, Joyleen and Lorraine was expecting her second child. Their place became my home away from home. Lorraine would prepare fine meals and Glow would ply me with beer. Lorraine and Joyleen escorted me around the "must see" places in Washington such as the Capitol and the National Archives.

When Marie was eight months pregnant, my mother and Marie came to Washington to visit. They rode the train and traveled by coach. During the war years the trains were always crowded. It was not unusual for some passengers to stand up for miles and miles, if not their entire journey. They stayed at Lorraine's apartment during the four or five days they were in the area. On two occasions, they traveled to Quantico from Washington by train, and I was able to meet them and show them around the base, have dinner in the PX cafeteria and put them back on the train in the evening for their trip back to Lorraine's place. Marie seemed to bear up quite well during all this traveling, but when we talk about it today, we wonder why she ever made such trip in her late stages of the pregnancy. I got to stay over with Marie at Lorraine's one night. It was an experience I will not forget. It was the first time I ever slept with a *very* pregnant woman. I did have an opportunity to feel the baby kicking and that was quite a thrill for a soon-to-be Daddy!

Left: Marie and me in front of apartment of cousin Lorraine Snyder in Maryland suburb of Washington, D.C. in February 1945, just one month before the birth of our son!

On April 28th 1945, we were in the field all day and I had taken the "RP" (Required Problem, same as a test) on the 81 mm Mortars in the Attack. It turned out to be the only RP that I failed in the whole course. After returning to the barracks, I found I had a telegram waiting for me. It was a message from my father informing me that I was a "father of a baby boy…and mother and child were doing well". I don't remember if I tried to telephone or not, but I do know that I wanted to celebrate. I couldn't make too much of a fuss about being a new "daddy" so I only told a few of my closest buddies. We didn't have liberty to leave the base, but I needed to do something special!

It so happens there was a band playing at the base that evening, Blue Barron and his Orchestra. He didn't play my kind of music. His music is what I used to refer to as the "Mickey Mouse" sound. Guy Lombardo, Sammy Kaye and a few other bands were of the same ilk. However, we did go and listen a bit, but it wasn't much fun, so I returned to the barracks and proceeded to tell more of my friends about my new status in life.

When I signed up in the USMC Reserve Class IIIb, the Marine's Officer Candidate program, the regulations forbid marriage before commissioning. In fact, several Marines were kicked out of the program during the Michigan V-12 days, when it was discovered they were married. Consequently, when Marie and I were married, we attempted to keep the news of our marriage "close to the vest" so I would not suffer the same fate. So, here I was with only a week or so to go before receiving my commission and I was not only married, I was also a father. It looked like I was going to keep our marriage a secret all the way, but something unexpected happened.

A few of us in the 7th PLC had been selected to go to the Officer's Field Artillery School after graduating and being commissioned. The Field Artillery school was located at Quantico, but on the other side of the base. There was a BOQ (Bachelor Officers Quarters) located directly across the street from the Field Artillery school. It was called the "Cinder City" BOQ for reasons unknown to me. The BOQs in Quantico were fairly crowded and the Cinder City BOQ was always filled because of its desirable location near the schools.

Our Lieutenant Scotcher, doing his best to help his men, had reserved several rooms at the Cinder City BOQ for those men in his platoon who had been selected to attend the Field Artillery school. He was quite proud of his accomplishment and he was telling some of the others who were selected of their good fortune. One of the members of the group was Joe Fox from Chicago. Joe's families were the Foxes of the Fox Deluxe Beer, which was popular in Chicago in those days.

Lieutenant Scotcher had just said "I have a room for you, and you and you and Harris and..." when Joe Fox blurted out, "Oh, Harris won't need a room, he is going to live in Fredericksburg with his wife and child". This surprised the Lieutenant and he told them to let me know he wanted to see me as soon as possible.

When I returned to the Barracks, I learned of Fox's "misspoke" and I reported to the Lieutenant as ordered. I thought the "jig" was up. He asked me if I was married and I answered in the affirmative. Then he said something like, "Why in the hell didn't you tell me about it...we could have taken care of it...you could have been drawing money for your dependents...etc." Evidently the regulations had been changed or relaxed and I probably could have declared my wife and son as dependent and received some cash allowances for them.

However, I wasn't anxious to test the system and file any claims; I was more than satisfied to learn I was not going to be booted out of the program at this late date.

After I received notice I was going to be ordered to the Field Artillery School, I began spending my weekend liberty periods searching for a house to rent. The Field Artillery School class would be running from late June to late August. So I was looking in the neighboring communities for a small apartment to accommodate my new family. The best I could find was a large bedroom, with a shared bath with another bedroom on the second floor of an old house. The house was located on Charles Street in an older section of historic Fredericksburg, VA, about twenty some miles south of Quantico. Sounds rather strange but how it all worked out is another story!

While we had been measured and fit for our new officer uniforms for a couple of months, in the last days before commissioning the whole package was coming together. We each had an allowance of $200 for uniforms, but in fact the required uniforms and accessories ran about twice that amount. At the time we were required to have the winter uniform, a green elastique; the summer, a tropical worsted tan one; the hat with visor, with green and tan tops; six officer shirts and field scarves (ties) and an overcoat! The overcoat was of green elastique and tailored form fitting. It was a very fine coat, but was really a waste of money. But we were required to have it in our kit.

Finally on June 6th 1945, we marched to the main theatre in the PX building at Quantico. We were all wearing our new officer's uniforms minus the bars of a Second Lieutenant. We filed into the theatre and after a few unremarkable and unmemorable speeches by some high-ranking officers we rose to our feet and took the oath of office *en masse*. We all helped each other with the pinning on of the "gold bars" and once dismissed, we individually filed out of the theatre. There we were greeted by a number of Marines who were anxious to collect the dollar for each "First Salute" rendered to the new officers. I didn't want to break the traditional ritual, so I reluctantly surrendered a dollar bill to the first one to salute me. I felt like asking him why he wasn't somewhere were he was supposed to be, rather than standing outside the theatre "saluting for dollars" Bah! Humbug!

I don't know how I traveled to the Washington airport, but I know that I flew a Pennsylvania Central Airlines plane from D.C. to Detroit, where my father and mother, wife and son met me. What a wonderful day! A new officer and a new father all in one day!

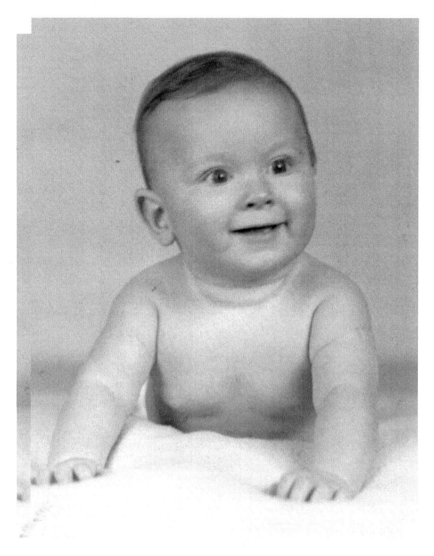

This is our son, Robert James Harris, born April 28, 1945 at Women's Hospital in Flint, Michigan. I saw him for the first time and held him on June 6, 1945 after flying to Detroit following my commissioning at the Marine Corps Schools, Quantico, Virginia.

Chapter 5   Fredericksburg, Our First Home

When I learned I was to receive orders to attend the Field Artillery School and stay in Quantico, VA after commissioning, I began to search for a house in the nearby communities. It would be the first chance for Marie and me to have our own "home". And now with our little baby boy, we looked forward to being a family.

Every weekend for several weeks prior to commissioning, I would look for a suitable place to rent. It was especially difficult to get around without a car. The first place I scoured was the little town of Quantico with no luck. I even found the apartment where Tyrone Power and his wife, Annabella, rented while he was stationed at Quantico. But, like all the other apartments in the small town, it was not available. However, I did get lucky in the city of Fredericksburg, about 20 miles or so from the base.

I was pleased to find a very large bedroom for rent on Charles Street in the historic section of the city. In the backyard of this house was a large oak tree with a sign saying George Washington had planted the tree. This neighborhood had survived the Union attack during the Civil War. It was a street of very large and very old houses.

A widowed lady, a Mrs. Pearson, was the owner of the house, and she was renting out three of her unused bedrooms. We were fortunate to be able to rent one of the two upstairs bedrooms. .

After a short leave in Michigan, Marie and I, with our infant son, flew back to Washington and took a train to Fredericksburg. It was after dark when our cab pulled up to the house at 1210 Charles Street. It was obvious Marie was not prepared for what she found. Somehow my description of our "new home"…our first home…led her to believe it was more than it was in actuality. She was shocked. I thought she was going to cry. She seemed to be in that "go home to Mother" mood or perhaps it was just the "shock". It didn't get any better when we finally made our way up to our room.

The room was furnished with a huge four-poster bed. It also had a chest of drawers, an antique wardrobe and a couple of chairs. We had access to the bathroom through a door from our bedroom. However, we were required to share the bathroom with the occupants of the second bedroom. Thankfully, the occupants of that bedroom had to use a door off the hallway.

We were traveling very light compared to how people travel today. The fact is we had very little in the way of clothes or other possessions. Mrs. Pearson provided a crib and she had already placed it in the room. The crib fit nicely along the side of the huge ante bellum four-poster. Later, when we acquired a baby buggy we were allowed to keep it in the foyer on the first floor of the house.

In spite of her disappointment with the lodgings, Marie soon had our "first home" in good order, even to the placement of a bottle warmer on the marble top of the ancient chest of drawers. It wasn't much but it was ours. The tears and the shock subsided and she made it work!

In the weeks prior to our arrival, I had another "big" problem to solve. Transportation! We didn't own an automobile! How was I going to get to and from Quantico every day? But here again, fortune smiled. There were four other new 2nd Lieutenants who would be in the Artillery School with me and they were living in Fredericksburg. Two of them had cars and they were willing to provide our transportation.

Cassius DeRahm and Clint Murchison, Jr. both had cars. DeRahm's was a big 1941 Desoto and Murchison had a 1941 Chrysler Station Wagon. Three of us, Fred C. McGlone, Joe Davis and me were *sans* vehicular transportation, and we were happy to be their passengers.

"Bud" McGlone and I were fraternity brothers at Michigan State College and we had moved together through the V-12 at Michigan, "Boot" camp, OCA and PLC. "Bud" and his new wife Ann had been married in Michigan during the leave following our graduation from PLC. He had not been able to find a place to rent and they were living in a hotel room in downtown Fredericksburg. While Marie and I were at their hotel visiting one evening, we told them about the "extra" bedroom at our house on Charles Street. It seemed to be as good, if not better, than a hotel room, and a lot less expensive, so they moved into the "room" next to us.

Our two-month old son had the "colic" most of the time we lived on Charles Street. Night after night, he would wake up screaming.

Marie and I would take turns walking the floor with the young fellow. It was very disruptive of our sleep, and I know Bud and Ann in the next room must have found it very disturbing too. Perhaps that is why they found another place to live about a month later. If so, I don't blame them, but there was little we could do about the problem.

In 1945 young mothers didn't have the convenience of paper diapers or diaper service. Marie had to deal with the cotton cloth diapers, which had to be washed, and dried every day, including Sundays. The only place she had to wash the diapers was in the large bathtub. So she would wash these diapers, leaning over the tub. After rinsing and wringing the diapers with her hands, she would take them to the backyard and hang them on the clothesline to dry. But look at the bright side. There aren't many kids who can say their diapers were dried on a clothesline attached to a tree planted by George Washington!

It was necessary to eat all of our meals in a restaurant. However, it wasn't all that bad. We would put Bobby in the buggy and walk about a block down Charles Street than left another short block to the Kenmore Inn. The inn was on the basement level of the corner building. We would place Bobby's buggy at the foot of the cement stairs leading down to the restaurant. We were usually joined at dinner by other young Marine couples who lived in the area and were living under similar circumstances. The people who ran the restaurant were extremely friendly and accommodating. The food was excellent and the menu choices varied from day to day. And best of all, the prices were reasonable. Our experience with dining at the Kenmore is one of the best memories of our time in Fredericksburg.

There was a very old lady living across the street from our place on Charles Street. Marie would take Bobby for a walk in his buggy and on occasion would stop and visit with the woman as she sat on her porch. She would tell Marie of her remembrances of the Civil War. When she was a young child she lived in the very same house during the battle for Fredericksburg. She recalled the bombardment and the occupation of the city by the Union forces. Her parents hid themselves and their children in some spaces above the ceiling as the Union soldiers searched the rooms below them.

Fredericksburg was a treasure for American History buffs. Unfortunately, we were too busy at the time to really spend much time visiting the historic sites that surrounded us. James Monroe's law offices were only a two blocks down Charles Street from where we lived, however, I hardly recall going inside to look at the items they had on display. I do remember visiting a stonewall behind which you could still see the shallow trenches that had once been occupied by Confederate soldiers during the battle for the city. A couple of streets over from Charles Street is the historic Kenmore mansion. It is a walled residence with several out buildings where the slaves did the cooking and laundry and cared for the horses and carriages. We did visit the Kenmore and after the tour, we partook of their famous Gingerbread.

Soon after the McGlones left Charles Street, we found a small apartment on Winchester Street and for the first time we had our own kitchen, toilet, front room and a separate bedroom.

The one story house had a covered porch across the front and our front door, along with the owner's front door, opened on to the porch. You might say the house was a "duplex", however it was not originally built to be a two family house. I suspect the war-created housing shortage induced the owner to modify the structure and create a rental unit. In any case, it was a very pleasant change from living in one room. Now, in addition to the task of caring for a three-month old son, Marie had the opportunity to cook and clean. More work, it would appear, but I think she enjoyed having the new jobs.

Our kitchen was the passageway between the bedroom and the bathroom. Talk about galley kitchens! It was very narrow with just enough room for a stove and a small kitchen table. We shared a refrigerator with the owners. It was located on the back porch. Since neither party had a lot of food that required refrigeration, there was amble space for both parties. The apartment was furnished and the bedroom and the front room, while small, were very comfortable for our small family. There were two incidents, which occurred in that apartment which fix my mental picture of the front room.

One evening while I was still on duty, probably on a night exercise, Marie was sitting on the couch in the front room. It was a warm night and she had the front door open and the screen door locked. All of a sudden she saw a man's face in the window directly in front of her. The window was on the side of the house and a bit higher than the normal house window. She screamed and ran next door to the owner's apartment.   The owner searched the premises with no success. Marie and Bobby stayed with our landlords until I returned home later that evening. Marie still shudders when she remembers and relives that terrifying experience with a "peeping tom".

The second incident was not as frightening as Marie's. It's easy for me to say that, but I don't know if Bobby would have agreed. This occurred as I was attempting to be a "good father" and helping the mother. I was in the process of trimming young Bobby's fingernails with a small clipper. After I had successfully clipped several of the nails on his tiny fingers, and started on the next one, he suddenly screamed as if I was killing him. I soon learned I had taken a small piece of the skin along with his tiny nail. It just made me sick. Even today, when I am trimming my own nails, I think about the time I almost "guillotined" one of my son's fingers

Joe and Jennie Davis were very good friends of ours. They were from a town in the "boot heel" section of Missouri and Joe's family was in the cotton gin business. They had a one-year-old child living in Missouri with one of the grandparents. Jennie would often accompany Marie as she walked around Fredericksburg pushing Bobby in the buggy. After moving into our apartment, Joe and Jennie would join us in the evening to sit with us on the porch of our new home. Our favorite beverage during those warm Virginia nights was the "Tom Collins". We would sit and talk while enjoying a few relaxing drinks. My recollection of one such get together is very vivid. The decision made that evening changed all of our lives.

It was a few days after VJ day. The school had posted a notice on our bulletin board. It requested those officers interested in applying for a "regular" commission in the Marine Corps to indicate their interest by putting their name on the list. Most, if not all, of the officers in our class were commissioned as "reserve" officers. The opportunity to begin a career as a regular Marine officer was presented to us. Joe and I were the only officers to sign the sheet indicating our interest in becoming regular officers.

The four of us sat on our porch that evening, partaking of our favorite beverage, and discussing our intention to stay in the Marine Corps as "regular" officers. Most of the men in service during World War II had this great urge to return to civilian life. Everyone seemed to want to "go home". Even those of us, who thought about making the military service a career, could feel the pressure to "get out". There was this "herd instinct". If everyone else was getting out, why should I stay in? There was this "band wagon" going down the hill towards home and it seemed only a fool wouldn't jump on the wagon. Marie and Jennie were evidently quite persuasive that evening or it may have been the quantity of gin we consumed. In any case, the next day, both Joe and I removed our names from the list.

At Fenton High School, one of Marie's classmates and a friend of ours was Ione Rounds. Ione had married a Marine aviator, a Major named William Bachelor. It so happened that the Major was stationed at Quantico and they lived in Fredericksburg. Ione became one of the "girls" with whom Marie would get together during the days when all the "hubbies" were doing their Marine Corps thing. The Bachelors had rented a whole house. I figure if I had the pay of a Major plus flight pay, I would have rented a house too!

While we Lieutenant husbands didn't associate with the Major, Ione did not wear his rank and she hosted the ladies on many occasions. On those afternoons at Ione's, the ladies would partake of the generous bar maintained by the Major. Marie said there were a few days after their afternoon "tea" when it was a bit difficult to push the buggy back home and get the dinner cooked before I arrived. I think she was exaggerating because I never noticed any impairment. It was a pretty stressful time for young wives and especially young mothers. They deserved to relax and enjoy the good times with their friends.

Many years later, Marie and I visited Ione and Bill Bachelor at their home in Pasadena. He was then a pilot for Pan American and was one of the first to navigate the polar route to Europe from California.

The automobile owners, Cassius DeRahm and Clint Murchison, Jr. were from wealthy families. DeRahm's father was a New York banker. Clint's father was a famous Texas oil and cattle kingpin.

At the time, I knew Clint came from a wealthy family, because he had also rented a whole house and he had this large Chrysler station wagon. However, it wasn't until years later I realized just how rich he really was. I believe I learned about his family from a cover story in *Time* magazine that told of Clint Murchison and Sid Richardson, the Texan Multi-Millionaires. I recall Clint telling me on one occasion about spending his summers as a youngster on the coastal islands off Texas, where his family had some cattle ranches. Regardless, Clint was a regular fellow, a genuinely nice guy.

The duty as a student at the Field Artillery School was very enjoyable. We were officers and we were treated as officers. For the most part our instructors were officers. We studied all aspects of Field Artillery during our course of study and spent a liberal amount of time in the field. Being an artillery officer was exactly what I wanted to be in the Marine Corps. To me it was the perfect combination of duties requiring both leadership skills and technical knowledge. Probably because of my education in mathematics, the fire direction and surveying aspects of artillery were the most interesting. I was very anxious to finish the school and join a Marine artillery unit in the field. However, it didn't work out that way until several years later.

The war in Europe had been over for sometime and our forces in the Pacific were on a "collision" course with mainland Japan. Okinawa had been seized and the United States was preparing for the invasion of the Japanese home islands. It promised to be a very rough time for all, because the Japanese were expected to fight to the death in defense of their homeland. On this day in August, we were conducting a field exercise which, involved artillery on the march. My particular assignment on the exercise was to provide security for the unit along a road leading to the gun position. I had set up a 105mm Howitzer along side of the road just below the crest of a hill. In this defensive position we were ready to counter any "enemy" movement down the road towards the "friendlies". It was in the mid afternoon, when suddenly a Jeep, traveling at a high speed came over the crest of the road. The driver and his passenger were waving their arms and yelling. When they reached our position we learned of Japan's surrender. After that news, no one wanted to continue "playing war" so the command "C-S-M-O" (Close Station, March Order) the Artillery's equivalent to the infantry's "SECURE", was given and we all returned to base and took off for home.

That evening, Marie and I put Bobby in his buggy and walked to downtown Fredericksburg where we thought we would find the citizens on the street celebrating the end of the war in the Pacific. To our surprise, there were very few people on the streets and there was no evidence of any celebration. We returned to our apartment, happy with the news, but disappointed with the absence of a celebration.

On October 3rd 1945, I graduated from the Field Artillery School and I was granted 14 days of leave. Following the leave period I had orders to report to the Commanding General, Camp Lejeune, NC for further assignment. Since I had indicated I did not want to be considered for a commission in the regular Marine Corps, I didn't know what to expect. I could be assigned to any vacant Lieutenant's billet in the Corps anywhere in the world.

The three of us were flying back to Michigan and we planned for Marie and Bobby to stay with her parents until I knew where I was going to be stationed. Then, depending on the location and living conditions at the new post, they would join me there.

On graduation day, one incident occurred immediately following the ceremony that, even today, has us dumbfounded. Soon after the ceremony ended, we were asked to come to the school's office. The officer there told us our former landlords had phoned the school and reported they had inspected our apartment after we had left and found we had "ruined" a mattress. They said it had been extensively damaged and stained by urine, probably baby's urine. Our former landlords were asking the Marine Corps to hold up our transfer until they were reimbursed for the damaged mattress.

We had maintained cordial relations with the owners, even though they had not been overly friendly. Marie swore she had never placed Bobby on our bed and further, she had changed the sheets regularly, even that very morning, and she never observed any staining or damage to the mattress. The officer was inclined to believe our statement, since it was a common "trick" by landlords to demand reimbursement for damages just as their tenant was about to be transferred. Whether their claim was justified or not, it appeared to be a "racket"...a way to extort some easy money. We were certain their claim was unjustified, so we continued on our way to Michigan.

Our plane was to leave the airport in Washington, D.C. and a classmate, a Dutch Marine Captain, drove us to the airport. Following graduation, class members went in separate directions and for the most part we never saw each other again. I saw Bud and Clint about eight months later at Great Lakes, but that's another story!

Chapter 6   Goose Creek

After a short stay in Michigan, I left Marie and our young son, Bobby in Fenton with Marie's parents and I made my way to Camp Lejeune, North Carolina as ordered. The flight from Detroit to Washington was a miserable ride, there were those summer storms in the East and the sky was not very friendly. In fact, the flight was diverted to Baltimore and I had to take a train to Washington. It was a very early morning train and the only passengers in the car with me were members of the King Cole Trio! But, that's another story!

I was able to get a ride in a small Navy aircraft from NAS, Anacostia to one of MCAS, Cherry Point's outlying fields. The Marines at the airstrip there arranged for someone to take me to nearby Camp Lejeune.

It was mid-morning when I finally reached the office of the Casual Company where I was to report for duty. It soon became obvious there was nothing but confusion in that office! The job of the people in Casual Company was to log you in, put your name on a list and then get you assigned to some billet as soon as possible. But from what I observed and heard from others there was a big backlog. More officers were arriving then were leaving. The barracks, which under normal conditions would house the enlisted personnel with about fifty Marines in a squad bay, were now filled with officers. Most of the officers were of Company grade, Captains and Lieutenants. However, there were also a couple Majors.

Marine organizations were transferring officers to Camp Lejeune for further assignment or separation from service. These officers were of three types: "Short Timers"; "Not-so Short Timers"; and career or "regulars". After the cessation of hostilities in WWII, the armed services devised a "point" system to determine the order in which their officers and men would be discharged. The "Short Timers" were those with sufficient points to warrant immediate release from active duty. The "regulars" were not concerned with "points", since they had made the Marine Corps a career choice. Those of us who were "Not-so-Short Timers" were not even close to having enough points to be released, but unlike the "regulars" we were just "killing" time waiting to accumulate the required points for discharge.

The Marine commands in the Eastern half of the country were sending their "Short-Timers" to Camp Lejeune for separation. As officers in these commands were transferred, vacancies would be created and the command would make these officer vacancies known to Camp Lejeune who in turn would fill the billets with either "Career" officers or "Not-so-Short-Timers". There was an apparent "lag time" in the system. The detached officers were arriving at Camp Lejeune faster than the replacements were being sent out.

Everyone was griping about the time it took for the processing for separation from service or obtaining orders for a new duty station. Some of the officers had been there for weeks. They had no duty to perform, but they had to kill time awaiting a call from the office.

While "checking in" I was standing in front of a personnel Sergeant's desk in this very large, crowded and noisy office. Some Marine clerk to the rear of the desk was loudly asking, "Did you get a Lieutenant for the Charleston slot? I said to the Sergeant, "Are you looking for a Lieutenant to go to Charleston?" He looked at me and nodded affirmatively and asked, "Do you want to go to Charleston?" Without hesitation, I said "Damn right I do!" He said "OK", and he started typing up my orders to the Marine Barracks, Naval Ammunition Depot, Charleston, South Carolina. About an hour later, I was on my way to South Carolina. I didn't even unpack or eat a meal before I was "in" and "out" of Camp Lejeune.

By the time I arrived at the railroad station in Wilson, NC it was late in the evening and I had to wait for the next train to Charleston for several hours. Consequently, I didn't get into Charleston until the middle of the next day. I found myself in the vicinity of the "Old Slave Mart" where I waited for a ride to the NAD, which was north of the city. While there I found a wonderful bar where I enjoyed a few beers and was introduced to boiled shrimp! And that is another story!

The Naval Ammunition Depot was located several miles up the Cooper River from Charleston. There were about 1000 sailors on the base and the Marine Barracks had about 150 Marines.

Major James (n) Ackerman commanded the Marine Barracks. (The Marine Corps uses an "n" when an individual does not have a middle name). Having the Major as my "first" Commanding Officer was an extraordinarily fortunate occurrence. Once I have told you about this exceptional individual you will appreciate, as I have, how lucky I was to have known the Major. He was the "old Corps" and in the times I had to visit with him it was like stepping back and viewing pieces of American and Marine Corps history from the "inside".

Major Ackerman had served in World War I as an enlisted man, a Sergeant, and had earned a commission while in France with the American Expeditionary Forces (AEF), commanded by the Army's General John Pershing. Following WW I, he had served in Haiti as an officer in the Guarde d'Haiti and then again in Nicaragua as an officer in the Guardia Nacionale, the Nicaraguan National Guard. When WW II began, he was too old for combat duty, so he spent the war commanding small barracks in the southern part of the USA.

Not long after I had been aboard, I was reviewing some correspondence in the Barracks office and noted the clerk had typed the Major's rank and name followed by his file number as is customary on Marine documents. He had typed: Major James (n) Ackerman 01. My officer's file number was 045803. This meant I was probably the 45,803th Marine officer commissioned. The clerk had typed 01 for the Major. No way, Jose! It was obvious the clerk, PFC Jungle (how could I ever forget his name?) had left off a few digits. "PFC Jungle, I think you have an error here", I said as I pointed to the Major's file number on the paper. However, PFC Jungle said he hadn't made a mistake. Believe it or not, but the Major's file number was 01. I just couldn't believe it, so I knocked on the Major's office door and after he responded, I went into his office to ask him about this 01 file number.

Major Ackerman explained that it wasn't until after WW I that the officers of the services were assigned numbers. The Army assigned 01 to their hero and ranking General, John J. Pershing. However, the Marine Corps decided to assign their officer numbers alphabetically and **A**ckerman happened to be at the top of the list. Hence **01**.

Major Ackerman was a cigarette smoker and he had the habit of rolling his cigarette between his fingers as he smoked. One day as he was at his desk and smoking, he told me of an incident which occurred in Haiti in the late 1920s. The Marines had established a base camp in the outback jungle and were sending out patrols from this camp in search of the rebels. The patrols would be out for days at a time before they would make there way back into camp. On this occasion, the officers in the camp had been playing poker most of the night, when one of the patrols came back into camp. The patrol had been led by then Captain Howland M. Smith, later the famed General "Howlin' Mad" Smith who commanded the Marines during the Saipan operation in WW II. The Major recalled the poker game was about to break up when Captain Smith came into the room and sat down and wanted to play poker. The players were "bushed" and said, "No we've had it...we're not playing". With that, "Howlin' Mad" took out his 45 pistol, laid it on the table and said, "I said we're playing poker!". They knew he meant it and they all returned to the table.

He told me of the red-headed Marine Captain of German descent who was a bit crazy too! I cannot recall the Captain's name, but I remember him saying he was very difficult to understand since most of the time he was speaking in German. He said he was a very stern person and at this time was very upset since his unit had just been ambushed while on patrol and he lost a few of his men. After coming back to camp he set up a machine gun just outside of the gates to a stockade where they were keeping some rebel prisoners. He ordered the gates open and as the prisoners fled through the gates he mowed them down with the machine gun. Obviously the Marines in Haiti at that time were unhampered by the "rules of engagement" which later tied their hands in Vietnam.

In the 1930s, he served in Nicaragua with the Guardia Nacionale. He was still a Lieutenant in the Marine Corps, but he was a Major in the Guardia Nacionale. He spent a couple years chasing the rebel General Sandino through the rugged hills and mountains of that country. As he related the episodes of transporting materiel and supplies via donkeys along the mountain trails, he told a joke I have heard in various versions several times in the years to follow.

It seems that every piece of equipment had to be accounted for to the Quartermaster General of the Marine Corps. During one of these mountain operations, a heavily loaded donkey made a misstep and fell into the abyss below. The Marine in charge had to file a report and list all of the equipment that had been lost due to this mishap. The officer seized upon the opportunity to include several other items of equipment, which were previously missing as having been lost in this accident.

Once the Quartermaster General had the opportunity to review the report, he sent a message to the Marine officer who had filed the report which read something like this: "I have this date reviewed your report of January 15th and have come to this conclusion. It is of no wonder this unfortunate donkey fell into the canyon since he was carrying one-half of your unit's total equipment allowance."

Not only was Major Ackerman my C.O., but he was also our neighbor. Marie, Bobby and I lived in a townhouse on the base directly across the street from the Ackermans. Since we didn't own an automobile, Mrs. Ackerman would take Marie with her when she went into the Naval Base in Charleston to shop at the Commissary and the Post Exchange.

On occasion, Marie and I would take Mrs. Ackerman with us when we went to the movie at the small recreation building on the base. The Major would never go to the movie. His reason for not attending had a lot to do with Navy tradition. In the Navy, the enlisted men sit in the front seats and the officers' section is to the rear of the enlisted men's seats. The Major would not attend the movie on the base because he could not stand to look at all those hairy necks on the sailors who obviously needed haircuts.

Every Saturday morning the Major would inspect the Barracks. That meant every Friday night we had a "field day" in which the Barracks floors were scrubbed and the heads (toilets for civilians) and every bit of our space was cleaned and made ready for his inspection. As I would accompany the Major on his tour of the Barracks, I learned after a few inspections exactly what he would say as he inspected the head: "This place looks like a shit house".

There were generally three company grade officers in the command at any one time. A couple of Captains were on board when I first arrived, but they were transferred within a few weeks after I reported for duty. One of the Captains was the owner of a large Ford dealership in Brownsville, Texas. He was a very kind fellow and an easy person to work with in the barracks. In fact, since I didn't have a car, he was kind enough to take me to the Charleston airport to pick up Marie and Bobby when they arrived.

The one officer I remember the best was a First Lieutenant Royce Lassiter. Later, while stationed at Camp Lejeune in 1946-48, I would visit with Royce on occasion. He was then attached to the Division Recon Company. (Recon is short for Reconnaissance). Division Recon folks were the ones who were prepared to land from submarines via rubber rafts behind enemy lines during wartime.

They would now be part of our "Special Forces". Frequently, Royce and his troopers would be away from the camp on some special exercise of which he was not free to speak, Suddenly, I discovered Royce was no longer around. I made some inquiries and it seemed as if he had never been stationed at Camp Lejeune, at least that was how I perceived the situation. No one seemed to know anything about him. I suspect his Recon team may have made a landing on the north coast of Russia and never made it back.

Another fellow I remember was an older Warrant Officer "Bucky" Harris. I don't know why, but many Marines named Harris always seemed to have the nickname, "Bucky". It was the same way with all Rhodes who were nicknamed "Dusty". Fortunately, I had several nicknames during my life, but none of them was "Bucky".

"Bucky" used to follow me on the Officer of the Day duty roster. During the day of duty, the OD was required to sleep at the Barracks. I often forgot to take my toilet articles with me after I completed my tour of duty. I would come back to retrieve my gear and I would find everything in order except my shaving lotion bottle would be empty. I figured "Bucky" was a bit of an alcoholic and he would take more than a few "nips" of my Aqua Velva.

During the 24-hour tour of duty, the OD was required to visit each guard post during each four-hour watch. We had several guard posts, which were quite a distance out in the "boondocks". The Ammunition Depot covered several hundred acres and the "boondocks" were filled with row after row of ammunition bunkers. There was a lot of activity at the Depot during this period of time as Navy Destroyers were coming up the Cooper River and docking at the Depot for the purpose of unloading their ammunition before moving to those ports where they would be decommissioned. So we had a few sentries in those bunker areas which had the activity.

Nothing is so uninteresting as getting up sometime between midnight and 4 AM, dressing, getting in your Jeep and driving ten miles out in the country to see if the sentry is walking his post and alert. Terrible job, but it had to be done!

I had many job titles during my stint at Goose Creek. I was the Training Officer; the Police Officer, the Mess Officer; the Base Fire Marshall, Recreation & Athletics officer and the judge advocate for the Summary Courts-Martial.

Fortunately we didn't have any Marines with charges serious enough to warrant a Courts-Martial, however the Navy Captain had his court in session continuously. Normally, that would not have affected me since the Navy had their own command structure to take care of their own. However, I was asked to be the Defense Counsel for one of the sailors and I accepted. I was successful in getting a "Not Guilty" verdict from the Navy court and the word spread among the sailors on the base that this Marine Lieutenant was a regular "Perry Mason"! Subsequently, I had the opportunity to defend several sailors who found themselves in trouble.

A Captain G. C. Logan, USN commanded the Depot. The story was that he was the most senior Captain in the Navy and his chances of ever being promoted to Admiral were between zero and none. He once had command of the battleship Maryland, but it ran aground in the Chesapeake Bay and in the Navy this is a "Cardinal Sin". Perhaps that is why he was such a difficult person?

Captain Logan's quarters was a beautiful two-story white plantation style home on a prominent point overlooking a bend in the Charles River. It was removed from the Main area of the Depot, where the Marine and Navy Barracks were located. The Captain kept three stewards, all of Filipino heritage, working at his quarters. They said he needed three stewards because he always had one being Courts-Martialed, another in the Brig serving his sentence from previous Courts-Martial and the third was working at his quarters, awaiting the release of the one in the Brig, so charges could be filed against him!

In any case, I had the opportunity to defend one of the stewards. The charges were ridiculous. One charge was for disobedience of orders. Specifically, the steward was alleged to have served Orange Marmalade after he had been ordered to serve Strawberry Jam.

It was a ticklish situation for me to be defending this young fellow, since the Navy officers were frightened to death of appearing to oppose the Captain. I did my best; completely destroyed the Governments case, however the Navy officers on the court found him "Guilty as charged" and the steward did a couple days in the Brig.

I was required to prepare a training schedule for the Marines for the time they were not standing sentry duty. All of the Marines at NAD had seen service in the Pacific theatre during WW II. When they were in uniform there was a lot of color showing from the ribbons they wore. Among the ribbons were many Purple Hearts. These fellows had seen combat in the War. Then there was 2nd Lieutenant Harris, with one lousy service ribbon, awarded for being in the military service during the war period. Most of the time I avoided wearing the single ribbon, it was so embarrassing! However, I was the one who conducted many of the training classes for these veterans.

One morning I had my class of about 30 to 40 Marines on the screened-in porch of the Barracks. I was conducting a class on "Scouting and Patrolling" I paused as a Corporal in the back row raised his hand to ask a question. He said "Lieutenant, is this the way they do it in combat, or is this the way they teach it at Quantico?" It was a difficult job, but someone had to do it!

With only a few exceptions, I did not have any problem with insubordination or any disrespect from the older more experienced NCOs or other enlisted men. I had been there only a week or so, when I was assigned to conduct an inventory of supplies. During the inventory the Supply Sergeant responded on a couple of occasions in a contemptuous manner. I let a remark or so pass by, but then he went too far and I jumped on him (figuratively speaking) and let him know the bars on my shoulders trumped the stripes on his sleeve. It was the best thing I could have done. I had no trouble with that NCO or any of them from that day forward.

Major Ackerman in his early days in the Corps had been a Mess Sergeant; consequently he had a special interest in the Mess Hall. As the Mess Officer, I was required to review the menus, check the supplies and be certain that we lived within the rations allotment. It was an easy job because we had some really good Marines running the Mess Hall and because the Major visited them regularly too!

The most interesting job was that of the Base Fire Marshall. The Marines ran the Depot's Fire Department and when you are moving ammunition around on and off ships, truck and whatever, the possibility of fire is downright scary! But before, I tell you more about the job as Fire Marshall, you need to know about Marie, Bobby and our living quarters.

Marie and Bobby flew to Charleston and my Marine Captain friend from Texas drove me to the airport to pick them up. They had had a terrible flight from Detroit to Washington, going through some very severe turbulence. Bobby became ill and vomited over his mother and it was terribly frightening for both of them. Fortunately the flight south was less disturbing, but to say the least, Marie was very happy to see that trip "from hell" come to an end.

I was fortunate to find a two story, two-bedroom townhouse available for rent on the base. It was a government subsidized housing project of four buildings each located on this short street right inside the main gate of the Depot. I had also been able to purchase the essential pieces of furniture from the previous occupants. We put Bobby's crib in the second bedroom upstairs and we had a double bed for our bedroom, a couch for the front room downstairs and a kitchen table for the breakfast nook off the kitchen. The stove and oven were "built ins" and the refrigerator came with the rent.

One afternoon, Marie had put Bobby in his crib for his afternoon nap. As was his habit, Bobby would fuss a while before he finally gave into the need for a rest. His favorite "fussing" activity was standing in his crib and shaking it's side, As Marie listened to the crib being shaken, it finally stopped and she thought Bobby had given up and laid down to sleep. A few minutes later, however, she heard some other noise coming from his room upstairs. She went up the steps to his bedroom to find out what was going on. As she looked into the room, here was Bobby sitting on the floor, outside of his crib, pulling on the cord of the window shade. He was having a lot of fun and laughed as she came into the room. The side of the crib was still up and locked securely. There was no evidence he had fallen out of this crib. How did he get out of the crib and onto the floor? Did he climb over the top of the side? If so, he had never displayed the strength to do that before. To this day, some sixty-five years later it is still a mystery. And Bob still refuses to tell us how he did it!

Since we did not have an automobile, the transportation problem was largely solved when I was assigned the job as the Base Fire Marshall. The Fire Marshall was provided a cargo jeep so he could get to a fire or anywhere else he needed to go during the night or day. I kept the jeep with me at all times. It became my personal vehicle.

When I had the duty, I would come home for a hour or so in the evening. It was only a mile or so from the barracks to our townhouse. On some of the warm summer evenings, I would put Marie and Bobby in the front seat and we would tour the "boondocks" on the roads that honeycombed the ammunition bunkers. It was a very delightful trip out into the country. We used the jeep to travel to the

Base recreation center for the evening movies, except when Mrs. Ackerman joined us, and then we would use their car.   The Ackermans occupied a townhouse, just like ours, albeit better furnished, in the building directly across the street from our building. Fortunately we didn't have one fire during the seven months I was stationed at the NAD.   That jeep was a Godsend.   I can't imagine what we would have done without it.   I may have been stretching the regulations a bit by using it for my personal needs, but the Major looked the other way and no one else ever suggested I was out-of-bounds.

I organized a flag-football team to play in a service league, which included a Navy team from the larger Naval Station at Charleston.   At first I served only as their coach, however, we were being out manned at every game, so about half way through the schedule; I started playing as a lineman.   Our record didn't improve and I was quite frustrated on many occasions.   I recall playing against that Charleston Navy team when the opposing linemen were manhandling me quite easily.   I have to admit I lost my temper after one of these fellows "pan-caked" me to the ground.   It was not acceptable officer conduct, but I was really upset, more like furious.   Later we found out many of the sailors on that team had come right out of some V-5 units, which were being disbanded.   Many had college and professional football experience.   That made me even madder!   I hate to lose!

Following the football season, it was basketball and our habit of losing games continued.   I believe we ended the season with a 3-17 record.   With the coming of baseball, my hopes for a winner were high.   There were several former minor league professionals in the Barracks including a pitcher from an International league club. However, just as the season was about to get underway, I was ordered to the Separation Center at Great Lakes for release from active duty. But that's another story!

Chapter 7   Civilian Life

My days as an active duty Marine were numbered. I was soon going to join the thousands of others who had returned to civilian life after years in uniform. In a few more days, I would have my "ruptured Duck" lapel pin and I could put the Marine green uniform away and don the multi-colored duds of the civilian. We were aboard the Southern Limited traveling from Charleston to Detroit. We were on our way home.

As we traveled through the southern states that first day, we passed by several abandoned Army camps. There were rows and rows of barracks, all empty. Some doors had been left open and they swung back and forth in the breeze. The office buildings and the repair facilities were abandoned. There were no jeeps or trucks moving down the company streets. The sight of this emptiness where once there were thousands of energetic young men filled me with sorrow and pensive sadness.

After a day in Michigan, Marie and I traveled to the home of my Aunt Olive in Hammond, Indiana where Marie stayed while I went on to the Naval Training Center at Great Lakes, Illinois. The Marine Corps had established a Separation Center at Camp Robert Small at the center and were processing hundreds of Marines for release from active duty.

When I reported into the Separation Center, I was surprised to find my old friends, Bud McGlone and Clint Murchison as part of the regular company. I can't recall where they had been since we went separate ways following graduation from the Artillery School in October of 1945, but they were doing their last days in the Corps processing other Marines for discharge. We had a pleasant albeit brief reunion. We never saw each other since that time. Fred Jr., Bud and Ann McGlones son was at Michigan State at the same time as our son and daughter, and they became acquainted, however we never managed to renew our friendship with the McGlones. I did have a phone conversation with Clint Murchison as I passed through Dallas several years later, but again we never saw each other again.

Immediately following WW II, there was a severe housing shortage throughout the nation. It wasn't any different in Fenton. There was absolutely "no room in the Inn". This required our family of three to move in with my parents. The house was very small for so many people for any extended length of time, but it had to do and everyone made the best of the situation.

I found employment almost immediately at the AC Spark Plug Company at their facilities on Dort Highway in Flint, Michigan. I became a member of the Plant Layout group in their Works Engineering department. At the time, the two major divisions of AC were the Production Department and the Works Engineering Department. My uncle, Leo Tobin headed the Production Department and his office was in the same building where I worked. On occasion I would pass my uncle in the hallway, and in his usual "gruff" manner he would make some sort of a growling greeting as we passed. It didn't bother me, because I knew that under all that "gruffness" was a very kind and generous man.

I found the work in Plant Layout very interesting since we were rapidly converting the factory from the production of war materials to products for the automobile industry. My particular area was in the new production lines for fuel pumps. By this time, Marie and I had purchased a used 1941 Ford Club Coupe and I recall going to the test stand at the end of the line where they were producing Ford fuel pumps and having a worker get me one which tested especially well. It soon found a place on our "new" Ford.

While working in Plant Layout, I had a lot of contact with the representative of the J. B. Webb Company in Detroit. J. B. Webb was the prime manufacturer of overhead conveyors and we had a lot of them in the AC plant. The J. B. Webb representative seemed to like the work I was doing and he asked me if I would be interested in working for his company. They offered a much higher salary but if I accepted we would have to move to the Detroit area. Both Marie and I were anxious to move out of my parent's home so we asked her sister Jean if we could move in with her and her family in Ecorse, Michigan. Jean and Cam Loucks were very willing to share their apartment and so we made the decision to accept the J. B. Webb offer and move to Ecorse.

Jean and Cam were more than gracious hosts, since they gave Marie and me their bedroom and they moved to the convertible sofa in the front room. Bobby joined their young children, Diane and Lynda in their bedroom. We were tight and cozy but we had a "fun" time in that apartment. Cam was working everyday as a welder and would generally come home after I returned from work at J. B. Webb's. Marie and Jean enjoyed being with each other and the only members of the group that didn't get along were our Bobby and their Lynda. Of course, we think it was Lynda who was the troublemaker. Smile!

Lynda was almost a year older than Bobby and while they played together nicely most of the time, there were those times when one or the other, or both, were out of control! It seemed as if Lynda would go ballistic whenever Bobby went into the bathroom. All of a sudden she would have to go to the toilet and she had a fit because Bobby was in the only bathroom. Diane, being a couple years older, was the kind and gentle person then as she is today. She was a doll.

Robert Cameron Loucks, AKA "Cam" was one of the nicest, easiest going fellows you would ever want to know. Cam loved to have the late evening coffee sessions and was obsessed with the Canadian stock market. It was a common occurrence for Cam to leave the apartment, which was on Jefferson Avenue, catch a bus going to downtown Detroit, and return within the hour with the evening edition of the Toronto *Globe and Mail*. He couldn't go a day without knowing what was happening to his Canadian stocks.

Cam was also obsessed with "gold". He would buy inexpensive stock in Canadian gold mines. They were only pennies per share and he would buy several thousand shares. More often than not, he would sell these shares when the price of the shares would suddenly escalate. Some how or another he seemed to get tips on what was going to happen in these gold mine stocks and he would profit on the "inside" information. A few years later, while I was stationed at Great Lakes, Illinois, Cam convinced me to put some money in a Canadian gold mine named "Gillies Lake". I believe I bought the stock for something like ten cents a share and I "invested" $1,000.

About a year later I found myself in need of a new car. I had taken my 1952 Buick to the dealer in Waukegan, Illinois for servicing. After I picked the car up, my drive home was interrupted when the engine overheated and the car stalled. The dealer had failed to put new oil into the engine after draining the old. The engine never ran well again. We had come to Michigan for a few days and I was telling Cam about what had happened. Before I knew it Cam had me in the local Buick dealership buying a new 1955 Buick Roadmaster.

At the time Gillies Lake stock had risen to twenty-eight cents a share and according to Cam the bottom was about to drop out and I should sell! I sold and used the profit towards buying the new car.

Cam had worked as a Millwright for years, but eventually specialized in welding. He was certified as a welder for some exotic metals and as such was in great demand in many industries, such as chemical refineries. One day while welding inside of a chemical tank, he received an electrical shock that knocked him off his perch and sent him falling to the bottom of the tank. He was in serious condition for several days, but not long after he was back on the job.

One memorable incident occurred with Cam and the kids during our stay in Ecorse. Marie, Jean and Diane had gone shopping and left Lynda and Bobby at home with Cam. I don't know where I was but I heard all about what I am about to relate when I came home. It seems that Cam fell asleep on the sofa in the front room while Lynda and Bobby found the flour canister in the kitchen. When the women returned home they found Cam asleep on the sofa and the two little children covered with flour. More than that, there were tiny

footprints on the floor running from the kitchen, down the hallway and into the front room. They led directly up to the side of the sofa where Cam had been sleeping. Evidently, the two little tikes had made several trips from the kitchen into the front room to check on whether or not Cam was still asleep.

In this picture, on the left is Cam Loucks with my father, Bill Harris.

After Lynda's birth, Jean began suffering from crippling arthritis. In their efforts to find a way of alleviating her condition, they tried several unorthodox treatments. Cam had learned of a "Doctor" in Windsor, who had developed a treatment that "cured" the disease. It involved taking a series of injections of a substance that was derived from the urine of rabbits. Just from that information alone, I suspect one should have known the fellow was a "quack". However, Cam was convinced the treatment had some merit, so Jean began receiving these injections each night. No one in the house wanted to perform the injection, so I ended up doing the deed. I don't like needles, especially when they are being pushed into my flesh, but after a couple injections I found I could do it very well. Unfortunately, both that treatment and the many others Jean tried were unsuccessful and the crippling continued. Both her hands and her feet were severally deformed and the arthritis was very painful. However, Jean was a very good trooper and rarely complained about her fate. She continued to drive her car, maintained her house and enjoyed her family throughout her life.

Some of the most delightful days of our lives were spent with Jean and Cam during the time we lived together. We played a lot of card games, visited with the neighbors (especially after they bought a new TV), hopped on a bus and went to the Tiger night baseball games (Cam loved those $1 bleacher seats), went to Del Ray for Marshall's pizza, drank many pots of coffee late at night and in general had a marvelous relationship.

As it turned out my job at J. B. Webb was working as a draftsman on a board. My leader was a very kind and helpful person; however I couldn't see myself working as a draftsman the rest of my life. While the pay was good, I was a leader, not a follower and the prospects didn't look very good from the seat of a junior draftsman. I missed the Marine Corps!

While living with Jean and Cam was much more enjoyable than it was living in Fenton with my folks, this kind of living could not continue. We needed a place of our own. However, rental houses or apartments were still very scarce and very costly.

I wrote a letter to the Commandant, U.S. Marine Corps expressing my interest in obtaining a commission as a regular Marine officer and returning to active duty. I had retained my commission as a reserve officer and had investigated joining a reserve unit at the Naval Armory in Detroit, but I didn't like what I had observed. At the time, it seemed more like a social club than a military organization.

I submitted my application for a regular commission and finally in the late fall; I received notification I had been accepted, subject to passing a physical examination. My orders were to report for the physical exam at Great Lakes and if I was found physically fit for active duty, I was to report to the Commanding General, 2nd Marine Division at Camp Lejeune, North Carolina.

Having decided to return to active duty after a brief period as a civilian, I am reminded of a story told of an old Marine Gunnery Sergeant who after twenty some years in the Corps decided to give civilian life a try. Within a week of his discharge, he returned to the Marines and reenlisted.

When queried about his decision to return to active duty, he remarked, "Well, it was like this. On my first day as a civilian I went downtown in the city and while I was standing on the corner, I observed all these people, all going in different directions, all out of step and wearing different clothing in various states of disarray…and most of all…there was no one in charge…I just couldn't stand the idea of being one of them…It was the Marines for me"!

It's difficult to be a Marine, but it is also difficult being a civilian. In both societies there are "orders" given by those in authority. However, there is a noticeable difference in how those receiving the "orders" respond. It's clever and humorous to note the difference when it comes to an order to "Jump". The Marine asks "how high?" the civilian asks "Why?" In fact, civilians even reject the use of the term "orders". They prefer "suggestions", "directions" or something sounding less threatening. However, even Marines react more favorably to orders when they have an understanding of "why" and have had an opportunity to participate in the formulation of the plan. However, Marines obey and react regardless, mainly because of their training and their understanding of the need to obey orders promptly and willingly. It's a different culture and after a brief experience as a civilian, I wanted to return to the Marine's world again!

Part II It' Sweeter, The Second Time Around

For a young officer, no duty is as rewarding as FMF duty! Here the neophyte has more authority, more responsibility and a greater opportunity than with any other assignment. Here the new officer will learn whether or not he has the "right stuff" to lead men. It is very unlikely any position in civilian life would place a young man in an equivalent position of trust and responsibility and with a greater potential to learn than being a new Second Lieutenant in the Fleet Marine Force.

Because I had indicated I was not interested in staying in the Corps and the exigencies of the service at the end of World War II, I was not given an assignment in the FMF after artillery school. Instead I was sent to a small barracks at a Naval station where I served until being separated from active duty in April of 1946.

After about eight months as a "civilian" I received a commission as a regular officer in the Marine Corps. So, it was not until then, after I returned to active duty, I had the opportunity to serve in the FMF. I joined an artillery regiment, the 10th Marines of the 2nd Marine Division at Camp Lejeune.

Duty with the 10th Marines provided a blend of "troop duty" and the more "technical" duties required of an artillery officer in providing fire support for the infantry. A shortage of officers meant each officer was required to wear several "hats". Consequently; the learning curve was much steeper than it would have been under more normal conditions when there would have been one officer assigned to each position.

I was assigned to Battery "B", a 105mm Howitzer Battery. After a few months, a Captain Lawrence L. Graham joined as our new Battery Commander. This began a friendship that lasted throughout my Marine Corps career. We served together again at Fort Bliss in 1958-61. Marie and I became very close personal friends with the Grahams and particularly enjoyed being with them in their home.

The photo above is the center portion of a large photo of the entire Battery "B" taken in June of 1947. I am standing second from the left and WO Holman and I are holding our Battery Guidon in front of Captain Lawrence L. Graham. To the right of WO Holman is our First Sergeant Smith and to the right of 1st Sgt Smith is Corporal Whipple. Corporal Whipple was one of the best Marines in my charge and played an important role on March 27, 1948. But, that's another story!

During my two years in this billet, I participated in three off shore exercises including two amphibious operations in the Caribbean and one cold-weather operation in Newfoundland. It was a great learning experience and it provided a "real life" understanding of "duty with troops". But, that's another story!

Chapter 8   Welcome Back
Jack!

It's odd but I can't remember whether I reported to Great Lakes in uniform or in civilian clothes! Regardless, I had them all off soon after my arrival as I submitted to a complete physical examination by the Navy doctor. It's difficult for me to believe it today, but I weighed in at 195 pounds and my waist was only 37 ½ inches. Even at that the Navy doctor indicated I was 31 pounds overweight for my height at 71 ½ inches. Even though he indicated it was "well distributed" I can't imagine how I would have looked at 164 pounds, because I weighed more than that in high school! In spite of being "overweight" I was found to be "…physically qualified for appointment in the regular Marine Corps as a 2nd Lieutenant and to perform all the duties of his rank at sea or in the field". This meant I was back on active duty and I was to proceed to Camp Lejeune and report to the Second Marine Division. When I arrived at Lejeune in December of 1946, I found the camp quite different from when I had been there before as an OCA (Officer Candidate Applicant) in December of 1944 and again when I passed through the processing unit on my way to the Naval Ammunition Depot, Charleston, SC in September 1945. During those two previous instances, the camp was very busy and loaded with Marines. In December of 1946, the streets in the barracks area of the camp looked like a "junk yard" and the level of activity was noticeably low. Those of you who are familiar with the layout of Camp Lejeune will recall that the Camp's main area was divided into five regimental areas, with the area streets running parallel to each other. These regimental streets were full of trucks and trailers of all types and sizes and they were in terrible condition.

What had happened was the Second Marine Division, upon their return from occupation duty in Japan following the end of the war, had moved their vehicles and assorted other wheeled equipment into Camp Lejeune and parked them end to end, bumper to bumper and just left them.   Most of the men of the Division were hastily demobilized and sent home.   What remained was a skeleton of a Marine Division and the "junk yard". This "junk yard" existed for months before the materiel was processed and the camp streets were returned to normal.

I was assigned to the 10th Marines, the artillery regiment, barracked in Area Five. I was further assigned to Battery "B", 1st Battalion of the 10th Marines where I found I was not only the sole 2nd Lieutenant in Battery "B", but I had the dubious distinction of being the only 2nd Lieutenant in the whole Regiment!

It was clear the whole Division was under-staffed.   The Division was really only a "skeleton" of its authorized strength. The 10th Marines consisted of a Regimental Headquarters and two of their four authorized Battalions. These two battalions, both direct support battalions with 105mm Howitzers, had only two batteries instead of the authorized three.   As a result of being under strength, each officer had to do more than one job to ensure that all the necessary tasks were completed.

So it was for Battery "B".   There were only three officers, a Captain, 1st Lieutenant and a 2d Lieutenant in the battery, which was probably authorized for at least seven or eight officers.   Our commanding officer was Captain Lawrence L. Graham and 1st Lieutenant William Reynolds served as the Battery Executive Officer.

In an artillery battery, the "Exec" runs the "guns".   He is the one responsible for the movement and placement of the four howitzers and once in place, the firing of these weapons.   The other officers handle the functions of fire direction; forward observation and liaison with the infantry units being supported.   Fortunately, for the only 2nd Lieutenant in the battery, two Warrant Officers joined our battery and were assigned as forward observers.   WO Henry and WO Holmes were the ones who had to live and move with the infantry units during maneuvers.

I was fortunate to be assigned the job of fire direction. The title for the job was Reconnaissance Officer or RO.   The primary responsibility of the RO was to organize, train and operate the fire direction section of the battery. This section was called the "Battery Fire Chart". It contained the same elements as that of the Battalion's Fire Direction Center (FDC). The FDC computed the fire commands for all the batteries of the battalion.

The infantry battalions at the time had a similar situation when it came to working with reduced manning levels and equipment. Our battalion, the 1st Battalion was in direct support of the 8th Marines. (Be reminded that in the USMC, the title "Marines" is synonymous with "Regiment"). The 8th Marines had only two infantry battalions at this time instead of the three, which were authorized.

Consequently, our Battery "A', commanded by Captain Hilliard supported their 1st Battalion, and our Battery "B" was in support of the 8th Marines' 2nd Battalion. At this time, a Colonel Ridgely commanded the 8th Marines. I considered Colonel Ridgely to be a very fine officer and with whom I enjoyed a fine professional relationship. (Which would hold me in good stead at a later date. but that's another story!).

In March of 1947, this "skeleton" Division was ordered to conduct a training exercise, including an amphibious landing, on the island of Culebra, just east of Puerto Rico. We were to move to the island of Culebra, execute a landing and seize the island from the "enemy". It was a "live fire" exercise for the Navy. Prior to our landing they would conduct a naval gunfire exercise in the island's impact area. Following the Navy's "live fire", the Marine landing force would come ashore and begin their maneuvers.

Since our artillery was not to conduct any "live firings" during the exercise, the role of our Battery Fire Chart was diminished. However, another aspect of my assigned job (wearing two hats!) was to provide liaison with the infantry. This required me to act as the Artillery Officer at the infantry battalion headquarters, where I would advise my "grunt" brothers on the use of artillery in their planning.

My team consisted of about 8 Marines, with a radio "jeep" for communications. The senior NCO with my section was Gunnery Sergeant Ira Basto. "Gunny" Basto was a real character. His accent was obviously US East Coast, either Brooklyn or Philadelphia is my guess looking back.

He didn't know much, if anything, about fire direction, but he was a very effective troop leader and the young Marines responded promptly to his directions. I know the "ol' salt" that he was found it difficult to be surrounded with intelligent hard working young men. It was certainly not what he had experienced in his 20 some years in the Marine Corps. But underneath that "crust" was one sweet, gentle old fellow that secretly enjoyed this "new breed" of Marines.

One evening while ashore on Culebra, after the day's exercises had been completed, our little group was sitting around a campfire on which Corporal Tony Sideris was brewing some coffee in a gallon size can. The coffee grounds were in a sock that was tied at the top and tossed in the boiling water. (I never knew or asked whose sock it was, or whether it had just come off someone's foot!)   After the coffee had boiled for a time, the can was removed from the fire and the sock removed from the brewed coffee, everyone's "tin" mess cup was filled with hot steaming coffee. After the Gunny had taken a few sips, he made a statement that has remained in my memory for over sixty years. He said, "This coffee reminds me of two lovers on a lake".   One of the troopers asked, "How is that Gunny?"   Old Ira Basto then said, "Fucking near water". Yes, it is a bit obscene, but in all truthfulness, it is one of those memorable moments that have stuck with me all these years.

This little group of Marines, with whom I served for about two years, were, for the most part, young men just out of high school, who enlisted for two years under a special program that allowed them GI Bill benefits for their service. They were of above average intelligence and consequently they learned the various tasks involved in fire direction with relative ease. Working with these young men made my work interesting and enjoyable. They were self-starters; learned complex tasks readily and never presented a disciplinary problem. They truly were the "new breed" of the Marine Corps.

Let me digress to say something about this idea of the "new breed" or "the Old Corps". It seems every generation of Marines looks at the "new breed" and shakes his head disparagingly and says," Nothing like the Old Corps". They tell the story about the first Marine recruited at Tun Tavern in Philadelphia in 1775. After signing up, the new Marine was assigned to go aboard a Navy frigate moored at the nearby docks. Once aboard, the new Marine went up into the ship's riggings and "hung out" with a couple sailors and made idle conversation with his new shipmates. In time, the second Marine recruit was coming up the gangway. The first Marine took one look at him, shook his head and said to his sailor friends, "Nothing like the Old Corps".

Three of the young Marines whom I remember to this day are Corporals Sideris, Whipple and Cornett. The sharpest of them was Corporal Whipple. He was the leader of the fire direction team. In those days, the fire orders would come from the Forward Observers who were with the infantry on the frontline. Through the use of a chart (a map for ye unwashed civilians!) and some computing with the use of a "slide rule" device, these orders were converted to fire commands to the guns. Corporal Whipple was a whiz at all these tasks and took over the leadership of the group. He did most of the instruction and ran the drills that made our unit the best in the Regiment. It was difficult to keep the Battalion and Regimental fire direction officers from "stealing" our men for their organizations. I best remember Corporal Whipple for the assistance he provided me on March 27, 1948, the day our daughter Patricia was born. (But that is another story!)

Tony Sideris (pictured below with me on Culebra) was one of the best-liked individuals in our Battery. He was intelligent and hard

working, but easy going, he kept everyone in good spirits. Sideris came from Nashville, Tennessee where his family ran a restaurant, which one might expect because of his Greek heritage. When he was discharged and leaving, he told me to remember to look him up if and when I came to Nashville. About twenty years ago, Marie and I were in Nashville on vacation, and we did look in the telephone book for a Sideris, but having no luck, we never had the opportunity to meet again.

Corporal Cornett (pictured to the right of me on Culebra) was another story. He was from Harlan County, Kentucky. His father operated a bar in his hometown and Cornett would work in the bar while on leave. And…this *truly* is another story!

Several years ago, I read the notice of Ira Basto's death in the bulletin that HQMC sends out to the Retirees. As for the others, I have no idea what ever became of them. I sure would like to know!

Note: Just for the sake of historical accuracy, when I first joined the 1st Battalion, 10th Marines, for a short time, my Battery Commander was a Captain Peter Hahn. "Pete" Hahn was a likeable but a distant person. We never had a personal relationship. In fact, I recall that during a Battery Officer's meeting in his office, I must have spoken out of turn, because he really "blew up" and I thought for a moment he was going to throw me out of the window! It was a terrible experience for a new Second Lieutenant. However, later in my career, when I was assigned as the Artillery Officer on the Marine Corps Equipment Board at Quantico, Virginia, my immediate superior was Colonel Peter Hahn. He must have forgotten the incident in his office in 1945, because we had a fine professional relationship during his tenure at the MCEB. But, that's another story!

Chapter 9   On Being The Only Second Lieutenant

The day I lost the distinction of being the only 2nd Lieutenant in the 10th Marine Regiment came when a small boat arrived alongside the LST in which our unit was embarked. I had transferred over from the APA *Cambria* to an LST, the landing ship which had transported the bulk of the men and equipment of our artillery battalion.

We were lying off Culebra and it was a beautiful sunny day and a very calm sea with a nice easy rolling motion. I was enjoying a cup of coffee in the Officer's Ward Room when I was alerted there were some Marines about to come aboard. I was dressed in the green herringbone utilities uniform of that period. I had on the loose fitting coat, not tucked in, as became the style in later years. I didn't have the insignia of rank on my collar and I was not wearing a cover at the time.

I arrived at the gangway area just in time to witness about a half dozen new Second Lieutenants come over the side. I can't recall, if there was an Officer of the Deck present or not (things were quite loose aboard this LST), and I may have been the only Marine in sight. This tall gangly Second Lieutenant approached me and saluted and said, "Sir, I am Lieutenant Reese and I am the senior officer of this group". I was a bit flabbergasted, and I don't recall what my response was to this introduction. Regardless, in short order, we were all enjoying coffee in the Ward Room and we began an acquaintance that lasted for years. Later, I often kidded "Howie" Reese about announcing he was the "senior" 2nd Lieutenant of the group, since I had heard that seniority among Second Lieutenants was often compared to virginity among whores.

It seemed the Division personnel people took an easy way out in making their assignments when this large group of new officers descended upon the Division. The new officers were assigned to the various Division units according to the first letter of their last name. "A-C" goes there, D-F" goes to another unit, and so on.   Our Regiment received officers whose last name began with "R" and "P". In addition to Reese, I can remember William "Bill" Plaskett, Dave Rapp, Will Patton and other fellows named Peabody, Peck and Piedmont.

My most vivid recollection of Howard Reese is about his new automobile. During those years, it was almost impossible to purchase a new automobile. Somehow or another, Howie was able to buy a brand new Nash sedan. He was very proud of the automobile, especially how the back seat could be turned into a bed.

As I remember it, Will Patton was an Annapolis graduate. While at the Academy, he had set a collegiate record with the javelin. Years later, in December of 1948, Marie and I had dinner with Bill Patton and his wife at Ft. Bliss, Texas. This was when I was a student in the Guided Missile Course there and he was with the Field Artillery class from Fort Sill who were visiting Ft. Bliss.

Bill Plaskett and I became very good friends, as did our wives, Katie and my Marie. For a short period in 1948, the Plasketts had quarters at Camp Lejeune directly across the street from us. When I was assigned to coach the Regimental football team in fall of 1948, Bill became my assistant. Bill had played football while a student at Rice Institute. Because I chose to go into the Guided Missile field, I had limited duty with artillery units in later years, so I did not have many occasions to serve with the "Lieutenants of 1946". In my memory, they remain very young boys, "gung ho" and eager to be good Marines.

The last time I saw Bill Plaskett was in Korea in the latter part of 1951. Bill was with the 11th Marines at the time and I had occasion to visit him at his unit. It was a period of high activity for his battery and I recall Bill appeared to be very exhausted. He had been out on a night reconnaissance and had fallen into a hole and wrenched his back. He was experiencing a lot of discomfort at the time. In about 1970, I remember reading in some publication that after his retirement, Bill had joined the staff of Rio Grande College in Ohio.

A couple years ago, about 1998, I was saddened to read of his death in the *"Retired Officer"* magazine.

Dave Rapp and his wife Jean also became good friends of ours. About a year after Dave and the others joined our Regiment, in February 1948, we were scheduled to leave on another training exercise to the island of Viegues, east of Puerto Rico. Dave and his wife Jean lived in a community called Midway Park.

Midway Park was a government housing area just outside the main gate at Camp Lejeune. It was an area of small wood frame houses, for the most part duplexes, and was the home to hundreds of Marine families of all ranks. Many of the families of civilians employed at the Camp were also living there.

At the time of the scheduled maneuvers, Marie was about eight months pregnant and we were living in Holly Ridge, about 15 miles south of the Naval Hospital at Camp Lejeune. Dave's wife Jean, kindly invited Marie and our son Bobby, to move in with her and her child in Midway Park while Dave and I went off on maneuvers.

So, while Dave and I were "basking in the sun" in the Caribbean, our wives and children were living together in Midway Park. As it happened they were also suffering through one of the worst ice storms to hit the coastal regions of North Carolina in years. They were without electrical power for days and moving around in an automobile for the first couple days was very treacherous. The Rapps had a large St. Bernard dog, (Bruno by name!) which is fondly remembered for coming into the house when wet and showering all those within range. What part he didn't wet by shaking, he would cover with slobber. However, in spite of the terrible weather and Bruno, they all survived and got along quite well.

We had been on the waiting list for Midway Park housing for some time, and finally we made it to the top. We moved from Holly Ridge to Midway Park soon after our daughter Patricia was born on March 27, 1948 but we lived there for only a few months, before accepting government quarters on the base at Camp Lejeune.

After our days at Camp Lejeune, we never saw or heard from Dave or Jean Rapp again. Occasionally I would hear something about him, but our paths never crossed again. This was true of most of the young Lieutenants with whom I served in those early days. While we may have heard about each other from other Marines we were never stationed together through the remainder of our Marine careers.

A word about that LST we were aboard during the Culebra exercise is in order. The Captain of the LST was a very young Lieutenant j.g. and the ship's Executive officer was also a very young Lieutenant j.g. It was apparent they didn't get along too well and the way things were done on the ship reflected this lack of cooperation.

When Marines come aboard a Navy ship as "passengers", one gets the feeling we have "invaded" their space and they wish we would go away. This is quite understandable, when you learn that when the ship is without "passengers", the crew has lots and lots of space However, when a few hundred Marines arrive, the crew has to move back into the crew's quarters, and everyone has less living space.

So it is understandable, when Marines come aboard, life becomes more difficult for the ships crew. What they forget is that the only reason for the existence of the ship and its crew is to transport the Marines and their equipment.

The way this particular ship operated could have been why the acronym SNAFU came into being. While we were aboard, they demonstrated how not to run a ship. On one occasion they pumped salt water into the fresh water tanks. But the big "boo-boo" occurred during our landing.

The general scheme of operation of an LST during a landing is to run the ship onto the beach, open the bow doors lower the ramps and allow the vehicles and tanks to move onto the beach over the ramp. During this operation, the LST needs to drop an anchor from the stern as it approaches the beaching. This allows the LST to extract itself from the beach after it has discharged its vehicles and tanks. With the stern anchor firm and off shore, the LST uses a winch to pull the ship from the beach. Once afloat and the anchor retrieved, the ship can move out on its own power. Everything went well with our landing, the LST beached and we all went ashore. However, they had forgotten to drop the stern anchor during their approach to the beach and they could not get off the beach without assistance.

Needless to say, this was the cause of much laughter among the Marines. Later that year, we heard that "our" LST was seen in the Norfolk area with its ensign flying upside down. That story was probably not true, but if anything could go wrong, it went wrong on that ship! It was always an adventure when you went aboard ship. Something interesting was bound to happen. But, that's another story!

Chapter 10   About Ships At Sea

It was in March of 1947 and the exercise on the island of Culebra was coming to a close as we packed up out gear, boarded the landing craft and returned to our transport ship, an APA named the *Cambria*. The hull number on the ship was 36, which meant it was one of the older troop ships in the Navy. The *Cambria* had seen a lot of action in the Pacific during World War II as it moved both soldiers and Marines around the south Pacific. The quarters were typical of the troop transports at that time. The ship was rated to carry 80 officers and 1146 enlisted men, and we had a least that many aboard for the trip. The enlisted spaces were forward in the bow or aft in the stern areas. The officers had small "staterooms" below deck, which were located amidships.

All the quarters were one or two decks below the main deck and were entered by steep ladders (Navy lingo for 'stairs") with heavy link chain running through rings at the tops of the upright "pipes" attached to the sides of the ladders. One had to watch his footing when coming down these ladders, especially if the ship was rolling and heaving in a heavy sea. The enlisted men were bunked about four levels high, not more than a couple of feet vertical space between bunks. When one would lie flat in a bunk, one's face would be less than a foot below the canvas bunk above. When you would enter one of the troop quarters, you would find all the space was utilized. It seemed as if every nook and cranny was jammed with gear. When a Marine came aboard, he carried a full pack, a rife and a full duffel bag. All this had to be stored in this already crowded space.

The "heads" (the Navy's name for toilets) for the troops were near their sleeping areas. In the bow, the head was all the way forward in the bow. The forward head was a triangular space with the toilets (metal troughs) running along the outside walls (or bulkheads). Washbasins lined the third side of the triangle. Even in smooth seas, it seemed the decks were always wet and therefore slippery. In heavy seas, it was very difficult to move about the troop spaces. During bad weather, many of the troops were found in their bunks trying to sleep and just "ride it out". In some ways, our troop accommodations were not much better than those of the old slave ships. Well, at least we didn't have the chains and leg shackles!

The officers had it much better. While the space was limited, you had only two bunks to a room, each with mattresses and a pillow. Officers generally carried a locker box aboard, in which they had packed their clothing. Their packs and weapons were stowed wherever one could find a vacant space.

Amidships and in the very bowels of the ship, one would find the Brig. This is where those subject to disciplinary action were kept. One may find a sailor or two incarcerated in the brig, and when Marines were aboard, it might be necessary to imprison one or two "jarheads" too. (Jarhead is an affectionate term for a Marine when used by another Marine…but a "fighting" word if used by others). It is a practice, if not a regulation, that those locked in the ship's brig were to be provided a period for physical exercise each day. Aboard the *Cambria*, the practice was to take the prisoners up on the main deck and back to the fantail (the rear of the ship) for this exercise.

We had embarked at Morehead City, North Carolina, and had been at sea for a couple of days as we headed south to an area east of Puerto Rico. There were several ships in our convoy. As I recall there was an LSD (Landing Ship Dock) and a couple other ships in line behind us.

On this particular day, while at sea several hundred miles east of the Florida coast, the prisoners were brought up for their exercise period. The prisoners were lined up in a couple rows across the fantail and they began doing the "side saddle hop" exercise. This is where one brings their arms up and touches their hands at the same time they extend both legs outwardly and then reverse the movement. After they had done a dozen of so "side saddle hops" one of the prisoners (a Marine) just took a dive over the side! (His leap was in perfect cadence!). Of course, all hell broke loose. "Man overboard" everyone seemed to be shouting. The ship blew its whistle (horn) and began a large turn. The Marine could be seen bobbing along in the wake of the ship. Luckily he didn't drown and he was picked up by a boat from the LSD that was a couple ships behind us in the convoy.

I understand the Marine had a few extra charges added to his sheet. Such as "Leaving the ship without permission" and being "Absent without Leave". I wasn't a witness to the attempted escape, but everyone on the *Cambria* heard all about it!

Another interesting thing occurred within a day or so of the "great escape". An amphibious airplane approached our convoy, circled a couple of times and then landed on the ocean surface a few thousand yards to the starboard. The ship came to a stop and they sent a small boat out to the seaplane. It seems someone aboard the *Cambria* was in great need of hospital care and the Navy had sent this plane out to pick up the one in need. For a landlubber on his first cruise, the whole episode was all very exciting.

Movies at sea! Then Marine PFC Coroneos aboard the *USS Bexar* took this picture in December 1946 on its return voyage from operations in Newfoundland. Coroneos, now an Army Lieutenant at Fort Bliss in 1959, gave the picture to me. Looking to the center of the photo, I am seated directly behind the Navy officer in blue uniform with white cap. I am wearing green jacket with cap. Lt Tim Holt (later in 1969, my son's Regimental CO) is to my right. Col. Ridgley is to right of Navy officer.

While cruising along, there was not much to do for those of us who were "passengers" along for the ride. Each day was a "work" day for the Navy crew, but for the Marines, it was mostly a "lazy" day. After the morning inspection of the quarters and a personnel inspection of the troops, the rest of the day was "free". If you didn't like to read, you could play cribbage, hearts or play poker. During these days at sea, I was introduced to the game of Cribbage. I was surprised at the popularity of this game. It seemed as if every Marine had brought his own Cribbage board with him. It was played everywhere on the ship.

Gambling was against regulations, however there were several poker games going on most of the time and I suspect those tokens on the blanket had some monetary value. I don't know what the stakes were in the enlisted quarters, but the games in the Officer's area were "too rich" for me.

About a year later, in January of 1948, we found ourselves heading south again. This time the 2d Division was to land on the island of Viegues, to the east of Puerto Rico. We were embarked in the *New Kent,* APA 217. As the larger hull number suggests, the *New Kent* was a newer transport and of a different layout, as far as troop accommodations were concerned. The general pattern of enlisted quarters fore and aft with officers amidships existed. However, the officer quarters were on the main deck. This meant those officers who were housed in the "staterooms" along either bulkhead had portholes. Not a big thing really, but for those junior officers with seniority, it provided them with the opportunity to "put their finger on their number".

In those years, the Navy and Marine Corps published a book with all officers listed according to rank. We called it the "Blue Book" because of the color of its cover. When a group of officers were commissioned or promoted, they were listed in order of rank. All officers in the group would share the same "date of rank", however not the same rank. For example, one 1st Lieutenant with the lower number would have rank over all the other 1st Lieutenants with higher numbers. There was this saying, often uttered in a derogatory manner, when an officer, particularly a junior officer, was overly concerned about who had the lower number. Such a person was considered to have "his finger on his number" as he checked the Blue Book to see if he was junior or senior to a fellow officer. For some reason having a porthole was a reason for some of the junior officers to check their number. Since I was only a 2nd Lieutenant, I didn't bother. Besides, who needs a porthole anyhow?

Again, most of the days aboard the *New Kent* were "lazy" days. We went aboard ship at Morehead City, NC on January 17, 1948 and didn't make our landing until February 9th. We had fairly good seas for the most part, and when we arrived in the vicinity of Viegues, it was exciting to find the battleship Missouri in the area.

On this trip as before, I was the Artillery Liaison Officer to the infantry regiment, the 8th Marines. One of the battery officers with me on the *New Kent*, was WO Marvin G. Myers, who was serving as a Forward Observer

Again, as it was the year before on the *Cambria*, poker and cribbage was a major activity for both the officers and men

My Warrant Officer Myers was a very active participant in these games. It was obvious to any observer that he was an experienced and "serious" gambler. He was a big winner on this "cruise", picking up several hundred dollars from a number of the less experienced junior officers aboard. You might say he taught these youngsters a lesson!

W.O. Myers and I served together again many years later when he was assigned to Battery "G", 3rd Battalion, 12th Marines, shortly after I became the Battery Commander.

He was always a competent officer and did his job very well and he hadn't changed much in the five or six years since we were aboard the *New Kent*. When we shipped out together for Japan in June 1952, I didn't notice whether or not he was gambling again, but I would wager if there was a big game going on, he would find it!

During our rehearsal activities preceding D-Day on Viegues, we were required to off load into landing craft over the side of the ship. The method of off loading was by throwing a large cargo net over the side, with the bottom end of the net in the landing craft. Then each Marine would go over the side, climbing down the net into the boat. Each Marine is carrying his weapon and his pack and in some instances various items of equipment, such as a radio or ammunition case.

The first two or three Marines to go down the net were required to grab the cargo net and hold it taught into the boat. This would move the net out from the side of the ship and make it better for the Marines coming down the net. As each group of Marines entered the boat, they were supposed to assist the Marines who had held the net for them. And so this procedure of holding the net continued until all the Marines scheduled for the boat were aboard.

Climbing down the net and holding the net was a strenuous workout. It was particularly difficult if the boat was tossing with the sea and you happened to be in the first group of Marines to enter the boat. It could be quite exhausting, however once everyone was aboard, and the landing craft left the ship, there was amble time to recoup your spent energy.

On this particular occasion, my small group of Marines was to off load down the net and into the waiting landing craft. The seas were particularly rough that day and the boat below was bouncing around like a cork.

Since I was the officer-in-charge of the unit, I was the first one to go down the net. Along with a couple other Marines who accompanied me going down the net, we grabbed the net and pulled it into to the boat. With each wave, the net would become slack and then almost pull us up and out of the boat. It was a real struggle to keep the net taut and help the other Marines coming down the net. Every time the net slackened, the Marines on the net were slammed into the side of the ship. The three or four of us that came down the net were fighting to keep the net in the boat and it was exhausting.

Finally, the last of the Marines had traversed the net and we were loaded. About that time the Coxswain (the Navy fellow in charge of the boat), reported the landing craft was "taking water" and everyone had to leave the boat.

So the Marines started climbing UP the net. The last ones down were positioned in the boat closest to the net, so they were the first ones to go up. As each group started their climb, those remaining in the boat were tasked with keeping the net tight and away from the ship's side. Since I was one of the first to come down, I was one of the last to go up! I was also, one of the last to hold the net. I was exhausted by the time I began my climb. There was no one in the boat to hold the net for me when I started my climb. The boat continued to bob around and once I had cleared the boat's gunnel I was on my own.

The net was hanging very close to the side of the ship, which actually caused my feet to be closer to the side of the ship than my arm and shoulders. The climb was very difficult since I have never had exceptional upper body or arm strength. I had to put my arms through the net on several occasions during the climb to rest a moment before resuming the climb.

Each time I would stop to rest, some Navy crewman would yell derisive remarks at me from above. I was not only getting tired, I was also getting mad! As I finally reached the deck of the ship and threw my leg over on it, I started to look for that SOB in the blue dungarees with that silly white cap. I wasn't able to locate him and that was probably for the best. I was in no condition to fight...or even yell. I was "pooped"!

Finally on "D-Day" we went ashore and for the next couple weeks conducted a really good exercise. During periods of inactivity, we were able to use a beautiful white sandy beach for swimming and snorkeling. If there was nothing going on with the exercise, our evenings were free to relax. On one occasion, I was able to obtain a jeep and along with three other Lieutenants, we went into the nearby town of Isabella Segunda for a bit of libation. As of today, I don't have any recollection of the visit, but in my letter to my parents, I tell of us all getting fairly inebriated and having a wild ride back to our encampment.

During the maneuver, I did a few days with the 65th Infantry Regiment as their Artillery Liaison Officer. This Army regiment was from Puerto Rico and most all of the officers and men of the regiment were Spanish speaking Puerto Ricans. I had a wonderful time with this unit. Best of all, they had the latest of the combat rations. The USMC was still issuing the rations left over from WW II. The story was that the Army gave our Quartermaster General an "offer he couldn't refuse". So the USMC bought up all the WW II canned rations the Army had left over in order to save a few bucks. I don't know if there is any truth in this tale, but the canned rations we had were in the WW II gold cans while the Army had the new "Green" cans. The "Gold" rations offered three choices: Ham and Lima Beans (as I remember they were very greasy); Franks and Beans; and something else equally uninteresting. The Army had a variety of meals. The one I remember best was the Chicken and Rice, which happened to be the "national" dish of the Puerto Ricans.

Once again aboard the *New Kent* on March 3rd we were underway for San Juan for four days of liberty. After leaving San Juan we didn't take the direct route home, but made a one-day stop at the

Naval base at Quantanamo Bay, Cuba. Then it was directly home to Morehead City. We arrived in Morehead on March 18th.and our daughter Patricia was born on March 27th! But, that's another story!

That was the last of my winter time "touring" experiences with the 2d Marine Division. I had had two pleasant excursions into the Caribbean during the coldest months of the year. I only regretted leaving Marie and Bobby back in the States. Whether it was Michigan or North Carolina, it was winter and it was cold. While they were shivering, I was enjoying the warm sunshine of the Caribbean. It was a dirty job, but someone had to do it! But, that's another story!

During the maneuvers on Viegues Island in the spring of 1948, Marie and Bobby stayed with Mrs. Jean Rapp, the wife of fellow officer, Lt. Dave Rapp, in her home in Midway Park.

The Rapp's dog "Bruno" was one of Bobby's favorite playmates...except when he was wet and would shake...and when he slobbered!

Bruno and Bobby (at about 3 years of age) are shown in the photo at the left.

Chapter 11 The Taxi From
Harlan County

During our field exercises on Culebra Island in early 1947, I operated as the Artillery Liaison Officer to the infantry regiment, the 8th Marines, commanded by Colonel Ridgley. My small group of about four or five enlisted Marines included a radio operator whose last name was Cornett. Corporal Cornett was from Harlan County, Kentucky. Just prior to leaving on this maneuver to the Caribbean, Corporal Cornett had been home on leave and, while at home, he worked in his father's tavern.

If anyone has ever read or heard about Harlan County, Kentucky, you will recognize it as being real "Lil' Abner" country. As I understand it, it is like the habitat of "The Hatfield's" and "The McCoy's", where "Moon shining" is one of the most prosperous enterprises.

As it was told to me, it seems while Corporal Cornett was home on leave, working at his fathers tavern, a couple of the moon shiners were attempting to persuade Cornett's father that he should be stocking their product rather than the one he had been using. The moon shiners were becoming more threatening as they continued to pressure the senior Cornett to agree to buy their product. At one point Mr. Cornett was in danger and his son, Corporal Cornett, lifted a shotgun from behind the bar and shot and killed one of the Moon Shiners

Evidently, there was no immediate action by the police or the local authorities, because at the end of his leave, Corporal Cornett returned to our unit and embarked with us for the exercises in the Caribbean.

I was not aware of the incident in Harlan County during the exercise, in which Corporal Cornett performed his duties in an exemplary manner. It wasn't until a few weeks later, when we left the island and returned to our ship, the *U.S.S. Cambria* that the wheels of justice began rolling.

Soon after I was aboard, I received a message that Corporal Cornett had been placed under arrest and was situated in the ship's brig. I wasn't allowed to see the Corporal, but I did learn the ship had received a dispatch directing them to put the Corporal under arrest and keep him locked up until he could be turned over to authorities upon return to the United States.

At the end of the Culebra operation, the ship was at sea for about six days as it returned to the United States. All this time, poor Corporal Cornett was locked up in the bowels of the ship. All he received was three meals and fifteen minutes of exercise outside the cell. He had been charged with murder and when we disembarked in Morehead City, North Carolina, Corporal Cornett was turned over to the Marine Military Police who took him to the brig at Camp Lejeune.

On one ordinary day, a couple weeks after our return, a Military Police vehicle arrived with our Corporal Cornett. He was escorted into the barracks, where he retrieved his sea bag containing his belongings. I didn't have an opportunity to quiz him about his situation, as the MPs were all business and we were only allowed a few moments to ask, "How are you?" etc.

A few minutes later, an old Chevrolet sedan, orangish in color and with big letters on each side reading "TAXI" pulled into the barracks area. There was a chubby older man driving the Taxi. A chubby older woman accompanied him. We assumed the lady was his wife. The driver wore a fashionable summer straw; wide-brimmed hat and he had wide suspenders over his white shirt, with the sleeves pushed up to the elbows.

We learned the Taxi driver was also a Deputy Sheriff from Harlan County, Kentucky. It was obvious he was an old friend of our Corporal Cornett, because when the MPs turned him over to the Deputy/Taxi Driver, both the Deputy and his woman warmly embraced him. Soon it was time to leave, so with a wave to all the assembled Marines in the area, he threw his sea bag in the trunk and climbed in the back seat and away they all went. I don't know what happened in the murder trial of Corporal Cornett, or whether or not there ever was a trial. However, I would wager what ever happened, he was cleared and set free and now is one of the best distillers of Moonshine in eastern Kentucky. But, that's another story!

Chapter 12   Not All Cruises End
With A Beautiful
Sunset

At the conclusion of our exercise on the Island of Viegues in March of 1948, the troops were given four days of liberty in San Juan, Puerto Rico. After a week of so on the island playing war, eating "C" Rations held over from the "Great War" and sleeping on the ground, this "vacation" was well deserved and very much appreciated. This was a new and exciting experience for most of us. The majority of the troopers had never been out of the USA let alone traveled to Puerto Rico. In my case, as with a few of the "veterans", I had visited the southern port city of Ponce just before the maneuvers on Culebra the previous year.

Within a few hours of making port and the sounding of "liberty call" there was hardly a place in the city you couldn't find a group of Marines. The merchants and the bars had a "field day". Most everyone visited the historic fortress El Moro, which guarded the entrance to the harbor, and the other tourist attractions. Souvenir shops did a land office business, and a goodly number sought out one or more of the many "cantinas". Many Marines tasted the "Demon Rum" for the first time in their young lives.

On our last day in port, some of us were still on board the ship relaxing when the chaplain came into the officer's quarters and told the few of us who were there that he had "Guest" tickets to the Ron Rico Company's demonstration bar. Since we had nothing planned, another 2nd Lieutenant named Joe "Bull" Fisher and I picked up the two tickets. It was a good way to spend our last few hours in San Juan before the ship pulled up the gangway and shoved off for home.

So we took off, headed for the "demonstration" bar. It was a very hot and humid day and in the early afternoon the conditions were particularly stifling. In those days, the uniform of the day consisted of cotton khaki trousers and cotton shirts with long sleeves. The "field scarf" (what civilians would call a "tie") was required to be worn. It was so hot and humid that, even with the minimum of exertion, it wasn't long before our shirts showed large wet areas under the armpits and in the lower back. We were soaked!

The Ron Rico Company was and is one of Puerto Rico's leading producers of rum. Their "demonstration" bar was located on the second floor of a building on a square in an older section of the city. We found the entrance, climbed the one flight of stairs and walked into the cool of an air-conditioned barroom. What a relief!

We were surprised to find we were the only "customers" in the bar. Just the bartender and the two of us occupied this wonderfully cool spot. For the next several hours, the bartender mixed about every kind of Rum drink one could imagine. Joe Fisher and I could hardly keep up with him. We sat on a couple of high barstools at the bar and we had the bartender's undivided attention. I particularly remember his *"Rumbanna"*. It was creamy and made with bananas. They never had milk shakes like it in Fenton, Michigan!

We were enjoying our "demonstration" so much we actually lost track of the time. I don't remember the exact time the ship was scheduled to depart, but let's say it was 6:00PM (1800 in military time). We had left the ship about 1400 (2 PM) and arrived at the bar about a half-hour later. One of us happened to look at our watch and to our amazement found it was about 5:30 PM. We only had about a half-hour to get to the ship before they pulled up the gangway and shoved off. What a disaster it would be to "miss the ship"! I don't think we even thanked the bartender as we headed for the door, ran down the stairs and out onto the street looking for a taxi!

As soon as we burst out into the street, the heat hit us hard. We had consumed a considerable amount of rum while sitting at the bar. We were enjoying each and every drink and, up until then, we had not experienced any noticeable effect from the rum. But plunging into that hot humid air changed all of that. Fortunately, we found a taxi in short order and ordered him to get to the pier area "mucho pronto".

When we arrived at the ship, they were just starting to pull up the gangway. Yelling to the sailors to "hold it", we leaped on the gangway and made our way up to the deck. Needless to say, once aboard, we were very, very relieved. If we had missed the ship, I doubt if either one of us would have had much of a career ahead of us in the Marine Corps. We were so relaxed we decided to stay on deck as the ship left the pier and the harbor of San Juan.

We found a spot near the bow and watched the whole procedure of casting off the lines and the tugboat operation. We stayed there as the ship moved out of the harbor, past the old fortress El Moro and into the open sea. It was a beautiful site as we left the island behind. By the time we went below to our quarters it was getting quite dark and we had "sobered up" completely. But with our appearance another "crisis" was set in motion!

It seemed they had taken a muster soon after the ship left the docking area, and we had been reported as "absent". Everyone there assumed that we had "missed the ship". So we immediately went to the Commanding Officer's quarters to do some explaining.

Before I tell you what happened next, let me relate more about the ship, the CO and "Bull" Fisher.

We were aboard the *U.S.S. New Kent,* an APA, and a troop transport that was typical of that class. Troop quarters were fore and aft, in the bow and stern. Officer's quarters were amidships. The *New Kent* was newer than the old *Cambria* that we rode to Culebra the year before. The Officers quarters were on the main deck level and those that had "rooms" near the bulkheads also had portholes. There were two or three officers assigned to each stateroom.

I was the only artillery officer aboard, since I was serving as a Liaison Officer for the Artillery to the infantry Regiment, the 8th Marines. Colonel Ridgley was the Regimental CO. As I remarked in another story, the Colonel and I got along very well. I enjoyed his confidence and respect. Similarly, I held him in the highest regard. He was one of the finest officers I knew during my Marine career.

I recall that Joseph "Bull" Fisher was commissioned on the same day I was commissioned, June 6, 1945. However, that may be our only commonality. Joe Fisher was commissioned in the field. That is sometimes called a "battlefield" commission. Joe was a veteran of several of the Pacific battles with the Marines. He was a stocky, strong looking fellow and that is probably why he had the nickname "Bull". Joe was an officer with the 8th Marines. I never served with Joe Fisher again and we never were close personal friends. However,

I did follow Joe Fisher's career from afar during the next twenty years or so, and I recall that he attained the rank of Lieutenant Colonel before he retired. And I was sad to see the notice of his passing a couple years ago in about 1998. Well the rest of my story is anti-climatic. When we found Colonel Ridgley in his stateroom, he had already received the muster report that showed us to be absent. He really got a "kick" out of our story and how we "almost" missed the ship. He waved us off and corrected the report. I know that being with a highly decorated fellow like Joe Fisher and having had a good relationship with the Colonel in the past stood me in good stead at the time. It was quite exciting and I still remember those *"Rumbannas"* But, that's another story!

Photo Album

My father, William G. Harris on far right. Taken in 1919 in Germany where he and his friends served in the Army of Occupation. Note the "Indianhead" patch of the Army's 2nd Division at the shoulder and the "Service Stripes" on the lower sleeve. One stripe for each six months served overseas. My father is wearing two stripes, which indicated he is in his second year of overseas duty.

Chapter 13   March 27, 1948
What A Day!

When we arrived for duty at Camp Lejeune, we found there was no housing available on the base or in Midway Park, a government housing community just outside the camp entrance. There was a long waiting list for housing at Midway Park, but being the optimists we were, we added our name to their list. We were told about some ex-government housing available in the town of Holly Ridge about 15 miles or so south of Camp Lejeune.

The Army had closed their Camp Davis at Holly Ridge and some of the government-constructed apartment buildings in Holly Ridge, originally abandoned, were being renovated and made available.

We learned a group of Marines, in search of a place to live, just like us, had begun putting this housing back into a "livable" condition and were moving into these small apartment buildings. We went to Holly Ridge and rented one of these "apartments".

After we had cleaned and painted the three rooms, we were happy to move into our new home. Holly Ridge was to be our home for over a year, until we finally got the call from Midway Park. We moved to Midway Park but were only there for a few months before we were assigned Officer quarters on the base at Camp Lejeune.

We were living in Holly Ridge on the morning of March 27, 1948. Early that morning, Marie started to experience some labor pains. She was nine months pregnant and we were expecting the birth of our second child any day.

It so happened that even though this was a Saturday, I was required to go to the Regimental Headquarters Building to serve as the Judge Advocate (Prosecutor) in a Special Courts-Martial. The Courts-Martial Officer was a Major Marshall J. Hooper. Major Hooper was on the Regimental Staff and most of the junior officers in the

Regiment thought he was somewhat of a pompous ass.   My agreement with this opinion of the Major had been reinforced when he scheduled this Courts-martial on this Saturday morning, He wanted to get the trial over so he could begin his leave.   Our Regiment had just returned from maneuvers in the Caribbean, and most of us were still unpacking and getting to know our families all over again after an extended absence.

While on these maneuvers, the accused Marine had been apprehended in the act of stealing from other Marines while aboard ship. As the "prosecutor" in this trial, I had two Marines, who had witnessed the crime and they were to appear for the government. These two Marines were stationed at one of Camp Lejeune's outlying camps, called Courthouse Bay.

Courthouse Bay was in the southern end of the Camp Lejeune military reservation. The road from Holly Ridge to the Regimental area at Camp Lejeune passed right past the entrance to the Courthouse Bay installation. Consequently, I had made arrangements to pick up my two witnesses on my way in from Holly Ridge

Our Regimental Adjutant, a Warrant Officer Riley, who also lived near us in Holly Ridge, had asked to ride in with me on that Saturday. At the time I agreed, I did not know we would have the situation that was rapidly developing.

Obviously, I had not planned on Marie having labor pains that day. But, it soon became obvious that she could not be left alone in Holly Ridge. She had to go to the hospital right away. So Marie and our three-year-old son, Bobby, along with W.O. Riley joined me on our way to the hospital and the courts-martial!

We all bundled into our 1941 Ford Club Coupe. This model was called a "Club" coupe because it had a bench seat behind the front seat. This allowed two or three persons to ride in the coupe behind the driver and his front seat passengers.

Marie and I were in the front seat. I was driving and little Bobby was sitting in between us. WO Riley rode in the back seat alone for the first half of the trip until we arrived at Court House Bay where the two Marines witnesses crammed in the back seat with him.

All during the trip, I was aware that Marie was suffering a lot of discomfort. She was very quite, and it wasn't until later that I found out that she was experiencing severe labor pains.

We finally arrived at the Regimental Headquarters building and we dropped off WO Riley and the two Marines. We then proceeded directly to the Naval Hospital where Marie was promptly admitted. Soon, she was taken from us, placed on an elevator and whisked away to the maternity section of the hospital. In 1948, fathers and sons were not allowed to be anywhere near the maternity area. After Marie entered the hospital, we were "persona non grata" anywhere beyond the lobby area.

However, we did get a chance to wave to her, when she came to a second floor window as we stood below in front of the hospital entrance. The next time I saw Marie was after the birth of our daughter, Patricia, in the late afternoon of March 27, 1948. I was allowed to visit her and Patty in her room; however Bobby was barred by the "No Children" rule. He didn't get to meet his baby sister until the day Marie was released to come home, almost a week later.

After Marie left the window, Bobby and I returned to the 10th Marines Regimental area. After all, I had a courts-martial to run and the time for the trial to begin was rapidly approaching.

I took Bobby over to the barracks that housed the men of my unit, Battery "B". I was fortunate to find Corporal Whipple who agreed to take care of Bobby while I did my duty at the Courts-Martial. Needless to say, we gave the guilty bastard a fair trial, Major Hooper took off on leave and I returned to the Barracks to pick up my young son.

From all reports, he had a wonderful time with the Marines. He had quality time jumping on the bunks and he enjoyed getting a lot of attention. I believe Corporal Whipple and the other Marines there that day enjoyed the diversion provided by having a young visitor for a few hours.

After checking at the hospital, only to find that Marie was still in labor, we went to visit an old friend who had been assigned as NCO in Charge of the Service Club in the area nearest the USNH. Master Sergeant Henry had until a short time before been Warrant Officer Henry, and a colleague in Battery "B". With the return to the peacetime Marine Corps, Henry had been returned to his permanent enlisted rank of Master Sergeant.

Bobby and I "hung out" with Henry for most of the day, periodically going over to the hospital to find out if there was any change in

Marie's status. While at the service club, Bobby was getting his fill of pop and candy, and had the run of the whole place, which was essentially empty at the time.

Finally, about 5 P.M., Patricia Marie Harris was born and I had a brief opportunity to greet her and her mother. Everyone was very happy. We were especially pleased to have a little baby girl!

It was dinnertime and night was approaching. At that time, the Bachelor Officer Quarters had a surplus of empty rooms. Any officer could have a room assigned just for the asking. Consequently, I had a room at the BOQ at Paradise Point (Officer's country at Camp Lejeune). So, Bobby and I went to the BOQ and shared a single bed that night.

I can't remember either one of us eating dinner, but I do remember Bobby in his underwear jumping up and down on the bed. This was one exciting adventure for him. I don't know how either of us slept that night, but we both rested after one "helluva" day. I now look back on that day of confusion, complications, frustration, apprehension, exhilaration, boredom, anxiety, joy and happiness with a smile and a fond recollection. March 27, 1948. What a day!

Patty at one-year in Ysleta, Texas

Marie and Patty in
Oxnard, California at age 4

Chapter 14   Cold Weather Maneuvers

In the fall of 1947, we received the word that elements of the 2d Marine Division were to conduct "Cold Weather" maneuvers. Now we all realized that one of the stanzas of the Marine Corps Hymn was "...from the snow of far off northern lands to the sunny tropic scenes you will always find us on the job the United States Marines..." But weren't they carrying it a bit too far? We had begun the spring on a tropical island in the Caribbean and now we were going to bring in the winter somewhere up north. But we knew they were serious when we began receiving cold weather clothing.

As it turned out, the "trip" was full of events and surprises, which made indelible impressions on my memory. The overall plan was for the units involved in the exercise to move to the U.S. Navy Amphibious Base in Norfolk, VA in mid-October 1947. The officers and men of the Marine units would be attending various schools related to amphibious operations for a week or so and then we would go aboard the ships that would move us to our maneuver area. The hinterlands behind the Naval Base at Argentia, Newfoundland had been selected as the maneuver area.

While we were in the "school" phase of the operation, we had our evenings free. Several of the officers, mostly those of field grade, had brought their wives to Norfolk for the time we were "schooling". Consequently, at the Officer's Club in the evenings we would observe these officers and their wives enjoying dinner and some drinks after dinner.

Our Battalion Executive Officer was a Major Ed Dzura. Most of the junior officers in the Battalion often referred to him as Major Zero. Major Dzura was a graduate of the Naval Academy and I suspect he was the class anchor...or very close to being it. Whether it was true or not, the one thing people said about the Major was that on one occasion he granted a Marine an extension of leave while that Marine was AOL.

Major Dzura was a small person, slightly built. His wife, to the contrary, was a very large woman. She wasn't fat; she was just big and muscular. One evening while at the club in Norfolk, we observed a disturbance occurring in the party that included the Major and Mrs. Dzura. We later found out that Mrs. Dzura became upset with her husband and took him to the toilet, put his head in the bowl and flushed the toilet. So much for being the "man of the house"!

The last time I saw Major Dzura was at Camp Pendleton in 1953. The 4th Marines, an infantry regiment of the 3rd Marine Division, was conducting "war games" in the rear areas of the base. I had been assigned as the Artillery Liaison Officer to a battalion of the 4th Marines. A large group of us were standing around on the top of one the many hills in the reservation awaiting the arrival of the umpires for the upcoming "game". It seems the Amphibious School at Coronado, near San Diego, were providing some of their officers to serve as umpires.

After considerable delay, an old black hearse came driving up the road to the hill. After it came to a halt, the rear door opened and a half-dozen or so Marine officers jumped out. As the driver left the "car", I recognized him as our old friend, Major Dzura. Those of us who knew him or his reputation were not surprised!

At the completion of our schooling, we were to conduct practice landings. Now remember, this was late October and the Atlantic Ocean, which is never really warm, is particularly cold during that part of the year. A Lt. Colonel Nutting who was considered the Marine Corps' "Guru" when it came to cold weather operations led the preparation for this cold weather exercise. He was tall, lean and his face was weather beaten. He looked like he had spent his life on the tundra. And, he was tough and demanding. If it was up to him, the landings would "separate the men from the boys"

Soon we experienced exactly what he meant by that expression. We had gone aboard the APA-44, the *U.S. Fremont* on the 28th of October. On the day of our landing on the beaches of Little Creek, VA, the temperature was in the high 30s or low 40s, sky overcast and the sea ran a little rough. I embarked in an LCM with the regimental Headquarters group. Lt. Colonel "Northern Lights" Nutting, our cold weather expert, was also aboard the landing craft. There were many in the Headquarters group who were carrying radio packs as well as their weapon and other necessary items. (The load is never light!).

As we approached the beach, the LCM ran aground on a sand bar that was a good thirty yards from the shoreline. Almost immediately after we hit the sand bar, "Northern Lights" ordered, "Drop the ramp". The Navy Coxswain responded immediately and the ramp splashed into the water, exposing a lot of water between the beach and us. Regardless, the Lt. Colonel was the first off the ramp as he leaped into the frigid waters of the Atlantic. Of course, the rest of us followed. The depth of the water over the sand bar was at least four feet and maybe five in some places. Several of the Marines, went in over their heads as they jumped into the water. Every one of us was totally immersed at one time or another as we made our way towards the beach. Needless to say, the rest of the day was equally miserable, few of us dried out during that period, but it is surprising how much more comfortable you are when you keep on moving and generate some body heat. We all were hoping that our landing in Newfoundland would not be a repeat of this practice one. Fortunately, they canceled the amphibious landing at Argentia and we all off loaded the ships like "civilians", moved through the populated area and into the hills where we began the maneuver.

While I was sailing on the *U.S. Fremont* with the headquarters people of the 8th Marines, my artillery battery was embarked on an LST. After leaving the Norfolk area, the convoy headed in a northerly direction. The convoy formation is best described as two parallel lines of ships. We could see an LSM, Landing Ship Medium, abreast of us in the formation. The LSM should not be confused with the LCM. The LCM is a landing craft, used to move large equipment and men from ship to shore. The LSM is a seagoing vessel, designed to carry heavy equipment for the landing force. In this case this LSM had an engineering unit aboard and you could see the beam of a large crane protruding from the open deck of the ship.

It wasn't long before the seas became ugly. I estimate we were east of Boston, when we ran into one of those infamous "Nor'easters". The sea became exceptionally rough. Looking amidships from the *Fremont* you would lose sight of the LSM, even the extended crane, as the swells of the sea seemed to swallow the ship from time to time.

The senior Marine on the LSM was a Warrant Officer known as "Cowboy" Moore. I only knew the fellow by reputation. He was well respected and was one of our Marine Corps characters. During the peak of the storm, we learned that the CO of the LSM had become incapacitated and most of the crew was very seasick. It seems that "Cowboy" was the only one who was on his feet and he was manning the wheel.

In the heavy sea, our LST with all the artillery had suffered some serious damage. A large seam across the deck had separated and the heavy seas threatened to do more damage. Our LST was ordered to the Port of New York for repairs. While entering New York harbor a Pennsylvania Railroad barge rammed them, causing more damage.

As it turned out, my small group was the only representatives of the artillery that made it to Argentia. Fortunately, it didn't snow, but the weather in Newfoundland was very monotonous to say the least. We played as if the artillery was ashore, but it was not a very rewarding experience.

Two things occurred that might be considered fortuitous: My fellow artillerymen aboard the LST were allowed liberty in New York City for about a week, before they returned to North Carolina and after we celebrated the Marine Corps Birthday, November 10th, in the boondocks, I developed a toothache.

The dentist took me to the *U.S. Bexar* where he did not one, but two extractions. The *Bexar* (pronounced BEAR) was lying in the harbor, awaiting the return of their complement of troops. Since I had two "open sockets", the Doctor would not let me return ashore. So I joined the *Bexar,* APA 237, for the return trip to the States.

The port of Halifax, Nova Scotia was chosen as a "liberty" stop on our voyage home. We were allowed a couple of days ashore to absorb the local culture. While shopping, I bought a wonderful snowsuit for young Bobby, who was 2 ½ years old at the time. I thought I could estimate his size, but when Marie saw it she could hardly stop from laughing. If he ever wore that snowsuit, it was not for a couple more years. I thought he was a really BIG boy.

Chapter 15   The Rifle Belt And Bayonet People

In the fall of 1948, shortly after I was promoted to First Lieutenant, I received orders to report to the U. S. Army Air Defense School at Fort Bliss, Texas for the purpose of attending the Guided Missile Systems Officer Course. After a couple years in the Second Division at Camp Lejeune, I had the 'itch" to move on and do something different. My duties as an artillery officer had been very interesting and I enjoyed the people and the duties I had been assigned, but I was looking to do something different and leave North Carolina.

Marine Corps Headquarters had requested applications from junior officers for the Guided Missile Systems Officer course. The basic academic requirements were mathematics through calculus and one year of college physics. The Army had set these prerequisites based on the course work of a military academy graduate. I had taken all the courses that were required, even though I had not yet received my Bachelor's degree. I jumped at the chance because I have to admit I liked being a student and this Guided Missile business was something new. I was very pleased when I learned I had been accepted and we would be moving to El Paso, Texas. It was all quite exciting.

Only a few months previously, I had been recommended and accepted to attend the Aerial Observer's school at Quantico, Virginia. It would have been about an eight-week school in Quantico, and upon completion I would have expected to have been sent back to the 10th Marines or, possibly assigned to the other Marine artillery regiment at Camp Pendleton, California, the 11th Marines. Every artillery regiment has billets for a number of AOs and at that time the only AO with the 10th Marines was Lieutenant Vincent J. Robinson. When an opening in the school presented itself, "Vinnie" had recommended me for the job. I think the AO job's main attraction to me at the time was the Flight Pay an AO received. Living on a Second Lieutenant's pay was not living "high on the hog", and the extra dollars paid for flying was very attractive. Of course, the Guided Missile selection took precedent but I do wonder what my career would have been if I had opted for the Aerial Observer school.

At the time, Guided Missiles were something very new. The German V-2 was the world's premier ballistic missile and the German V-1; the "buzz bomb" of London blitz notoriety, was the "cruise" missile of the day. The rethinking this new weapon brought with it was exciting and different, and at the time, "mind-boggling".

I have often wondered whether or not it was to my advantage to "specialize" and enter the Guided Missile field rather than continue to serve in the more traditional role of a Marine officer. The artillery had provided a nice blend of duty with troops and the technical aspects associated with fire direction. I don't think I would have enjoyed being an infantry officer, which is about 100% troop duty. I needed to have some technical "problem solving" along with the command of troops.

I should explain that every other tour of duty, or a least every third tour, a Marine officer expected to be assigned to the FMF. FMF stands for "Fleet Marine Force". The tactical units of the Marine Corps make up the FMF, principally the Marine Divisions and Marine Air Wings, and their supporting units. Consequently, I knew that after one or two tours of duty in "Guided Missile" billets, I would be returning to the FMF and a Marine Artillery Regiment in one of the Marine Divisions.

I recall what a Captain told me about becoming "too specialized". It was while I was attending a reception for the newly appointed Commandant, General Cates, at the Officer's Club at Paradise Point, Camp Lejeune in 1948. I was standing with a group of young officers at the bar and I had just told them of my new orders to the Guided Missile school. This Captain (whose name and face I do not recall), was a Company Commander in one of the Infantry Regiments, said I was making a "big" mistake. He said the "rifle belt and bayonet" people ran the Marine Corps and if one ever wanted to be successful in the Corps, he should not become "specialized". He said to "make it" in the Corps one must stay with the troops, i.e. infantry or tanks…. or not any further away than engineers or artillery.

I didn't experience any disadvantage with being "specialized" until the fall of 1963. Headquarters, USMC convened a special selection board at that time to establish a special promotion zone from which to select a number of Majors for early promotion to Lieutenant Colonel. Since it was a "special" selection zone, those who were in the zone and were not selected would not be considered to have been "passed over". I was in the zone and I thought I would be one of those selected. However, I was not one of those to receive an early promotion. While it was not an official "pass over", I felt as if I had failed.

I was living in the "Cinder City" BOQ at Quantico at the time, having recently returned from a tour of duty with the 12th Marines, 3rd Marine Division in Okinawa. Marie and the children, Bob and Pat were still living in Fenton, Michigan, where they had moved before I departed for Okinawa. A friend of ours, Major Bob Smith and his wife Jane, invited me to dinner at their home along with another Major and his wife. I can't recall the other Major's name, however I do recall he had been in the University of Michigan V-12 unit after I had left the unit and his wife was from Hartland, Michigan. He was an infantry officer and very junior to me in rank.

The dinner date was only a few days after the Special Selection Board had published the names of those to be promoted. During the visit, it became known that this young Major had been selected, and in fact had "passed over" me. All during the evening, I kept asking myself, why was he selected and I was not? After all, I was one of the relatively few officers in the Marine Corps who were specialized in Guided Missiles and weapons development. In addition to the school at Fort Bliss, I had graduated from the U.S. Naval Postgraduate School, with a Master of Science in Electrical Engineering. My record was "outstanding". I had received several commendations from Marine and Army commands for the performance of my duties. I was one of four officers who developed a new weapons system for Marine aviation! What goes? On the other hand, my fellow dinner guest was strictly a "rifle belt and bayonet" officer, whose primary duty had been with infantry regiments and Marine detachments. Granted he must have been an outstanding officer, however, his principal duty had been with infantry units, he was a couple years younger and he had much less time in the Corps and as a Major. What goes? It really bothered me! It still does!

You should know that, our friend Bob Smith was a Marine aviator and he was lost in Vietnam and listed as a POW. His wife Jane was very active in the POW organizations in the late 1960s. Bob was a Naval Academy graduate, either the Class of 1948 or 49. Bob and Jane were with us at the Naval Postgraduate School in Monterey. It is my understanding that Bob's remains were recovered a few years ago, after an intensive search in North Vietnam for the remains of MIA pilots.

There was a relatively small group of officers who were the "Guided Missile" people. Most of us knew each other, having either served together, attended the Naval Postgraduate School at the same time or if we didn't know each other personally, we knew of each other by reputation or through mutual friends.

Sometime later, I found out that all of the "guided missile" Majors who were in that Special Promotion Zone were "passed over". It also became known that the "rifle belt and bayonet" people controlled the selection board. They didn't consider these "Guided Missile" Majors as "real" Marines, deserving a special promotion.

You can imagine how pleased the "Guided Missile" people were when we learned that the upcoming regular selection board was to be chaired by a "technically oriented" General. This General was known as a progressive thinker, interested in advanced weapons development and new tactics for their use. We knew the General understood the need for officers educated and trained to work in these areas. Our confidence in his understanding was justified, when the Board selected every one of the "Guided Missile" Majors for promotion.

If I have any regrets about "specializing" and becoming one of the "Guided Missile" people it is that Marie and I did not have the opportunity to develop more lasting friendships with other Marine Officers and their wives. While we were serving at Fort Bliss with the Army (on two occasions) or NAMTC Point Mugu or Great Lakes NTC with the Navy, or being the only Marine in our office at the Pentagon, our Marine contemporaries were serving at the Marine bases: Pendleton, Lejeune or Quantico in various capacities. Those officers in the "band of Lieutenants" that served together in the late 1940s at Camp Lejeune who did not "specialize" were generally reunited every year or so and therefore were able to reinforce their friendships throughout their careers.

However, you must recognize that living a life is making one decision after another and you have to live with each decision you make! I have often used the following visualization to make this point. Let's say you are in a room. On one side of the room are ten doors. You are required to select one of those doors and leave the room. You make your selection and you find yourself in another room with ten more doors ahead of you. The door you used to enter the room is closed and you cannot go back through it. You need to make a decision and select a door and leave that room. And so it goes...decision after decision and no way to return and choose another door. So in a way, looking back is all right if you can learn from your previous decisions, however you cannot relive the day or return to the past. Make the best decision you can, but make the best of your decision. I can't help but think about what might have been, but all in all, I have had a variety of life experiences and each of the experiences have had their good times and their bad times, but, overall, there have been many more good times and I have enjoyed my life! But, that's another story!

1st Lt. Harris visiting an "old friend" in Korea. This is the 105mm Howitzer. . Most of my duty in Marine Artillery was with the "105s".

Here is Marie and our two small children. We were living in Midway Park, a small community just outside of the Main Gates of Camp Lejeune, North Carolina. Patty is only a couple months old and Bobby is only three years old. Picture was taken in the summer of 1948.

Below is Pat-spending Sunday at Aunt Ol's in Hammond, IN, 1954 Bob in backyard of Santa Ana home in 1952

Chapter 16   The Point Of
No Return

In the late summer of 1948, with transfer orders in hand, the young Harris family, myself, Marie, three year old Bobby and five month old Patty, packed into our 1941 Ford Club Coupe and departed Camp Lejeune, North Carolina. We headed for Michigan to visit with our parents. We had a few weeks of leave available before I was required to report to the U.S. Army Air Defense School, Fort Bliss, Texas to begin the *Guide Missile Systems Officer Course*.

This was the second time we had driven back to Michigan since I had returned to active duty in November of 1946. On our first trip back to our hometown, we experienced some heavy rain and stormy weather.

On that first trip, I had left directly after work and did not change into civilian clothing. I was wearing my uniform cotton khaki trousers and shirt. While driving a while in the heavy rain, we discovered the car was leaking around the windshield and a considerable amount of water was coming down inside the car from underneath the dashboard. The little "waterfall" was hitting my legs a little below my knees. After a few hours, my trouser legs were soaked from the knees down and the water had saturated my socks and filled my shoes. Those of us, who used to wear the cotton khaki uniforms, all washed and ironed with plenty of starch, remember how difficult it was to continue looking "sharp" in that uniform. After wearing a clean starched uniform for short length of time, it soon looked as if you had slept in it! If you sat down once, you caused a thousand creases in your trousers to ruin that "sharp" image. On Inspection Days, while dressing for the inspection, Marines would need to exercise great care while dressing. They would gently ease their legs into the starched trousers, carefully avoiding disturbing the razor crease. The shoes were laid out so that one could slip into them without bending over. After the shoes, they would put on their starched shirt, again easing their arms through the sleeves, ever so carefully, trying desperately to keep the edge on the creased shirt sleeves. Finally, came the tying of the field scarf (a tie for civilians!). In those days, the field scarf for the enlisted men was also made of cotton. It was laundered, starched and ironed in the same manner as the rest of the uniform. One had to be very careful in making the forehand knot with this piece of starched cotton. Tying the field scarf was very much like tying a thin piece of wood into a knot. A field scarf was good for one wearing, and then it had to be laundered, starched and ironed again.

Finally, after driving across North Carolina on a very dark night with heavy rain, it came time to stop for overnight. We were exhausted. We stopped at a very nice hotel in Roanoke. It was a very up-scale place; the entrance was on a large circular drive. We arrived very late in the evening, parked on the drive and entered the hotel and approached the desk. Picture this if you can. Here is a Marine Lieutenant in a very wrinkled cotton khaki uniform. From his knees down to his shoes, his trousers are soaked and he is dripping wet. In each arm he is carrying a paper shopping bag, loaded with pajamas, children's clothing and toys. Coming closely behind him is a young woman, carrying a grocery bag in one arm and dragging a sleepy little boy by one arm. Talk about the Beverly Hillbillies! Occasionally we think about it and have a good laugh, but secretly, I can't help but wonder if that embarrassing event didn't have something to do with Marie's reluctance to travel and stay in hotels?

But back to our second trip from North Carolina to Michigan, one of our many trips "back home" to Fenton from wherever we were stationed. It became the rule rather than the exception that each year, we would use our annual leave time, to travel to Fenton, Michigan. With two sets of Grandparents both living in Fenton, it seemed the right thing to do. On this particular trip, we were returning with two children since Patty had been born after our first visit. It goes without saying that the Grandparents were overjoyed to have three-year old Bobby and five month old Patty within their grasps. It was always fun to be in Michigan in the summertime. My parents lived on Lake Fenton, so there was the pontoon boat and swimming at their house. Our biggest problems were determining where to stay and where to eat. Each of the Grandmothers vied for the privilege of hosting and feeding us. We made an effort to "balance" our time between both parents, but it wasn't easy!

In addition to having a good time on this trip, we were able to sell our old Ford and acquire a "new" 1947 Chevrolet sedan. I use the word "new" even thought it was "pre-owned". My father, an employee of AC Spark Plug Division of General Motors, was permitted to buy a new car at a discounted price and then resell it after holding it for a specified period of time. His "holding time" requirement had expired so he was free to sell the auto and purchase a new 1948 model. Since we had a genuine concern about the reliability of our old Ford, we were planning on buying my father's car and having it available for our trip to El Paso. My father was inclined to help us so he "made us an offer we couldn't refuse". He offered us the car for $1000, just what he needed to complete his purchase of a new model. So, we sold our old 1941 Ford and bought his 1947 Chevrolet.

The Chevrolet was in excellent condition with very low mileage. Now, with our transportation problem solved, we were ready to make the 2 to 3 day trip to El Paso. When the day finally arrived we packed the "new" car with most of our worldly possessions, including a supply of diapers, and literally drove off into the sunset to begin a new adventure in America's southwest.

As was generally the case in those years, our orders had explicitly stated that no Government quarters were available. Therefore, our first task upon arriving in El Paso was to find a place to live. Our immediate needs were barely met with accommodations at Fort Bliss' Officers Guest House. The Guest House was one of the typical wooden barracks constructed by the thousands on hundreds of military bases throughout the world. The barracks area had been subdivided into rooms. The walls were not wall-boarded so the 2 x 4 studs were exposed. The floors were bare wood and the windows had some cloth pieces serving as curtains. The toilet facilities were "down the hall". The only good thing that could be said about these temporary quarters was that they provided a place for us to sleep and the price was right! In fact, downright cheap!

Each day, after getting the children dressed and fed our primary objective was to search for a place to rent. We did all the usual things, read the want ads, checked with the Base Housing office, talked to the real estate offices and drove up and down acceptable neighborhoods looking for "FOR RENT" signs. Several days went by with no luck at finding a suitable place.... really *any* place! One must remember that housing was in a critically short supply in most cities and towns in the United States. Basically, no houses had been built during the four years of the war. Servicemen had returned home, married, started families and they all needed housing

Each day, we would start our search again. The Guest House accommodations were beginning to get on everyone's nerves and there was a limit to the number of days we were allowed to stay in these wretched rooms. But our biggest problem was that we were running out of money.

Our dilemma was this. If we couldn't find a place, Marie and the children would have to return to Michigan and live with the grandparents. In that case, I would report for duty and move into the Bachelor Officers Quarters, BOQ. Our money situation was getting to the point where we were dangerously close to not having enough money to pay for the train tickets. We got to the point where I said to Marie, "If we don't find a place today, you and the kids will have to go back to Michigan". We were approaching the *point of no return*.

That morning we happened to go to a small town called Ysleta. Ysleta was a very "Mexican" town. Only the main street through town was paved. All of the side streets were dirt streets. If I recall correctly, the principal industry in the town was something to do with cotton, a cotton gin or something like that. We were inquiring of downtown business people about the availability of any rental houses or apartments and were delighted to learn there was an upstairs apartment for rent in the building across the street.

The first floor of this building was a grocery store and there were several apartments on the second floor. The entrance to the second floor was a door on the main street and a very steep stairway led to the second floor.

We found the owner, Jack Hughes. Jack Hughes' appearance was that of the stereotype Texan rancher, western shirt and jeans, cowboy boots and all. He was an older fellow, a very pleasant and decent man. He took an immediate liking to young Bobby and the feeling was mutual. Bobby took a real "shine" to Mr. Hughes, the first real life "Cowboy" he had ever seen. Mr. Hughes took us to the upstairs apartment, which was at the rear of the building, and we found our "home".

Once you climbed the steep stairs, from the street level entrance, to the second floor, the corridor made a turn to the right to the center of the building and then the corridor went down the center of the building from front to back. There were about five or six apartments entrance doors along the corridor. Our apartment was the last one on the right side of the corridor as you traveled from the front to the rear of the building. Fortunately, there was a second stairway at the rear of the building just beyond our apartment which went down to a street (or alley) which ran along the side of the building.

The apartment consisted of one bedroom, a bathroom, living room, dining nook and small galley kitchen. When you entered the apartment you entered the living room. To the right was the small dining area and to the left, the door to the bedroom. The bathroom door was in the far corner of the bedroom. The kitchen entrance was off the dining area and ran the length of the living room. The bathroom was quite large, large enough to accommodate our prize possession, a Thor washing machine. All the windows in the apartment were in the living room, bathroom and kitchen and all on the side of the building overlooking the alley below.

We soon got to know our neighbors across the hall, Army Captain James Hitchcock and his wife Maribelle. Jim and Maribelle had only three children at the time but were planning to have four to complete their family. Their goal was to have four children, each with a first name starting with the letters, J, K, L and M, those being the letters between James and Maribelle. John, Katherine and Leslie had filled the first three spots and only the M spot remained. Many years later, when we were again stationed at Fort Bliss, we had Major Hitchcock and his family as neighbors. They lived on the same street as we did and by then they had a complete set since Mary had joined the crew.

With no TV and no money we spent many evenings playing cards with the Hitchcocks. After our children were put to bed, we'd sit around the dining table and chat and play cards. It sounds quite boring, but at the time it was a pleasant way to spend an evening.

At about four years of age, Bobby wanted to go "outside" and play. The only space available to play outside was in the dirt street along side of our building. With little to no traffic, this was a relatively safe place to play. There was no grass, just dry dirt. However, Bobby found great pleasure in driving his trucks through this dirt.

Marie's practice was to take Bobby down the rear stairs leading to the dirt alley. She would find a place close to the building and get Bobby started playing in this restricted area. Then she would go back to the apartment to tend to the household tasks and young Patty. On one occasion, Patty was up and crawling around the front room when it came time to go downstairs and check on how Bobby was doing. As she closed the door to the apartment behind her she belatedly realized the door was locked and the keys were inside the apartment. For sometime thereafter, she found herself, trying to find Mr. Hughes with his master key, checking on Bobby and talking to Patty through the locked door. She was telling Patty to stay where she was, "Mommy will be right back" and anything else that would come to mind to keep the young child from crawling somewhere and getting into trouble or to begin panicking and crying for her mother. Finally, someone got the word to Mr. Hughes and he arrived on the scene and opened the locked door. All is well that ends well, but Marie remembers the incident with fear and trepidation to this day.

One day, Jack Hughes came to the apartment and asked Marie if he could take Bobby with him to do some shopping. He wanted to buy Bobby a pair of real cowboy boots. Not long after, Bobby returned wearing a pair of red cowboy boots and one of the biggest smiles you could imagine. It was difficult to get those boots off of Bobby's feet for months to come. Even today, some sixty years later, our son still remembers Mr. Hughes and the cowboy boots.

There was not a lot of "homework" from the course I was attending at Fort Bliss, but just enough to be annoying. Occasionally we would venture out to such places as the Carlsbad Caverns or some Mexican Restaurant, but for the most part our evenings and weekends would find us "at home". In the evening we could "pick up" Los Angeles, California radio and we would listen to a program where the fellow hosting the show would play the piano and interact with the audience, sometimes at the same time! He was a very entertaining and funny young newcomer named Steve Allen.

We had a comfortable and clean home and it was our first time of living in the high "desert" however, our next move was going to be to California and that's another story!

Chapter 17   Introduction to
Guided Missiles

Those of us who lived through World War II were somewhat familiar with the German's use of "guided missiles" in their efforts to subdue the British people. We generally knew the "V-1" and the "V-2" were those terrible weapons that terrorized the people of London during the "Blitz". Our movie news programs showed the V-1s cruising across the sky until their jet engine stopped and they began their plunge to the earth. We were told the V-2s were much larger and they struck without warning since they were "ballistic" missiles and their trajectory arched very high in the sky and they were not easily detected.

In spite of this information, Guided Missiles were quite mysterious to Americans in 1948 when I was assigned to study them at the Army's Air Defense School at Fort Bliss, Texas. I was a member of Guided Missile Class No. 5. The class was composed of officers from the Army, Navy and Marines. There were 25 Army; 15 Navy; and 3 Marines. While most of the officers were of Company grade (Captains and 1st Lieutenants) we did have some Navy Commanders, Lieutenant Commanders, a Lieutenant Colonel and four Majors.

The Air Force was just coming into existence and one of the Army officers, a Captain Crews changed the color of his uniform from Army khaki to Air Force blue during the term of our instruction. I remember we all kidded him about wearing the uniform of a Greyhound bus driver.

The course was divided into three areas: a review of college calculus and physics; introduction to guidance, propulsion, aerodynamics as related to missiles; and a field trip to major contractors in the field.

While I had been mathematics major in college, I experienced an epiphany in the calculus course taught by Marine 1st Lieutenant Cornelius "Corky" Sheffer. For the first time I really felt comfortable with the subject. He was a wonderful teacher. Marie and I became close friends with "Corky" and his wife Sybil and later, we were stationed together on several occasions. Upon retirement Corky became an instructor at Cuyahoga Community College in Cleveland, OH. I used to visit them occasionally when on business trips to the Cleveland area. Corky was a Naval Academy graduate, Class of 1944, and as such was a classmate of our dearest Marine Corps friends, Sam Dressin and his wife Sue.

As part of the program the whole class was occasionally taken to a lecture by one of the notables in this emerging field. Werner Von Braun, one of the "liberated" German missile experts spoke on one such occasion. With what we know about missiles today, I am a bit embarrassed to admit that one of his statements actually startled me. It was as if a light went on in my head. When he was talking about the range of ballistic missiles, he mentioned the maximum range need not be more than one-half of the earth's circumference. If we found the range to the target was greater than that we could just attack the target by turning the missile 180 degrees and come into the target from the other side. I used that nifty bit of information on at least two occasions when, while on leave in Michigan, I spoke on Guided Missiles to the Flint Kiwanis and to the XX Club in Fenton. Just as I was awed by the remark, I could see the "light bulbs" coming on in various members of the audiences as they got the idea!

We made field trips to nearby White Sands Proving Ground and the Air Force installation at Alamogordo, New Mexico. There we witnessed the firing of several different missiles, including the German ballistic missile, the V-2. One day we heard a V-2 fired from White Sands had gone out of control and landed in Juarez, Mexico, across the Rio Grande from El Paso and Fort Bliss. The word was that before the Army MP convoy could get across the border and cordon off the wreckage, the Mexicans had already been there and were hauling off pieces as souvenirs.

One of my best friends in the class was Army 1st Lieutenant James L. Hayden, better known as "Buster". "Buster" was an Army brat, a graduate of West Point and the son of a Colonel who was a long time member of the faculty at that institution. "Buster" and I traveled together on our three-week field trip to the West Coast. While in the San Francisco Bay area, we spent a weekend at a "dude" ranch in Carmel Valley owned by one of his relatives.

One of the activities available was horseback riding and "Buster", an experienced horseman, insisted we seize the opportunity to participate. Reluctantly, I agreed and we saddled up along with a group of about ten other guests. Most of the ride was uneventful as we moved over the hilly terrain in a single file. However, as we were approaching the end of the ride, we came out of the woods within sight of the stables. I was near the end of the line and when my horse saw the stables, he just took off at a gallop. There was no way I was going to regain control of this thundering beast! I held on for dear life and was greatly relieved when the animal reached his "home" and slowed to a stop. I have never sat on a horse since that scary ride. I am convinced a horse is much too powerful for any human to control, once it makes up its mind as to what it wants to do.

Three of my Navy classmates, Commander James Craig, Lieutenant "Nick" Evans and Lieutenant "Sandy" Knotts were transferred to the Naval Air Missile Test Center at Point Mugu, California following completion of the course at Fort Bliss. "Commander" Craig became "Captain" Craig and was the Commanding Officer of the Base.

I went flying with "Nick" Evans on several occasions and he and his wife went to the 1950 Rose Bowl Parade and game with the two of us. "Sandy" was a "submariner" and a bachelor, so while we were friends, we didn't do much socializing at Point Mugu. Both "Nick" and "Sandy" were also Naval Academy classmates of my best friend, Sam Dressin. Sam had been a member of Guided Missile Class No. 4 at Fort Bliss and he was at Point Mugu when I arrived in 1949. But, that's another story!

During our time at Point Mugu, we lived in a new house in Oxnard, California. Bobby started school at nearby Port Hueneme and Patty was anxious to do the same. Our new neighborhood was full of friends and "kids" which made our two years there very enjoyable. Below are some pictures of some of the activities that happened in our backyard.

Upper left: Bobby and Pat. Upper right: Bobby batting and Marie catching. Lower left: Marie with children at a Birthday Party. Lower right: Patty and flowers.

Photo Album

Bobby and Patty at Lake Fenton visiting Grandma Harris in 1949. The rowboat was a very big attraction for Bobby,

Marie and Pat in Oxnard, CA

Bobby is "hoisted" in Fredericksburg, Virginia in summer 1945

Sign on tree; upper right from Marie states that tree was planted by George Washington.

Photo Album

Top Left: Marie holding
Bobby in 1945

Top Right: :Bobby in 1952
Bottom: Marie and Patty 1948

Part III   The Mugu Marines

At the time of this writing, I am aware of only one other publication that tells the story of a small group of Marines, stationed at the Naval Air Missile Test Center, who developed and built an All-Weather Close Air Support bombing system, which became a tactical unit in the Marine Corps.   Lieutenant General Victor H. Krulak USMC Retired devoted a chapter of his book, *First to Fight* to this group. While the General's recounting is, in general, representative of what actually occurred, some of the details are close to the truth, but as they say, close is only good enough in horseshoes or hand grenades.

As one of the group of the original twelve Marines who worked on the project from its beginning to its deployment in combat in Korea, I suggest that the story related in the following pages is the most truthful recounting of events available.   They are derived from the available written records of the period and the best recollections of the three remaining members at the time of this writing.

The original members of the Marine Guided Missile Unit, who developed the equipment and the procedures for its employment, were four officers and eight enlisted Marines.   Then Captain M. Cranford Dalby was the Officer in Charge of the unit and was the prime mover in leading this group of Marines in this very unique program.

What is most amazing about the whole experience is how four company grade officers and eight enlisted Marines, on their own initiative, with no specific direction or authorization, could design, build and test a system, which would be accepted by the Navy and Marines as an integral part of their close air support weaponry.

In today's highly sophisticated military environment it seems inconceivable that something like this could ever happen again.

I joined the unit in August of 1949 and my prime contribution to the program was in developing the tactical procedures for the employment of the system in combat. I also became the "official" scribe for the organization. Most of the reports, especially the "Yellow Book" which was our most successful promotional piece of literature, was written and edited by me.

In his book, General Krulak labeled us as "The Improvisers". He writes, "We can drop a bomb from an aircraft at high altitude in closet darkness or in the worst of weather and be reasonably sure of hitting very near the target on the first try. We can do this, although neither the pilot nor friendly forces on the ground can see the target. *This is a monumental breakthrough, and one that has killed many an enemy at greatly reduced risk to our own pilots.*" (Italics are mine)

In today's arsenal, this system is obsolete and appears very primitive. However, in the wars in Korea and Viet Nam, the Marine Air Support Team using the original and, later, the improved "industry built" systems were very effective and provided the means to meet a real need in air support for the ground forces. But, there is more to the story!

On the right, I am with TSgt. John Seissiger, Sgt. Marvin Darrow with Cpl. Edward LeLouis peeking over his shoulder.
Below left are living quarters for unit on east central front south of Hill 854 on reverse slope of ridge. Below right is control tent directly behind Hill 854. Fall 1951

Chapter 18   The Improvisers

A few days after my 79th birthday, while sitting at my computer, my mind was wandering as I contemplated my feelings of getting older. In my mind, I was wondering about the ages of some of my old friends and comrades. I was thinking of my team leader in 1949, then Captain Dalby. I was only a First Lieutenant then, I was thinking, and he was a Captain. "Hell, he must be 80 something by now!" Being in that mental state, I was somewhat startled when the phone rang. I was even more surprised when the caller announced, "Hello, Bob, this is Cranford".

It was Colonel Marion Cranford Dalby, USMC Retired calling! Some people called him by his nickname "Dirty" Dalby. I never called him that; in fact, I never called him anything but "Captain" or in later years, "Colonel". As a young First Lieutenant, I was really in awe of this energetic, inspiring Marine aviator. He provided the leadership for a small group of Marines of which I was proud to have been a member. In recent years, we had talked to each other on several occasions, however, because of the circumstances, this call was different. Do they call it serendipity?

It turns out that "Cranford" was calling to ask my permission to provide my address and telephone number to a fellow who was organizing a reunion for "Point Mugu Marines". Once we disposed of that issue, I brought up the subject of leaving a record of our experiences at Point Mugu and in Korea with the Air Support Radar Team.

I told him our little group had an experience, which will probably never be repeated by any other Marines. In today's military climate, it is highly unlikely that twelve men, led by a mere Captain would ever again have the opportunity to develop a new and innovative weapons system. Our experience was truly only one of a kind. We had built the equipment, developed the tactical application and evaluated the system in combat. We needed to have the record of this unique adventure put down in writing before all of our little group had died. As far as we knew at the time, only three of the original twelve Marines were living. Later we were pleasantly surprised to find that Hal Leber was still among the living. However, Hal died a few months later, before he was able to contribute to our memory. Now, with the passing of Cranford Dalby in 2008, only John Seissiger and I survive.

It was then that Dalby told me that Lieutenant General Victor Krulak, USMC Retired had written a book entitled *"First to Fight"*[*] back in the 1980s, and he had devoted a chapter in his book to our enterprise. When I told him I had never seen the book, Dalby said he would send me a copy of the book. Within a few days, I received a copy of the book and found a whole chapter in a section entitled "The Improvisers" telling about our program. Upon reading the General's account, I found it flattering and, in general, a fair accounting of our endeavor. However, my problem was in his "details". I prize accuracy, and in several areas, his recounting of events was "not quite" right!. You might say that in some respect he was writing with an expired "Literary License".

However, he wasn't the only one whose memory confused some of the "details". Early in his tenure at Mugu, Captain Dalby developed an excellent relationship with Navy Commander Grayson Merrill. Commander Merrill is today considered the "Father of the Naval Air Missile Test Center" and at that time was one of the most important officers at Point Mugu. It was Commander Merrill that gave Dalby the go ahead on bringing all the Marines together to work on one project that was more related to Marine Corps tactical operations. However in his paper, written in 1984 and later republished in 2003, then Captain Grayson Merrill, USN Retired, at age 91 had the general story .correct, but had several details confused. Even the Captain was aware of what happens over time and wrote *"Please bear with an occasional embellishment of a sea story and lack of accuracy due to a fading memory"*. **

---

*"First To Fight", Victor H. Krulak, LtGen USMC Ret, Naval Institute Press 1984
** "The Birth and Boyhood of Point Mugu", Grayson Merrill, Capt.USN Ret

As a result of our telephone conversation of that day, the three known "survivors" of our group; Dalby, John Seissiger, and I began an exchange of emails in which each of us recorded our remembrances of our activities. The following is the history of our little group of "Improvisers". The Chapter entitled "Devastate Charlie", "Hot Showers And Near Misses" and "Hill 854" relate to our experiences with the MASRT in Korea

Upon completion of the Guided Missile Systems Officer Course at the U.S. Army Air Defense School, Fort Bliss, Texas in June of 1949, I received orders to report to the Commanding Officer, U. S. Naval Air Missile Test Center, Point Mugu, California for "on the job training in Guided Missiles". When I reported in to the NAMTC command, I was further assigned to the Navy's LARK Guided Missile project.

I cannot recall much about the LARK missile, since within a day or so, my orders were changed and I was directed to report to the Marine Guided Missile Unit for duty. The "Unit" was "officed" in a couple of small temporary buildings just across an asphalt parking area from the B.O.Q. and the Officer's Club. These buildings were on the south end of the "beach" area of the base. The northern part of this sandy strand along the beach was where the Navy had developed a complex of buildings. These buildings housed the radars and other guidance and tracking equipment used in the various missile projects being conducted at NAMTC.

I later learned the Marine GM "Unit" had only been formed a very short time and was not really an official USMC organization. NAMTC had a Marine Detachment under the command of Captain Howard Pittman that provided the Marine sentries at the Main Gate and other posts around the Base and performed the usual tasks of a Marine Detachment on a Naval installation. In addition to the Detachment Marines, there were a dozen or so other Marines, officers and enlisted men, who had been assigned to NAMTC for "on the job training with Guided Missiles". Up until the formation of the Marine GM Unit, these "guided missile" Marines were assigned to the various Navy projects and were scattered all around the base.

The senior "guided missile" Marine was Captain Marion Cranford Dalby, AKA "Dirty" Dalby. It was Captain Dalby's idea to bring all the "guided missile" Marines together and have them work on a project which was more likely to directly benefit the Marine Corps. I am also of the opinion that Captain Dalby recognized there was a chance that our Marines might be "corrupted" or, at least, learn some "bad habits" by working under the supervision (or lack thereof) of these Navy types. In any event, when I arrived, I found three Marine Captains and nine enlisted Marines as members of the Marine GM Unit. Two of the Captains, Dalby and Oscar Burston Johnston, were Marine aviators. The third was Captain Sam Aaron Dressin, a communications officer, a graduate of the U.S. Naval Academy and a graduate of the same Fort Bliss Guided Missile course, which I had just completed.

The enlisted men were for the most part Staff NCOs with technical MOS, primarily in electronics. There were four Master Sergeants in the group: Clark D. Hayden, Floyd A. Dickover, William L. Holtz and Elsden H. Reed. Master Sergeant Reed died within a couple months after I joined and, consequently he was not involved in the development program to follow. Others there at the time were Technical Sergeant John E. Seissiger, Staff Sergeant Robert F. Waggener, Staff Sergeant Hal T. Leber, Sergeant Marvin L. Darrow and Corporal Casimer J. Gramza. They were an extraordinarily well-qualified group of Marine NCOs. Later in their careers, Hayden, Dickover, Holtz and Seissiger were commissioned as Marine officers. Darrow rose to the rank of CWO and Hayden, Dickover and Holtz were promoted to the rank of Captain before they retired. John Seissiger retired as a Lieutenant Colonel in 1973.

Dr. Herbert A. Wagner

Just prior to my arrival, Captain Dalby had been talking with a Dr. Herbert A. Wagner about a guidance project that might be undertaken by the new Marine GM Unit. Dr. Wagner was one of the German rocket scientists who had been persuaded to come to the United States at the close of WWII to assist in our guided missile programs. Dr. Wagner had been closely associated with Germany's missile program and the development of the V-1 "Buzz Bomb". The V-1 was a cruise type missile propelled by a Pulsejet. The original German V-1 did not have a very sophisticated guidance system. The missiles the Germans launched from the continent were essentially aimed in the direction of English cities. A propeller in the nose of the missile was used to determine the distance to be traveled. When the number of revolutions of this propeller reached a set number a signal was generated that would shut down the pulse-jet, blow the wings off the missile and cause it to spiral downward to the point of impact. The Germans used the "Buzz Bomb" in their assault on London. To say it lacked "pinpoint" accuracy is a serious understatement. The Germans were satisfied if it landed somewhere in Greater London.

After the end of the War in Europe and as soon as the Air force was able to recover enough V-1 debris from the rubble of London, it hired Republic Aircraft to make some 1500 copies. Many of these missiles were delivered to the NAMTC, where the Navy renamed them the LOON and started working on the idea of launching the missiles from submarines. A hanger type structure was built on the deck of the submarine to accommodate the LOON. After surfacing, the LOON was removed from the hanger and launched toward a land target.

The guidance system for the LOON was only slightly improved from the original V-1. Dr. Wagner had designed a simple but more complex guidance system for the Navy's LOON missiles. This system was similar to the guidance of a radio controlled model airplane. After the launch, the directional guidance was provided by the radio signals to keep it on the course from the submarine to the land target.

Dr. Wagner had written a paper presenting a more advanced concept for developing a guidance system that would more accurately control the LOON, and thereby increase its effectiveness as a naval weapon.

Capt. Grayson Merrill
USN Retired

Captain Dalby was successful in obtaining the approval of Commander Grayson Merrill, to have the Marines develop this more advanced guidance system. Commander Merrill arranged for the NAMTC to provide the services of Darrell Wallace, a civil service electronics engineer, to convert Dr.Wagner's proposal into schematics and "hardware". Working with Mr. Wallace, the Marine's technicians led by Master Sergeants Holtz and Dickover began building this guidance computer. It wasn't long before they had a "bread board" model set up and working in the north beach complex, and ready to guide one of the Navy's LOON missiles. However, it was very difficult to get any time on the

Navy's radars or participate in any part of a missile launch. Simply stated, our program did not have much of a priority…or more like "0" priority…zilch!

The tracking radar being used by the Navy was the standard SCR-584 which was developed for use by the Army anti-aircraft artillery during World War II. As the Army and the other services began working with guided missiles following WWII, the SCR–584 was available and became the tracking radar of choice. There was a large inventory of the SCR-584s and it had been in service long enough that both maintenance and operational problems were minimized.

The Navy had several SCR-584 installed on the beach at Point Mugu and used them extensively in their missile projects. These were the radars we used when available. Our guidance computer was designed to accept the tracking signal from the SCR-584.

The problem of getting the opportunity to control one of the LOON missiles was a major obstacle in the testing and evaluating the performance of our guidance equipment. The LOON project people at NAMTC had their test program and the submarine people had other requirements. It is my best recollection that we had only two opportunities to participate in the guidance of LOON missiles.

For these controlling opportunities it was necessary for us to transport our "bread board" guidance equipment to San Nicholas Island and use the SCR-584 radar the Navy had located on the island. In these tests, we controlled one LOON which was launched from the "beach" and another which was launched from a submarine off the coast. Our radar would pick up the "incoming" LOON shortly after its launch and control its flight toward the target. And at the proper time, our computer would generate a command signal which would literally blow the wings off the LOON and cause it to plunge toward the target.

In both cases, the target was Begg Rock, a small cluster of rocks off the coast of San Nicholas Island. San Nicholas Island was part of the NAMTC and located about 65 miles off the coast from Point Mugu. There was a small airstrip on the island and the Navy had a small detachment manning the airstrip and other electronics equipment on the island. We didn't know it then, but San Nicholas was to play a large part in the development and testing of our guidance equipment over the next year.

I have no exact recollection of how accurate our system was on these two occasions, or how it compared to the Navy's guidance system for the LOON. However, I suspect that it was not any better or any worse than their system. I don't believe any LOON missile ever hit Begg Rock. Hitting within a mile or so was considered quite satisfactory at that time.

Since the LOON missiles were really not available in sufficient numbers to develop and test our system, we decided to use "drone" aircraft in lieu of the LOON.

As it was, NAMTC had a large number of F-5F aircraft which were equipped with an automatic pilot to serve as "drone" aircraft. The planes were painted red so as to distinguish the "drones" from other Navy aircraft. Radio control devices worked through these automatic pilots and allowed the controllers on the ground or in another aircraft to remotely control the "drone" aircraft. When not being flown as a "drone" the aircraft could be operated like any other F-5F.

The availability of "drone" aircraft for use with our project was a major breakthrough for the testing and evaluating of our guidance system. We were able to schedule the "drone" flights with little difficulty. Captain Johnston became our "test" pilot and he would fly the F-5F drone into position and we would acquire his aircraft on our radar. We would guide his aircraft to the Begg Rock target in the same manner as we did with the LOON missile. Just as we would send control signals to the LOON, we would send these signals to the automatic pilot in the drone aircraft and guide the "drone" on the course to the target. However, there was one big difference, between controlling the LOON and the piloted "drone". This difference was of considerable importance to "Obie" Johnston, the pilot.

With the LOON missile, at the proper time, a signal was sent to blow the wings off the missile, causing it to go into a spin and dive into the target. However, blowing the wings off of the F-5F, even without Captain Johnston in the cockpit would have been considered as unacceptable. Therefore, we loaded the F-5F drone aircraft with 100-pound water-filled practice bombs. At the appropriate time, our guidance system would send the signal that automatically dropped a practice bomb.

We were able to make numerous runs each time we operated with the drone aircraft. As we recorded the location of the bomb hits, we noted the bombs were falling very close to our target, Begg Rock. It soon became apparent that our equipment could control aircraft and drop bombs regardless of the weather, which might obstruct the pilot's view of the target. Using our guidance system, it was not necessary for the pilot to see the target in order to put bombs on the target.

We then realized we had developed an All-Weather Close Air Support system. Forget the LOON! It was now important to perfect this system, and take it to Korea, where a war had just begun.

However, the likelihood of experiencing success in combat with electronic guidance equipment that was sitting on open racks and still in a "laboratory" state and relying on fixed radars, or at best radars in large vans, was obviously not practical. The task before us was to repackage our system so it would function and survive in a combat environment. Further, if we were to provide close air support, all of our system, including the radar, must be able to move. setup and operate in a manner very similar to direct support artillery units.

Immediately prior to reporting to NAMTC, Point Mugu, I had been a student at the U.S. Army's Air Defense School at Fort Bliss, Texas. While at Fort Bliss, I had observed a large fenced-in area where literally hundreds of military vehicles and equipment were stored. I had assumed it was a yard where "surplus" equipment left over from the war was being stored awaiting the decision for its disposal.

Among the equipment, I had seen a number of SCR-784 radars. I understood that the SCR-784 was actually a repackaged SCR-584. Electronically it was the same as the SCR-584. However, while the SCR-584 was housed in a very large van type trailer, the SCR-784 was packaged in a relatively small two-wheel trailer.

The SCR-584 crew operated the radar from within this large van, and the antenna was mounted on top of the van. The antenna for the SCR-784 was mounted on top of this small trailer and the control panel for the operation of the radar was located at the end of the trailer. One needed to raise the end panel, extend a canvas cover to form a room-like enclosure. The crew would then operate the radar from within this enclosure, outside of the trailer. It is my understanding the Army repackaged the radar as the SCR-784 for use in amphibious operations. It was small enough to load off the landing craft being used at the time and appeared rugged enough to withstand the movement from ship to shore.

SCR-784 at Mugu with Lt. Harris and MSgt Holtz "faking" operation!

These features were attractive to one considering operating radar and associated equipment in an amphibious landing or a combat environment. And even more important, here were radars, which would meet our immediate requirement, sitting in what appeared to be a yard for the storage of "surplus" equipment. Upon hearing my tale, Captain Dalby decided we should fly to Fort Bliss and see if we could "borrow" one of these "surplus" SCR-784s.

A few days later, Captain Dalby and I flew to Biggs AFB, which was adjacent to Fort Bliss, to check on the availability of the 784.

Upon arriving, we were graciously received by the Commanding General, Fort Bliss. After explaining our need for a radar to use in our close air support project, the General called the appropriate supply officer on our behalf. With relatively little difficulty, we were able to arrange for the "borrowing" of an SCR-784. In the following week, Captain Johnston traveled to Fort Bliss with a Navy flat bed truck and picked up a complete SCR-784 for our use in the project.

Captain Dalby was not only our leader, but he was also our "politician" and a good one too! Once we had the SCR-784 in operation we gained some mobility for the system. Dalby was a very persistent salesman and he was able to "sell" some of the "right" people at HQMC and the Navy's Bureau of Aeronautics (BUAIR) on the potential of our system.

Our "politician", Captain Dalby, made several trips to Washington and talked to both Marine and Navy planners about our program. At Dalby's instruction, I was directed to prepare a document which explained our relatively complex system in "words any one can understand". My effort became known as the "Yellow Book"...a book of about 50 pages with photos and charts, but, with a minimum of technical terms. Dalby took a large number or the "Yellow Books" to Washington and dropped them on the desk of every Marine or Navy officer who would have any influence on deciding our future. Dalby's mission was accomplished! He was successful in arranging for a contingent of the decision makers from HQMC and the Navy to attend a bombing demonstration on the ranges of Camp Pendleton.

We brought our "breadboard" computer and guidance equipment back from San Nicholas Island and installed it in the van of a navy truck. Now with the towed SCR 784 radar we were able to travel the highway to Camp Pendleton and demonstrate the feasibility of the all-weather close air support system we had developed. Therefore, we moved our equipment to Camp Pendleton, setup and conducted operations for several days before the day of the demonstration for the "brass".

At the time, we had two F4U-5N Corsair fighter aircraft from a night fighter squadron at El Toro MCAS assigned to our project. Later we had two Navy F4U-5N flying for us for a couple of weeks. At the time, the F4U-5N was the only fighter plane in naval aviation that was equipped with an autopilot. Our airborne computer equipment was installed and incorporated with the planes autopilot in these aircraft during the time they were operating with us.

On the day of the "demonstration" a number of Marine Generals were on hand including General Gerald Thomas who had visited with us at Point Mugu several months earlier. With the large group assembled on an observation post close by our radar, the truck with the guidance and control equipment and our operations tent, the demonstration began with bombing runs on some pre-selected targets. The results were outstanding, including several direct hits by bombs dropped from aircraft flying overhead at about 10,000 feet. Our real test came, when Captain Dalby invited the visiting dignitaries to select any target they wished for us to attack.

Several of the high ranking officers selected targets and within minutes we were able to process the information, pick the aircraft up on the radar, set the aircraft on their initial courses and turn them over to the automatic control of our computer. At the appropriate time, our computer triggered the release of the bombs and the hits on targets were outstanding.

The exercise was a complete success. It clearly demonstrated the feasibility of our system. This marked a turning point in our program. Following this demonstration we were placed on the "fast track" for preparing the system for combat operations in Korea.

We were amused by the naivety of some of the observers. One of the observers remarked that the equipment we were using could not withstand the rigors of combat operations. Captain Dalby said he would never again allow anyone see our gear until it was it was ready for combat. We couldn't believe that anyone would think we expected to take a van truck with racks of exposed electronics into a combat environment. We knew our equipment needed to be "hardened" and repackaged for use in the field and we knew how to do it.

A standard 3/4 Ton Trailer was used to house the guidance computer and the radio control equipment linking us to the aircraft. The control panel at one end of the trailer provided space for two operators who would input the required data and monitor the system during the bomb runs.

Soon after the demonstration, we were able to procure the trucks and trailers and men and materiel needed to prepare the system for combat operations in Korea. Once this was accomplished we conducted several weeks of simulated combat operations in the desert near the NAS, El Centro, California.

We set up in Carrizzo Canyon in the hottest days of the early summer. It was so hot the resin filled capacitor cans in our computer were melting like candle wax. The terrain was very rugged so we used it for conditioning the troops for the upcoming tour in Korea. I was quite proud of my physical condition when I took my group on a short hike up and down some of those weird dessert rock outcroppings. At 28 years of age, I was about ten years older than these Marines who had recently joined our team. I recall feeling good about myself as I noticed some of them were dragging by the time it was over and I still had "gas in the tank".

Once we completed our exercises we returned to Point Mugu and began preparing for the move to Korea. Unexpectedly, we made a very significant change in radars. A newer tracking radar, the AN/TPQ-2, was made available for our team. It was more than a repackaged SCR-584; it was completely new radar. It was necessary to make some modifications to produce an output compatible with our computer. This was accomplished with the help of some outside contractors. We were also able to have this radar mounted on a 40 mm Antiaircraft Gun Carriage for better mobility. Once we had this completed and after a few trial runs, we were ready to load up the men and equipment and take off for Korea.

The Marine Corps had provided equipment and personnel for two "Marine Air Support Radar Teams" (MASRT), as we were officially designated. As with many successful ventures, there were several new officers assigned who were anxious to "take over" the operation. Fortunately, our leader, the "politician", was able to make some "end runs" and protect his position of leadership and the positions of those of us who had worked through the development of the system.

In June of 1951, the "originals" with Captain Dalby in charge, augmented by selected individuals and now designated the 1st MARST was ordered to Korea, to operate in support of the 1st Marine Division. We were to conduct a combat evaluation of the system, now known as the AN/MPQ-14. The 2nd Team was to remain at Point Mugu and continue to work with the system and hopefully be able to recommend modifications or improvements, which would enhance the system. Since the combat evaluation was to be completed in a relatively short period of time, in about four or five months, the training of replacements for the "originals" was not contemplated at that time.

We motored in convoy to San Francisco and reported to the Naval base at Treasure Island, where we parked our equipment and barracked our men while awaiting an assignment to a ship heading in a Westerly direction. A couple of days later we were scheduled to embark on a U.S. Naval Ship, the *General Howze*. The *Howze* was a rather large transport ship, unlike all the other Navy transports I had experienced during maneuvers.

The *Howze* actually had many luxury features. The staterooms and dining facilities would remind one of a cruise ship. The passengers aboard also included a large contingent of women and children, dependents of Army personnel stationed on Okinawa. We were at sea for about ten days, before we landed at Okinawa and the dependents disembarked. The *Howze* then took us to Japan where we disembarked at the Naval Station in Yokosuka. We were in Japan for several days before we boarded the U.S.N.S. *General Black* for the last leg of our journey. After an overnight voyage we arrived in Pusan, Korea.

Three of the four original MASRT officers
In the Bankers O-Club, Yokahoma on way to Korea.
L-R Capt. Sam Dressin, 1stLt Bob Harris and Major O.B. Johnston.
July 31, 1951

We moved from the ship to an airfield outside of Pusan designated K-1 and the location of the Headquarters of the First Marine Air Wing. We were actually a unit of the FMAW's Tactical Air Control Squadron, MTACS. We set up our tents and began checking out our equipment in preparation for our next move, the trip north to join the 1st Marine Division. The 1st Marine Division was in the rear area just north of Wonju and had been regrouping following the movement out of the Chosin Reservoir the previous winter.

Finally the day came, when we loaded our equipment on a railroad flat car and boarded a Korean train for the trip north. Most of us were traveling in a boxcar, while some remained on the flat bed car behind us with our equipment. The locomotive was a coal burner, and when the wind was toward the train, we would receive a generous amount of black smoke, with hot cinders intermixed.

As we traversed the mountains of South Korea, we went through numerous tunnels. While in the tunnel, the entire car was saturated with the hot dense smoke. Everyone tried to hold their breath until we came out of the tunnel; however in most cases the tunnels were too long and breathing was very difficult. The heat from the smoke while in the tunnels was another of the discomforts we had to endure during this two-day trip to Wonju. When we left the train, we were covered with the black soot and ashes.

We were positioned with the Division's Tank Battalion, where we were able to clean up, work on our equipment and enjoy their hot food. At that time the division had already moved north as the Fall Offensive of 1951 was underway. A few days later we took to the road and moved north to position ourselves where we could provide some close air support for our infantry.

As our small convoy was moving north, we had to pull over to the side of the narrow road in order to allow some trucks heading in a southerly direction to pass by. It was quite sobering when we realized the cargo of these trucks were the bodies of dead Marines, wrapped in what appeared to be camouflage ponchos.

We went into position up a small valley on the east side of the larger valley through which the So Yang Gang (River) ran from the north to the south. We placed the radar on the forward slope of the ridgeline and set up our living area and supporting equipment on the reverse slope. We had a row of about ten pyramidal tents which each housed from four to six men.

The Headquarters Battery of the 3rd Battalion, 11th Marines was in a similar small valley immediately to our south. We attached ourselves to their mess and we were able to enjoy hot meals most of the time we were in that position. Lieutenant Colonel Healy was their C.O. and Major Ed Fossum was their S-3. When I had free time from my duties with our team, I would visit with Ed Fossum and a Lieutenant Coons in the Battalion Fire Direction Center. Being an Artillery Officer, I felt very comfortable living near my *compadres* of the 11th Marines.

Once we were up and running we were able to conduct air strikes on a variety of enemy positions when aircraft was made available for our control. Newly commissioned 2nd Lieutenant Clark Hayden along with Major O.B. Johnston and TSgt Leber had moved to K-3, an airfield on the east coast of Korea in order to service the Marine night fighter squadron VMF (N)-513, who were equipped with our control devices. These were the only planes we could control automatically with our guidance system. In order to work with other aircraft, not equipped with our automatic control devices, we developed a "manual" procedure.

When an aircraft without the automatic capability would come up on station and report to us as ready for our control, we would conduct their bombing runs "manually". When operating in the "manual" mode, we would vector the aircraft out of an orbit on the approximate heading to the target. Once the radar had "locked on" the aircraft, the computer would determine the correct path and indicate the corrections in heading to keep the aircraft moving down the correct path to the target. These required course corrections were transmitted via voice radio to the pilot. The pilot would make the course corrections and maintain a level altitude. As the moment for the release of the bombs approached, the pilot was instructed to arm his weapons and standby for the "dump" command. The "manual" procedure proved to be almost as accurate as the automatic control. Most of the inaccuracies were introduced by the pilots who failed to follow the instructions or were not properly briefed before taking off on the mission. Using the "manual" procedure allowed us to control Navy aircraft flying off carriers, U.S. Air Force fighters from Korean airfields and B-29s coming from Okinawa.

The success of the MASRT presented some problems when it came to replacements and the length of the tour for the "originals". Even though the combat evaluation phase had been completed, the 1st Marine Division wanted us to stay in support of the Division. Major Dalby was the first to return to the States, and Major Ed Harper, who had joined us at Point Mugu before we left for Korea, became our team leader. A few months later, we began to receive one officer and several enlisted men a month as replacements for the "originals". Probably, because I was the junior officer of the "originals", I was the last officer to be replaced. I would like to think it was because I was the most experienced and qualified of the officers in the operations of the Target Information Center (TIC) and I sincerely believe that to be the case. The primary duty for an officer in our team was to control the aircraft and supervise the Marines operating the computer and working in the Target Information Center (TIC). The enlisted specialists did all of the technical work. Since I was the "original" who developed all of the procedures used in the TIC it fell to me to train each officer replacement in their duties in the TIC. After thirteen months in Korea, I finally received orders to return to the States and after leave, report for duty at the MTACs with the 3rd MAW at MCAS, El Toro, California. There I would join now Major Sam Dressin and now 2d Lieutenant John Seissiger in setting up the training for MASRT personnel.

I was promoted to Captain while at El Toro, but after only a couple of months, both Sam Dressin and I received orders returning us to duty with the "ground" Marines. Sam went to the 2nd Marine Division at Camp Lejeune, North Carolina and I was assigned to the 3rd Marine Division at Camp Pendleton, California.

When I arrived for duty with the 3rd Marine Division, I was assigned to the artillery regiment, the 12th Marines. Colonel Leonard F. Chapman, who later became the 24th Commandant of the Marine Corps, commanded the 12th Marines. I became the Battery Commander of the Service Battery of

Lt. Harris on his way to chow with HQ Btry, 3rd Battalion, 11th Marines, October 1951.

the 3rd Battalion. In my mind this was not the most prestigious command for a Captain in the Battalion, however the three Captains who were serving as firing Battery COs at the time outranked me. Our Battalion commander was Lieutenant Colonel Lonnie McCurry. Colonel McCurry was an outstanding officer and fine gentlemen.

I learned an MASRT from El Toro was at Camp Pendleton conducting some practice bombing runs. I asked Colonel McCurry if he would like to visit the MASRT and he responded affirmatively. So, I took him out to see the equipment for himself. When we arrived at the MASRT site, I was pleased to find 2nd Lieutenant John Seissiger still with the organization. We arrived after the close of operations and the CO of the MASRT had declared a "field day" and allowed the troops to have some beer and munchies on the site. Consequently, there were Marines moving to and fro as John and I tried to steer the Colonel through the control tent. A Marine carrying a case of beer came through the tent and accidentally drove the corner of the beer case into the short ribs of Colonel McCurry. I decided it was time to leave and we left with the Colonel rubbing his bruised ribs.

Within a few weeks things became more interesting as I became CO of "G" Battery, a 105 mm Howitzer Battery. I was very pleased to have my first "real" command of a combat organization. We were conducting a heavy training schedule that placed us in the field almost every day. At the same time we were joining personnel and rapidly getting up to the authorized troop strength. The same activity was happening throughout the 3rd Marine Division. Something was in the wind! But, that's another story!

As a Postscript to "The Improvisers" the following is the text of a magazine item, which appeared in either 1951 or 1952. There was another item in an edition of the *Marine Corps Gazette*. The article reprinted below is from an unidentified magazine, which my mother clipped and saved for me. Those of us in Korea were not aware of any public release about what we were doing at the time.

Robot Bombardier
An electronic "bombardier" that delivers bombs more accurately than any human airman was reportedly shipped to Korea. While the new weapon doesn't leave the ground, it guides planes to the target, and then releases bombs.

Photo was taken in Itami, Japan, while I was on a week of R & R from Korea. Since we were a unit of the First Marine Air Wing, even though we were attached to the First Marine Division, we were eligible for a week in Japan.

I flew by helicopter from the Division area to the Marine Airbase K-3 on the east coast of Korea. From there it was a short hop to the air station at Itami, Japan. During the week I stayed at the Miyako Hotel in Kyoto and lived very "high on the hog". The Miyako was a four star hotel and Kyoto had escaped war damage since it was one of Japan's holy cities.

One of the members of the 1st Marine Air Support Team decided we needed to have a "patch"...so one was designed, The "unofficial" patch for our Team uses the patch of the 1st Marine Division (Blue with Red One) and super imposes the outline of the Korean peninsula (light Blue), an aerial bomb (Black), and a radar (White) emitting electromagnetic pulses and the ribbon (Gold) with the letters M.A.S.R.T. in Black

Chapter 19   Hill 854

Hill 854 was the farthest north the 1st Marine Division advanced during the fall offensive of 1951. There was a terrific firefight for the top of the hill and Captain Frank Goff of our group witnessed it during its final phases. He told me of seeing this helmet-less young redheaded Marine leaping to the top of a mound and firing his BAR into the "gooks" entrenchment. It was a few ferocious minutes that will not even earn a footnote in the annals of the war. I'm reminded of this incident as I listen to the accounts of the encounters from reporters "imbedded" with our Marine and Army units in Iraq. What is reported as minor firefights or not even reported at all are at the time very "big" firefights for those engaged. They are life and death matters, and each such contact with the enemy is terribly serious for those involved. So it was on Hill 854 in the fall of 1951 in the mountains of eastern Korea.

One of my responsibilities with our Air Support Radar Team was to pinpoint the location of our radar and to obtain accurate position coordinates for our forward positions. This information was needed to more accurately determine the positions of enemy targets. During the years the Japanese had ruled Korea, they had executed a complete and very accurate survey of that country. Every hill of any significance in Korea had a Japanese Imperial Survey marker on its most prominent point. At that time there was no more accurate way of determining ones position than having it tied into the Imperial survey.

A few hours after Hill 854 had been secured; I took a couple fellows from our team up the trail toward the top of the hill. On the way up we encountered many of the Korean labor troops who were used to carry boxes of ammunition on their backs up the trail. The Koreans used their native "A" frame carriers and the weight they carried up the hill for such small people was truly remarkable. There was no way I could have carried a box of ammo on my back and negotiated the steep trail. The Koreans also had the task of tending to the dead North Korean soldiers. At that time so soon after the battle, they had covered some of the bodies with dirt.

On the way up the trail we came upon the body of one North Korean who had been only partially covered with dirt. His feet were sticking out from the pile on one end and his right arm with his hand upraised was protruding from the other. The feet had on the usual black tennis shoes the North Koreans wore, winter and summer. They looked like "Keds" with the inside round pieces to protect the anklebones when they are knocked together.

Resting on the way up Hill 854, fall of 1951

The outstretched hand of the dead fellow was what was most interesting. In the fingers of his hand someone had placed five playing cards. "Aces and Eights", the notorious "Dead Man's Hand", reminiscent of the tales of the poker hand being held by Wild Bill Hickok when he was shot and killed. Marines are known to be exceptional fighters, but perhaps not as well known for their unique sense of humor.

Another mental picture remains after all these years from the climb up and back down the trail that day. On the way up at one particular bend in the trail, one could see another dead North Korean soldier lying not far off the trail and a bit uphill from where we were standing. Later in the day, near sunset, as we traveled back down the trail, we came to the same spot. The soldier was still there, uncovered, only this time, several hours since we first noticed his body, his appearance had drastically changed. His body had taken on an eerie greenish hue. He glowed iridescently in the light of the setting sun. It was an uncanny sight I shall always remember.

When we arrived at the top of the hill, we began searching for the survey monument; however the battle activities or the "gooks" had destroyed or removed it. It was a common practice of the enemy (the "gooks") to remove the monuments because they knew the value of the survey to our troops. However, we were able to dig around on the

 spot where we suspected the monument would have been placed and were able to find the subterranean marker. The Japanese always placed a subterranean marker directly below the surface monument, just in case the surface monument was destroyed or moved.

On subsequent trips to the Marine positions on top of Hill 854, I had some experiences, which remain vivid parts of my memory. On one occasion I was able to visit with an old friend from my days at Camp Lejeune. Lieutenant Michael Sparks (on far left with cap in picture with me) had been one in the large group of new Second Lieutenants who joined the 2nd Marine Division while on maneuvers in 1947. Sparks was then assigned to the Military Police. At the time of our meeting, Michael was an infantry platoon leader. As I sat with him in his dugout, it was obvious he was very distraught. The reason he was in such a nervous state became clear as he told me about his experiences of the night before. He had led part of his platoon across the Soyang Gang River into "gook" territory. Once they had crossed the river, which was essentially the dividing line between the good and bad guys, he ran into a group of North Korean soldiers and they became engaged in a firefight as they worked their way back to the riverbank. Before crossing back into our territory, he did a head count to make certain that every one of his men was present. When the check verified all were on hand, he moved the unit back across the river.

Once they had made it across, he redid his headcount. Only this time one Marine was missing. With the enemy on the opposite bank, it was not possible to cross the river again, without risking additional casualties. The code in the Marines is that you never leave a fellow Marine, dead or alive, on the battlefield. The fact that he had lost one of his men was tearing up his "guts". He was terribly distressed by the thought of having left this fellow behind. No one in the patrol had any idea of what happened to the missing Marine. I have no idea what was ever learned about this unfortunate fellow.

Earlier, about a day or so after our Marines had seized Hill 854, the KMC troops were in the process of assaulting this hill to our east. It was like having a 50-yard line seat at a football game. We could watch the KMC fighters moving up the hill in attack and then being thrown back by the defending North Korean troops. This up and down the hill went on for the good portion of the day, until finally the KMC overran the ridge and took possession of the hill.

On Hill 854 in winter 1951-52

On another occasion, Major Ed Harper accompanied me on one of my trips "up the hill". Ed Harper had joined our outfit a few months before we were deployed to Korea. He was a close personal friend of our leader, Major Dalby and he was Dalby's successor as our O-in-C when Dalby left early for the USA.

Ed Harper was a decorated fighter pilot from WWII when he flew with "Pappy" Boyington's "Black Sheep" Squadron. He had a large ugly scar in his back from where a Japanese 50 caliber Armor Piercing round had exited his body. On his last mission he had been strafing some Japanese trucks, and on his final pass he was hit. The 50 caliber round .entered under his arm, passed through a lung, clipped his spine before exiting through his back. When he was hit he lost control of his legs and began bleeding profusely. He decided that ditching in Pacific was not an option and set a course to his home base on Green Island. He was experiencing considerable pain and was going in and out of consciousness, but he managed to land at his home airfield. It was over six months before he was able to return to limited duty.*

---

* "Once They Were Eagles", Frank E. Walton, The University Press of Kentucky

Majors Ed Harper & O.B. Johnston

While Major Harper had considerable combat experience in World War II, flying fighters in the South Pacific, being on the ground in a combat zone was new to Ed Harper. I was certainly no veteran of being under fire either, so when the position began taking some incoming mortar fire we both went for the shelter and protection of a "slit" trench. The "slit" trenches on the hill had been dug for two purposes. One set of the "slits" was for protection and the other was for defecation. In fact, the ones for defecation were of two kinds. One group of trenches was used by the Korean "honchos" and the other group by the Marines. In his haste Ed Harper made a bad choice and he ended up in one of the "honcho" toilets. He was covered from his shoes to his thighs. I asked him to walk behind me as we returned to our unit back down the hill.*

A month or so later I was returning from a week of "R&R" in Japan, and I had just disembarked at an airfield south of the Division's position. It was in the early evening and as I walked across the tarmac I passed several rows of stretchers occupied by wounded Marines awaiting the Air-Evac to Japan. Then I heard a call from one of the wounded, "Hey, Harris". I turned about and there I saw Michael Sparks lying on one of the stretchers. "What in the hell are you doing here Mike"? I asked. Sparks then told me he had received the "million dollar" wound. He had been shot in the leg and it broke his leg bone. The "million dollar" wound was one in which you received a broken bone that necessitated your return to "the world". Mike was transferred to a Naval Hospital in the New York City area, so he would be close to his family.

---

* Ed Harper retired from the Marine Corps in 1969 with the rank of Colonel.. Soon thereafter he began a successful career with McDonnell Douglas Aircraft retiring as their General Manager

Michael Sparks and I never met again, but after my retirement from active duty in 1965, I read the Marine's professional journal, *Marine Corps Gazette,* every month and was impressed by the many articles that Mike Sparks contributed. He was a full Colonel during the War in Vietnam and commanded an infantry regiment. I am sorry to report that Michael was killed in that war while on a reconnaissance flight in a helicopter. It was shot down and crashed.

In the valley to the immediate east of Hill 854 the river, the *Soyang Gang,* turned to the south. The river divided the fronts of the US and the Korean Marines. A road ran next to the river from north to south and southerly through the valley, which was occupied by the rear elements of the 1st Marine Division. One day, the new commander of the MTACS-2 and an aviator unfamiliar with the situation on the ground, decided he wanted to visit the "front lines". The Colonel and his driver traveled in his jeep up the road, heading north toward the front lines.

Hill 854 looking North into a cratered "Gookland"

Being unfamiliar with the terrain and the troop locations, they continued in a northerly direction and drove right into "Gook" country. They were captured. I have been told that months later the North Koreans displayed the Colonel on television as he confessed the use of "germ warfare" by the United Nations forces.

In the early spring, just weeks before the 1st Marine Division was ordered to move to a blocking position north of Seoul, we occupied a position just to the rear of Hill 854. The Marines were dug in on Hill 854 and they were the ones who separated us from the North Koreans. Occasionally, some individual or small group of NKs would sneak through the lines where they either surrendered or were caught before they could do much mischief. We had our own perimeter defense, but that's another story!

Photo Album

Our TPQ-10 Radar in position 1951
L-R Sgts. Brown and Darrow checking
positioning.

Sam Dressin with me in Korea,
During the Winter 1951-1952

MASRT Camp Site Sept 1951-Radar behind hill to rear

"Officers Row"- My tent second from right

My (with three others) "home"

Photo Album

Approaching Hill 854 looking ENE...note Marine tanks on top of ridge and road used to travel

On Hill 854 looking NE up Nam Gang Valley..."Gookland" to left of river..note craters

Looking to east from Hill 854...the Sea of Japan is on the horizon

Looking west from Hill 854...note USMC Pershing tank on ridge line with crewman standing outside at the rear

Chapter 20   Devastate Charlie

I sometimes wonder if there is the wreckage of an old jeep in a junkyard in South Korea hidden in a pile of scrap metal. Not any old jeep, but "Devastate Charlie". You could identify "ol' Devastate Charlie" by her name painted in gold on a red background on the panel below the front windshield. It had been painted there in the fall of 1951. It was the bright and bold colors of the Marine Corps. Once our team arrived in Korea, we confirmed the fact that we needed a cargo jeep. While outfitting in the States prior to embarkation, we were provided sufficient trucks to move all of our equipment and men and two "Radio" jeeps for communication. The radios in these jeeps filled the "rear seat" completely. There was only room for the radio operator and the driver. When it became necessary to make a "run" for something, the only option was to use one of the tactical radio jeeps or turn to one of the large trucks. We desperately needed a jeep to do the necessary runs, but one was not approved for our team in the initial outfitting and our requests for one from the command in Korea were still "in process". We didn't expect to receive favorable consideration even when it got to the top of the Supply Officer's pile of requisitions. We had been operating with the 1st Marine Division for only a few weeks when we began experiencing difficulties with our radar, the AN/TPQ-2. The only other outfit equipped with the AN/TPQ-2 in Korea was the Marine 90mm Antiaircraft Artillery Battalion stationed around the city of Pusan, in the very southern tip of the Korean peninsula. Consequently, it was decided to send Captain Sam Dressin and Technical Sergeant John Seissiger back to Pusan for the purpose of visiting with the Antiaircraft people to learn how they solved their radar problems. Upon arrival, Sam and John met with their technicians and learned a lot about keeping the radar working. While visiting with this group, they also learned the U.S. Army was unloading hundreds of cargo jeeps from a ship at the Pusan docks.

These were all new jeeps and as they came off the ship they still had the wooden crating around the windshields and a wooden box full of accessories in the back seat.

Even though U.S. Army sentries were on guard, Captain Dressin and TSgt Seissiger made a call on the docks, were passed through the sentry post with no difficulty and began to look over the row upon row of U.S. Army cargo jeeps. What in the world was the Army going to do with all these jeeps? They identified one of the jeeps near the head of the line that looked especially inviting. So they got in, with Sam Dressin at the wheel and John Seissiger riding shotgun.

They found that the combat switch was working and when it was turned on, the gas tank gauge showed a reasonable amount of fuel was in the tank. Once they had it going, they turned out of the line and moved down the pier towards the sentry. The sentry saluted the Marine Officer, who promptly returned the salute as he drove off into the streets of Pusan.

They continued driving through the city directly to the outskirts of Pusan to the Marine Airbase known as K-1. Once on the base and within the confines of the First Marine Air Wing, they found a maintenance area where they arranged for the rapid transformation of this "one in a million" U.S. Army ¼ Ton, Truck, Cargo into the one and only Marine jeep, "Devastate Charlie".

It wasn't long before the drab Army green was covered by Marine green paint. The panel below the front windshield, about 1 ½ feet wide and running the width of the vehicle, was painted a bright Marine Corps red. When the red paint dried, the letters DEVASTATE CHARLIE were boldly printed in a bright yellow, almost gold, color.

When it came to the markings for the front and rear bumper, the usual USMC was printed in yellow on one end. The vehicles serial number needed to be painted on the other end of the bumpers. What number should be used? Captain Sam A. Dressin, USMC volunteered his officer's identification number, slightly modified. Sam's file number was 023109. Devastate Charlie became 123109.

Once the title to the vehicle had been "transferred", the new owners drove their newly acquired jeep back across town to the USMC Antiaircraft Battalion area and began the preparation for their return trip up north to our unit with the 1st Marine Division. With the Captain at the wheel, the two Marines drove north until they rejoined our team, which was still in position in support of the Marines just north of the "Punchbowl" and the city of Wonju.

Fifty years later, John Seissiger told me of this ride through the Korean countryside. During their travels, they would arrive in some small town where the only military to be found was a Republic of Korea Army (ROKA) Military Policeman who could not speak English. In spite of John's offers to relieve Captain Dressin with the driving, Sam would not relinquish the wheel and he drove the whole distance.

Needless to say, Devastate Charlie became an essential part of our team. It was always on the run for spare parts, the mail, and rations and for almost every conceivable reason. There didn't seem to be anyone designated as the driver. Everyone seemed to drive the jeep on one or more occasion. However, I do think there was one Marine who assumed the responsibility to make sure "she" was running right, had oil and gas and had maintenance performed on a regular basis.

Sergeant John C. Roberts was the fellow. John was in charge of the generators, big diesel generators, which provided the power for radar operation. For the thirteen months I was in Korea with the team, John was our man. He lived with those generators. He made certain that they were "humming". Although it was one of the most important jobs in the organization, it was one no one else wanted to do! It was a terrible job! Regardless of the weather, those generators had to be maintained and fueled. Working with diesel fuel everyday was a very messy business. John Roberts was our living "Pig Pen"! He was a filthy sight. His clothing was saturated with diesel oil from head to foot. However, it was his job and he did it with great pride. He had the same attitude for Devastate Charlie. Others may have had the opportunity to drive her here and there, but she always came home to John.

John had another collateral assignment. It was John's job to routinely pour a little diesel in the "four holer" and "burn it out". The "four holer" we had during the winter months of 1951-2 was the pride of the camp. It was a very popular place for both the officers and men. Everyone made an attempt to visit the "four-holer" at least once a day. In the winter months, the "four-holer" was enclosed by a tent which added to the comfort of its users. On one particular day, John had not removed the tent and the wooden structure from the "hole". He poured in a generous amount of diesel oil into the hole as he prepared to ritualistically "burn it out". On this particular day, John had been a bit too generous and a huge ball of fire erupted from the ground. The tent and the "four holer" ignited and we all came out to witness this fiery spectacle. Fortunately, John was also a carpenter, and the new "four–holer" was even more spectacular, considering it was made from old ammo boxes.

A few months after Devastate Charlie had joined our outfit, the radar problems continued to persist, so the whole team was moved to Pusan, where we could use the test equipment the Antiaircraft Battalion had at their disposal. I was one of the fortunate ones in our group who flew south instead of driving in the trucks over those miserable mountainous roads in South Korea. We all enjoyed the "Florida" weather in the Pusan area while we were there. It was like going to Florida for the people of Michigan in the middle of the winter! I was assigned to live with a Battery away from the Headquarters of the Battalion, which made it even nicer. However, being away from the Headquarters resulted in me missing the opportunity to meet Lieutenant General Lemuel C. Sheppard, then Commanding General, Fleet Marine Forces, Pacific, during his visit to the unit.

Finally, the day for us to leave the "tropic climes" of southern South Korea arrived and we were to return to the 1st Marine Division "up north" where there was snow and freezing temperatures. It was decided that Captain Dressin and I would take Devastate Charlie and head out a couple of days ahead of the rest of our team and drive up to the Division area. When we arrived in the Division area we were to reconnoiter the various areas and select a desirable position for our radar and our team.

Sam and I started driving north from Pusan in the early afternoon and made pretty good time until it became very dark and rainy. Parts of the road were rather mountainous and we had to watch the road carefully to be certain not to miss one of the sharp turns that came up very quickly. Just as before, all offers to share the driving were not accepted and Sam stayed behind the wheel all of the way.

As we would enter one town after another, we would check our map to be certain we took the correct road from the town. On one occasion, in the middle of the night, hours before dawn, we were confused as to which road to follow so we talked with a ROKA military policeman as to what road would take us to the next town plotted on our map. We did our best to pronounce the name of the town correctly and he seemed to recognize the name and comprehend what we were asking. Smiling, he bowed and happily pointed us down the road and repeated the name of the town. We felt we had successfully communicated and we "happily" followed his directions.

As dawn came upon us we found ourselves in a more populated area, and upon further scrutiny we suspected we were not where we thought we were! It turned out we were in a small city south of Seoul. The spelling of the name of the city was very close to that of the town, far to the east, where we had intended to go. While I don't remember the name of the place, it was something like Suwon, while we had wanted to travel to Suwan or something like that. The "bottom line" was we had traveled all night and instead of being in the vicinity of our destination, we were half way across the Korean peninsula from "home". We spent most of the day driving east and finally we arrived in the Division area just before sunset. We went to the Headquarters for the MTACS-2 (Marine Tactical Air Control Squadron Two) where we found food and shelter.

We were so tired from our trip that after eating, we located a couple of cots in the "visitor's" tent and went fast asleep. The next morning, after having breakfast, we loaded aboard Devastate Charlie to begin our search for a new location. To our great consternation, we found the engine block was cracked! We had left sunny Pusan without antifreeze in the engine and after sitting in the freezing cold for about ten hours the water in the coolant system had frozen and cracked the engine block.

This situation presented us with a myriad of problems. First, the powers that be would look very harshly on anyone so negligent as to overlook the antifreeze. Second, this was a big repair job; it had to go to a higher level of maintenance, probably a U.S. Army maintenance organization in our Corps area. Thirdly, it was a stolen vehicle!

When they would start to check the serial numbers on the engine and the vehicle, it would become apparent that it was not a Marine Corps vehicle. The Army was starting to crack down on the problem of stolen vehicles.

I once visited with a U.S. Army survey team who was working in our area. They drove a ¾ Ton Dodge truck. This truck was peculiar to the Army. The Marines did not have the ¾ Ton Dodge anywhere in their inventory. However, their leader said, almost every time they came into the Marines area to do survey work for us someone would "steal" their truck. They would park their truck along side the road and invariably when they returned their truck was gone. After several hours they would generally find it where some "joy rider" had left it, but they were getting "sick and tired" of this thievery.

So we thought we're going to have some real trouble getting Devastate Charlie back in order and we thought we would have some serious explaining to do to someone higher up in rank. However, the "Old Sergeant's" network came to our rescue. It seemed that the Motor Sergeant for MTACS-2 knew someone in the Army Ordnance detachment and he arranged for a new engine to be installed without any questions and before the day ended. If you think the "Old Boy's Network" is something, you have no idea what some Staff NCOs can get done in their "shadow world"!

In the spring, the 1st Marine Division was ordered to move out of the mountainous area north of Wonju, along the So Yang Gang and move into a blocking position north of Seoul, just over the Freedom Bridge leading to Panmunjon.

If you have ever seen pictures of the Chinese 8th Route Army of the late 1930s moving on the road, it had nothing on the Marines of the 1st Marine Division on the road going west. Everything the Marines had built or accumulated during the months in the mountains was piled high on their trucks. On top of these piles the Marines were perched wherever one could find a spot. The road was very dusty and after a few miles everyone had a liberal coating of red and brown dust.

Sam Dressin and I were in Devastate Charlie for the trip and we led our small contingent of trucks westward across Korea toward Seoul. When we reached the city, Sam and I had the occasion to swing out of line and visit the Headquarters of the 5th Air Force. The 5th Air Force had occupied many of the buildings on the Seoul University campus in that city. There was one building, which had once been a Buddhist temple and now had been converted into the 5th Air Force Headquarters officer's club.

Having been on the road for some twelve hours or so, we thought that a drink would be just the thing to get the dust out of our throats. So we decided to make a stop at the Officers Club. Before I tell you what we ordered, you need to construct a mental picture of our appearances.

We had been traveling in an open jeep over a very dusty road behind thirty of forty large trucks for over twelve hours. Each of us was wearing an assortment of clothing. I recall I was wearing a brown long sleeve shirt that I had picked up at an Army shower unit weeks before and had found it very comfortable, if not regulation. We were into the "layering" of clothes long before they created the expression. We both had field jackets and steel helmets with the camouflage covers. Our utility clothing was both dusty and dirty. We were only company grade officers, a Captain and a First Lieutenant, and we could have easily been mistaken for our own "Pig Pen". However we were officers and we expected the Air Force would be pleased to have representatives of a sister service join them for a drink or two.

As we entered the Club, we immediately met the stares of about thirty or forty men in blue. It seemed that everyone in the bar area was dressed immaculately in their blue uniforms, blouses and all, and they were looking at us with big question marks all over their faces. Who dragged those bums into our club? It seemed as if they were all Majors and Lieutenant Colonels, with a full Colonel sprinkled here and there. I have never received such an "icy" reception before or since.

I think both of us had the same mental reaction. It was "Screw You" or something like that and we sauntered up to the bar, brushing the dust off our field jackets as we went. John Wayne had nothing on us! We had a couple of beers and they even accepted our military script in payment. Later, we found the office we were seeking and Sam more or less "reported in" to let the fly boys of the 8th Air Force know we would be operating in the area. I think they could not have cared less!

We moved into a position north of the river and directly behind the Marine infantry regiments. Our nearest "neighbor" was the Army's 555th Artillery Battalion. Their greatest claim to fame was that their Battalion, "the Triple Nickel", had been ambushed more than any other Army artillery unit in Korea. Regardless, they were nice to us and we enjoyed their cooking.

The months that followed found us very actively engaged in dropping bombs in support of the 1st Marine Division and finally the day came when Sam Dressin received his orders to return home. On the morning Sam was to travel to the Kimpo airfield, Sergeant Richard Maxwell and I went with him in old Devastate Charlie. As we moved south toward Seoul just after sunrise, we met a train of oxen drawn "honey" carts. The "honey bucket" people would go from house to house in the village and empty the disposable waste "buckets" from each house. They would collect this "honey" and take it to the countryside and spread it as a fertilizer for their crops.

As we approached this line of "honey bucket" carts, the stench became almost unbearable for Dressin and Maxwell. I was seated behind them and I could not smell a thing! I then realized I had lost my sense of smell. I could recall the stench of the corpses on Hill 854 only eight or nine months earlier. No one can forget that smell. I continued to have a diminished sense for years until I lost it all during an operation on the sinuses in 1997.

The only picture I have of our "Devastate Charlie" The jeep was painted in Marine green immediately following its "liberation". The panel directly below the glass windshield was painted bright Marine Corps red with gold lettering. The markings on the front and rear bumper of the Jeep had the letters USMC on left end and the "new serial number" 123109 was on the right. One of the" liberator's", (Sam Dressin) officer file number was 023109.

Not long after Sam went home, I also received orders to return to the States and Devastate Charlie took me the airport too. What happened to the old lady after that is unknown to me, but I suspect for many months to come, lots of Marines and others would be wondering, "what goes with that Devastate Charlie"? So, as to not keep you from wondering too, "Devastate Charlie" was our radio call sign. "Devastate" was the call sign for MTACS-2 and we were administratively attached to the Squadron. "Devastate Baker" was the unit with the 1st Marine Division which provided air support for the Division and also provided us with a nights rest during one cold winter night. They were "Baker" and we were "Charlie" but don't ask me about "Able". I never had the pleasure!

Chapter 21   Hot Showers And Near Misses

Hits and Misses...we certainly had a lot of both during our tour in Korea! One of the biggest hits was when the Army moved a Laundry and Shower Unit into our area! After bathing with a wet cloth for a couple months, you can understand why a hot shower was such a hit!

But seriously folks, the reason why the Marine Corps sent us to Korea was to test the reliability and the effectiveness of our newly developed all-weather bombing system under combat conditions. So, it wasn't long after our arrival in the 1st Marine Division area before we were set up and dropping real bombs on real enemy targets.

The intelligence people at the Division headquarters selected the targets we were to attack. Since we had a long-range capability, the targets selected were far beyond the range of our artillery. Consequently, our attack on these targets was not observable from Observation Posts on our front lines.

Because it was important that we observe the bomb hits in order to determine our accuracy, our early bomb runs were conducted in the daytime with clear skies. This allowed the pilots to observe the hits (and misses) and report on the accuracy of our bomb drops.

It was far from a perfect system in which to determine the systems accuracy. There were many opportunities for the introduction of errors. Our target information would be received as a map coordinate along with a description of the target, for example "Ammo supply dump". The accuracy of the map coordinates was questionable and the pilots' ability to identify the target and estimate the location of the bomb hits relative to the target provided another uncertain variable.

I suspect another concern of those in the Division providing targets for us to attack, was to keep them at a distance, where this untried system could not hurt any of our people. This safety concern was quite legitimate since all humans are error prone and dropping a 250 or 500 pound High Explosive Fragmentation bomb on some "friendlies" would have some serious consequences. Once we had demonstrated our ability to hit where we "aimed", many of the targets assigned were closer in to our front line troop positions.

In the beginning the only aircraft we controlled in the attack on these targets were from VMF(N) 513, the Marine Night Fighter Squadron which was equipped with our controlling devices. The number of aircraft they were able to provide for our "experiment" during the daytime was quite limited. Their primary mission required them to conduct operations during the hours of darkness, and they could not be expected to fly both night and day. However, in spite of this situation, they did fly about 20 missions for us in the first month of our operation.

This was not enough activity to provide an adequate evaluation. It was obvious that we needed to use other aircraft not equipped with our "automatic" control devices and conduct more strikes "manually". To further complicate our beginning efforts we were experiencing reoccurring technical problems with our new radar. Eventually, it became necessary to return to Pusan to fix our equipment problems. The Marine Antiaircraft Gun unit in Pusan had the same radars and the facilities to perform the necessary maintenance.

Once we had completed our repair, we returned to a position in support of the 1st Marine Division. At that time we began operating with a variety of aircraft. We were controlling aircraft from all services during the winter of 1951-52. We controlled F9F Panthers from Navy carriers, Air Force B-29s from Okinawa and several types of aircraft from the USAF and Marine Squadrons in Korea.

In spite of the difficulties in obtaining reliable target assessment information (distance from target, etc) we were receiving encouraging reports on the success of our bombing. For example, during night attacks on rear area ammunition dumps, the pilots were reporting "secondary explosions".

The first time we worked with the Air Force's B-29s is quite memorable. Our intelligence learned of a large supply and ammunition depot deep in enemy territory where they were actively working at night and "boldly" driving their vehicles with the lights on. This depot was in a deep valley and was protected with antiaircraft weapons as well as cables stretched across the valley designed to "snag" our night fighters attempting to strafe and bomb along the valley floor.

They asked us to control a B-29, loaded with 500-pound bombs on a bomb run attacking this target. We learned that the B-29s would only drop their bomb load in one "string", so we planned to have them fly the long axis of the valley and have the first bomb of their "string" hit at the beginning of the valley. In this way the bombs would be falling along the full length of the valley.

The night of the planned attack arrived and the B-29 reported on station as scheduled. The pilot was instructed as to the procedure to follow and we successfully flew him down the correct course and dropped his "string" of bombs as planned.

A few days later, I sat in on the interrogation of some North Korean Army defectors by our Division Intelligence people. It so happened that these prisoners had been in the vicinity of this valley on the night the B-29 attacked. They told our interrogators that everything was going along as usual that night when all of sudden a large number of "artillery" shells started exploding down the valley. This did considerable damage and much of their ammunition was destroyed in the subsequent fire and explosions. The time and date and location of the prisoners corresponded with our B-29 attack.

After the Division had moved to the west coast of Korea and established a blocking position north of Seoul, we experienced another interesting situation in which our unique system provided substantial dividends.

The negotiating parties at the truce talks had agreed to the establishment of a "no-fly" zone that encircled the North Korean city of Kaesong, the site at Panmunjon and the Capitol city of Seoul. The zone was in the shape of a "dumb-bell" with a circular bulge in the middle of the grip…that being Panmunjon, the site of the truce talks.

What our intelligence discovered was that the North Koreans had established a huge supply depot immediately adjacent to the "no fly" zone boundary. It was impossible to attack this depot using conventional tactics since it was outside of our artillery range and any strafing aircraft would need to fly through the "holy land" either in its approach to or departure from the target. You just couldn't fly in; drop your ordnance and then pull out in time to avoid penetrating the restricted area.

However, with our system, we were able to fly aircraft at 10,000 feet on a course to the target, release their bombs and vector the aircraft in a direction away from the restricted area, without ever over-flying the area. This was done and the depot was put out of commission. This attack was very significant and those who doubted the value of our system were diminished in number. We understood the North Koreans protested claiming there had been a violation of the no-fly agreement, but they were wrong! They didn't know what hit them!

With the arrival of each new officer replacement, it was my responsibility to train him in the functions of our Target Information Center (TIC) and specifically in the procedure of controlling the aircraft reporting to us for bombing strikes.

In brief, the assigned aircraft would report to us by radio and be directed to a "orbiting" position to the rear of the Division area. As the plane was orbiting, our ground controller would brief the pilot on the procedure to be followed. We would ask for his bomb load, number and type and the length of time he could remain on station. Once we had selected a target and had acquired the aircraft on our radar, we would command the pilot to come out of his orbit on a designated heading. He was to maintain a constant altitude and we would direct the required heading changes determined by our computer to keep the aircraft on the course to the target. Prior to reaching the "bomb release" point on the bombing run to the target, we would command, "Armstrong" at which time the pilot would "Arm" his ordnance. At the end of the run, we would give the pilot a "countdown" and at the drop point command "Dump". With that command the pilot would release his bomb(s) and reply, "Bombs away". Then, we would vector him to another heading to prepare for another run or release the aircraft for its return to base.

In the early spring, before we moved to the West coast of Korea with the Division, I was in the TIC tent with Captain George Knapp where we were both observing a new officer conduct one of his first missions. Our officer was doing exceptionally well, and the aircraft was on course heading for the target. Our controller directed the pilot, who was on his first mission with us, to arm his bombs...."Armstrong". The pilot responded with "Bombs Away"!

We immediately went to the chart where an operator had been marking the track of his course over the ground to see where he was when he prematurely released his bombs. We were then able to estimate where these errant bombs would hit.   Our calculations indicated that the two 250–pound HE Fragmentation bombs were going to land in the vicinity of the Division Command Post!

Both George Knapp and I walked outside the tent and prayed! Please God… don't let those bombs hit in the Division CP. It was out of our control, there was absolutely nothing we could do to intercept or redirect those errant bombs. All we could do was pray.

Fortunately the bombs landed in a small, unoccupied ravine some 200 yards north of the Command Post installation. The explosions were tremendously loud and threatening to those in the CP area. It was reported that some of the rear echelon lackies started running for slit trenches that they had forgotten to dig and were looking for their steel helmets that they had not worn since the last inspection. The life of a rear echelon soldier or Marine has a way of "softening" one and tends to make one forget some of the basics of military training.

It was also reported that at the Generals staff meeting the next morning they had some fun with the incident. The G-1 (Personnel) reported no loss of personnel. The G-2 (Intelligence) indicated it was "friendly" fire. The G-3 (Operations) reported it was not in the Plan of the Day.   The G-4 (Logistics) reported the expenditure of two 250-pound bombs. Thank God, they could have some fun with the incident.   It could have yielded some very nasty and tragic results.

Our projected period of four to six months for combat evaluation of the system soon extended to over a year. As each month went by, we would generally receive one officer as a replacement and a couple enlisted technicians. Most of the "original" Mugu Marines were stuck with the longer tours. In my case I was the last officer of the "original" group to leave for home.   The 1st Marine Air Radar Support Team, MASRT was now a combat unit and an integral part of Marine Ground-Air Warfare.

Meanwhile, a successor to our "handmade" system was being developed by a civilian contractor. In Vietnam, this successor, the AN/TPQ-10 was used with great success, especially at Khe-Sanh where poor weather made conventional CAS methods unreliable. The commander of the Khe Sanh defense, Col. David M. Lownds, said "Anything but the highest praise would not have been enough."[*]

---

[*] "First To Fight", Victor H. Krulak, LtGen USMC Ret, Naval Institute Press 1984

Not all of our contingent was involved in the operation of the system. We had a Gunnery Sergeant Pringle and several infantrymen as part of our team. Their responsibility was to ensure our security so the rest of us could concentrate on our jobs with a reduced concern for fighting off any intruders.

It was Pringle's routine to take a small group and "sweep" our perimeter each day about sunset, to flush out any "Gooks" who may be in our area awaiting the darkness to do us mischief.

On this particular occasion, we had moved our radar to a new position close behind Hill 854 and in that position; it was probably more likely we may encounter enemy infiltrators. Pringle and his men were walking a small trail on the periphery of our position when one of them caught a trip wire with his foot. Pringle heard the "pop" and immediately spotted the triggered grenade. Without hesitation he dove full length with arms outstretched and covered the grenade with his helmet an instant before it detonated. No one was injured and Pringle only suffered a numb right arm to his elbow. For his heroic action, GySgt.Pringle was awarded the Silver Star.

But that's not the end of the story. Over the last year, I have had a lot of communication with retired Colonel Dalby and retired LtColonel John Seissiger. At the time, we were the surviving members of the original group of twelve at Point Mugu. In Korea, John Seissiger was a Technical Sergeant and he bunked with the enlisted men. He had a different frame of reference as we talked about shared experiences. As we were reminiscing about our Korean experiences, I reminded him of the incident involving Pringle and the grenade. Seissiger said he heard that it didn't occur exactly as it was reported. So what is the real story?

Supposedly, the true story is that Pringle and his men were in their tent when one of the men accidentally pulled the handle off the grenade and dropped it on the floor of the tent. Pringle immediately reacted and covered the grenade with his helmet just before it exploded. Again, no one was injured and Pringle only suffered a severe numbness in his right hand and arm. Evidently, the "trip wired grenade" story was concocted to avoid an investigation and possible courts-martial action. Regardless, it did not distract from the quick thinking and the bravery displayed by GySgt Pringle. He deserved the Silver Star!

I am sometimes asked if I had any close calls while serving in Korea. As I think about it, I recollect I was most concerned about my safety and the welfare of the troopers who were with me when we almost became victims of "friendly fire".

On this particular day, I had a three or four of my survey people with me as we searched for some survey markers established by the Japanese Imperial Survey. We had moved to the west of the position of our front lines and were making our way back into our lines from the left flank and rear of our front line troops. It was a beautiful sunny day and we were moving in single file through a wooded area with some high ground to our immediate front when suddenly it seemed as if we were in the "butts" at the rifle range.

The bullets were flying over our head and we instinctively "hit the deck" and began to figure out what was happening. The fire was coming from the high ground immediately to our front. The firing would stop intermittently and then resume with the same intensity. During the pauses, we could hear the voices of the riflemen...they were talking American! We began shouting to "cease fire" and for a few moments we thought no one would hear us. Then it all stopped as suddenly as it began and a voice from the hill inquired..."is someone down there?" We all responded with variations of "HELL YES! ...CEASE FIRE!" The voice acknowledged our presence and commanded the troops "Hold your fire" and he told us it was safe to move on up the hill.

Once we reached the top of the rise, we learned that a platoon of a Battalion in reserve had come to the flank of their position and were "exercising" their weapons before they moved back into a front line position. They had no idea anyone was in the area...especially some of their own kind.

As I indicated in the first paragraph of this chapter, one of the big "hits" for us was the arrival of an Army Laundry and Shower unit in our area during the winter of 1951-52. We had been going for a couple of months without a real bath or shower...sponge bathing is what my mother would have called it and because of the winter weather, we had to do the "bathing" in our tent, by the oil burning stove. After a while, you begin to feel real "grungy" and unclean all over. So the day the Army moved a Laundry and Shower unit to the banks of the Soyang Gang it was a "beautiful thing".

At our first opportunity, a group of us went to the shower facility to learn if Marines were eligible to join the club? We figured that the Army Corps people had decided to share some of their "high living" facilities with us Jarheads, but we were uncertain about the rules. We were pleased to learn that the Army fellows were more than happy to have us use the facility.

This unit set up right next to the river and had thrown their intake lines into the river. They had the equipment to produce lots of hot water! The day we arrived to take a shower, we didn't expect to get clean clothes also, but that's what happened.

As we entered the shower tents, we first encountered the undressing room, where we disrobed and where the Army fellow collected all of our clothing except our shoes and outer garments. From there we entered another tent with a raised wooden floor and at least thirty shower heads gushing hot water. To describe the pleasurable feeling of standing in this flow of hot water is almost impossible. It had been so long since any of us had had this experience; it seemed as if it was our very first shower. We were not rushed, so we showered, washed our hair, over and over again. Finally it was time to move on, so we left the shower room to another tent where we found an abundant supply of clean towels. In this tent was an attendant issuing clean clothing…underwear, socks, and trousers…the whole works! At first I was disturbed by the fact that some of the articles were "Army"

togs. However, I soon recognized that the brownish sweater-like undergarment I received was much better than what I was wearing when I came in! (See left, Holding up a tree and wearing my prized "Army Brown undershirt")

After dressing, we put on our "old" boots and outer-garments and left the "paradise" club on the river to return to our campsite about a mile away. Later, we came back to the showers often and enjoyed the outings. I held on to my "Army brown undershirt" for the rest of my stay in Korea.

Chapter 22   Riding the Tiger Cat

You will recall that during the development of the Marine Air Support Radar system at the NAMTC, Point Mugu, California, we came to the point where we needed our own radar. Our testing program for our guidance computer was often delayed, postponed or cancelled because the Navy's radars were not available for our use.

Also, just prior to coming to Pt. Mugu, I had completed a course of study at Fort Bliss, Texas and I remembered seeing a large area where many SCR 784 radars were stored and I had suggested we make an effort to procure one of these surplus radars from the Army. Captain Dalby and the others thought the idea had merit, so we planned a trip to Fort Bliss to see if one could be made available for our use.

Captain Dalby was a Marine aviator and he was able to check out an F7F "Tiger Cat" for a trip to Fort Bliss. The "Tiger Cat" was introduced to naval aviation near the end of WWII It was a single-seat fighter with two radial engines, one tall vertical stabilizer and a low to mid wing configuration. This particular plane had been converted by providing another "seat" directly behind the pilot's compartment. The "seat" had no leg well. This required the occupant to sit with legs folded. The canopy was flush with the aircraft's skin and the wall that divided this "seat" from the pilot's area was solid. This meant that the rider could not see forward but only to the sides, where only the wings and the engines were in his view. The back seat rider could not see the pilot and the only means of communication was by the intercom. The intercom cord was plugged into the "dash" in front of the rider, and the cord was long enough to reach and plug into a set of headphones. The F7F had a reputation of being a very fast "bird" and one that landed "hot". It was also reported that some of the unfortunates who had to bail out of the F7F were caught up on the single "tail". So pilots were cautioned about avoiding the tail if and when they might have to abandon ship!

Since I was the one who had suggested the SCR 784 as a solution to our radar problem and I had the most recent experience at Fort Bliss, Dalby decided that I should accompany him on the trip to inquire about the availability of an SCR 784 for use in our project.

As we prepared to board the F7F, I remember it to be one of the few times in the numerous airplane flights I have taken, that I was required to wear a parachute. It went on as one would expect, straps around the thighs, over the shoulders and across the chest. Not a big thing, in fact I remember it was kind of a "kick". I was really playing aviator!

I got into the back seat, sat like a Buddha with my legs folded, put on my headset, plugged in the intercom and did a trial run with Dalby who was busy with things pilots do to get ready to move out. The crewman closed the canopy after pointing out the red handles on either side, to use when I wanted to move the canopy to the rear in order to disembark. It wasn't long before we rolled off the apron, taxied down to the end or the runway. Dalby did his final run-up and checked his gauges, turned onto the runway and whew! We were moving down the runway and into the air, climbing out in an easterly direction over the peak that is the real "Point Mugu".

It was a beautiful day for flying. Clear skies with great visibility, and while my view was limited to the sides, I could see a lot of the terrain below as we moved over the mountains northeast of Los Angeles. It was late spring and snow was still on the peaks below. The terrain below appeared to be quite rugged!

About that time as I was looking at the mountains below, the engines stopped running. The propellers of both engines were obviously slowing down. I could start to see the individual propeller blades. I knew that Dalby was busy doing something to get the engines going again, so I didn't want to bother him with a call, so I anxiously waited for him to contact me. It seemed like an eternity and I still didn't get a call from Dalby. I figured I might have to bail out of this plane. I didn't like the idea, but I found myself cinching up the straps on the parachute, checking the location of the handle to pull on the chute, checking the location of the red handles to release the canopy and at the same time looking to either side to see if Dalby was leaving the airplane. I wasn't going to leave before him, but if he went, I was going to follow!

Then, thank God, the engines started up again and soon we had regained some altitude and were sailing along as before. Again I waited for Dalby to contact me and tell me what had happened. No call. Waited some more. No call. So I decided to check my intercom connections. The plug was in the front panel OK, but I found that the plug was disconnected at my headphones. I re-plugged the headphones and gave Dalby a call. He responded, with something like "where in the hell have you been? I have been trying to talk to you!" After I explained my situation, he told me that the fuel pump had failed and it had taken him a few moments to get the backup pump working. He said it was best that we land at the Naval Air Station at Litchfield Park in Arizona and have the pump replaced.

Litchfield was just outside of Phoenix and was being used by the Navy as the storage facility for the thousands of surplus aircraft left over from WWII. As we entered the landing pattern at Litchfield it was absolutely amazing to see the hundreds, perhaps thousands, of planes sitting in rows. All kinds of fighters, torpedo bombers, patrol planes, transports…all makes and models were sitting in the desert. Here were row upon row of airplanes that once were crewed and flying in all parts of the world. Now they were sitting unused, unwanted, collecting sand. It made me feel sad and quite melancholy.

It turned out that we had to spend the night in Litchfield as they worked on the plane. Captain Dalby was from Arlington, Texas. He spoke Spanish like a native. Some said like a native Cuban. I do recall that some Mexicans thought he was Cuban. In any event, I recall that we did find an excellent Mexican restaurant in the Phoenix area and I let Dalby do the ordering in Spanish!

The next day we took off early and got to Biggs Air Force Base, adjacent to the Army's Fort Bliss, before noon. When we arrived at Biggs AFB, we changed into our service uniforms and I phoned the Visitors Bureau at Fort Bliss to arrange for some transportation from Biggs to Bliss. I recall telling the person who answered the phone "This is Lieutenant Harris. I am traveling with Captain Dalby of the U.S. Naval Missile Test Center and we require some transportation to Fort Bliss." The person acknowledged the request and said transportation would be provided in a timely manner.

Not long after the call, a nicely polished Army sedan arrived, with a driver and an escort officer. When we identified ourselves, it became obvious that they had thought the Marine Captain Dalby was actually a Navy Captain Dalby. (For those unfamiliar with military officer ranks, a Navy Captain is equivalent in rank to an Army or Marine Colonel.) The escort officer informed us that his instructions were to take us to the Commanding General. And that is what they did. In a very short time, we were being escorted into the General's office for introduction. To the Army's credit, they played it all out without giving much of an indication that they had made an incorrect assumption.

We were escorted into the General's office where he welcomed us to Fort Bliss. We sat in two chairs in front of the General's desk and briefly exchanged some pleasantries before the General inquired about our mission to Fort Bliss. This gave Captain Dalby an opportunity to "sell" our program and explain how this important work was being held up for the lack of a radar. Dalby then presented the idea of borrowing one of Fort Bliss' idle SCR 784 radars for use in our program. Dalby was extremely convincing in his presentation and the General seemed to be sincerely interested in what he had to say. After hearing us out, the General picked up his phone and called one of his officers and told them we would be over to discuss the loan of an SCR 784.

After leaving the General's office we went to the appropriate office and made arrangements for the loan of the radar. It was a very simple transaction. As I recall, it was almost like signing for a set of new mess gear. I suppose that without the General's call, we would have eventually found the "right" person with whom to talk, but it could have taken a day or so to work our way through the maze of offices at Fort Bliss. There is no doubt in my mind that the person we needed to talk with was more favorably inclined to meet with us knowing that the Commanding General asked for the meeting.

In any event, lo and behold, two Marine officers of company grade, not Colonels or Generals, "borrowed" a million dollar radar by signing a standard requisition form, which at the time in the Marine Corps was known as a "784"slip. (Just coincidentally the same numbers as the radar designation.) After an uneventful flight back to Pt. Mugu, we arranged for a Navy flat bed truck to travel to Fort Bliss and bring the SCR 784 back to our base. Captain "O.B" Johnston, an aviator and one of the four officers in our group, went with the truck to Fort Bliss and picked up the radar.

Soon after its arrival at Pt. Mugu, our fellows started reconfiguring the SCR 784 to make it more compatible with the other parts of our developing system. The word we heard was that several years after our "borrowing" of the radar, some supply officer at Fort Bliss having come across the record of the loan of the SCR 784 contacted NAMTC and requested its return. I don't know how the Navy explained the disappearance of such a large and expensive piece of gear, but I am happy I was not there to respond.

The development of the Air Support Radar system proceeded at a rapid pace with the availability of our own radar. It soon became obvious that we had a system that would not only guide LOON missiles launched at sea to land targets, but a system that could provide all-weather close air support. The development of the Close Air Support function soon became our primary mission. The Korean War had begun about this time, and in June of 1951, the system began its "combat evaluation" in support of the 1st Marine Division in Korea. In the preparation for deployment to Korea, we acquired different and a more advanced radar, a TPQ-2, which we mounted on a 40mm Gun chassis for better mobility. Our unit became known as the 1st Marine Air Support Radar Team or 1st MASRT and it remained in combat for the duration of the Korean War. Later MASRT became a unit in the Marine Corps Table of Organization and was active in the War in Vietnam. But that's another story!

SCR 784 at Point Mugu with TSgt
John Seissiger

TPQ-2 in position in Korea. 1951

The "Loon" Missile

The "Wildcat" F6F-5FK

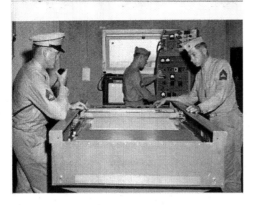

"Breadboard" with SSgt Hal Leber, MSgt Floyd Dickover and MSgt Wm. Holtz L-R

TSgt Seissiger and Cpl Grama Control Panel

Chapter 23   Mugu Miscellany

Rules for Pool....and for life

While at Point Mugu I was a member of the *Marine Guided Missile Unit.* The unit was housed in two temporary buildings on the south end of the beach area.   Directly across the street from these two buildings was the Navy's BOQ. As it is with most BOQs, there was a pool room

On occasion, at lunchtime, our little group of officers would go across the street and play a few games of pool. I don't remember anything about who won or lost, but I do remember the "Rules for Pool" someone had posted on the wall. I always thought the "Rules" were one of Captain Dalby's creations, but some fifty years later, he had no recollection of having been the author.   However, I still suspect it was him; it was the type of humor and the thing we would have expected of our leader.

I thought there were *Ten* Rules *for Pool* but again, after fifty some years, Dalby and I could only remember five. In any case, five will suffice to relate the message of my story. As we remember them, the *Rules for Pool* posted on the wall of the BOQ poolroom in 1950 were:

1. Never Shoot Easy
2. Always Pick Off a Cripple
3. Don't Give Up Hope Until the Balls Stop Rolling
4. Always Keep A Straight Face
5. And, Most of All, Remember Fortune Favors the Stout of Heart!

Regardless of the total number, Rule 5 has stuck with me ever since. In fact it has become one of my "words to live by" kind of thing. When I began my tenure as the President of Johnson County

Community College, I placed a small placard on my office door that read: *Fortune Favors the Stout of Heart.* It remained on my office door throughout my seven years at the college. During my tenure I cannot remember one person asking about the sign. No why? what?, when?, where?, or how? On several occasions, during public speeches, press interviews or in general conversation, I would use the phrase to exemplify the spirit I worked to infuse in the college staff and faculty. However, I often wondered why there seemed to be so little interest in the sign on my office door.

One of the original faculty members at Johnson County Community College was Li Ren Fong. We had hired Li and his wife Lorraine in the very early days of building the college. Lorraine became the victim of an automobile accident and at that time, Marie and I had rushed to the hospital to see what we could do. When we arrived, Lorraine had already passed and Li was very distressed. On that occasion, Li and I became good personal friends. Years after I had left the college, Li moved to take a position on the faculty of a college in southern California.

In the early 1990s, Marie and I spent a month in Lake Forest, California visiting our daughter Patricia and her family. We contacted Li and arranged to have lunch with him. While conversing during lunch, Li told me one of the things he remembered about me was the small placard I had posted on my office door. *"Fortune Favors the Stout of Heart".* Finally, after all, there was positive evidence that at least one person had noticed my sign!

I had to tell Li of the origin of the sign, which prompted some laughter. However, regardless of its origin, you couldn't do much better if you are seeking "words to live by". Let me suggest you consider adopting Rule 5. Set your goals and objectives. Pursue them in a bold and positive manner. Never give up! And always remember, **Fortune Favors the Stout of Heart!**

*****

.If you can't trust the Disbursing Officer…whom can you trust?

While stationed at the Naval Air Missile Test Center, Point Mugu, California, the Navy Disbursing Officer at NAMTC issued our monthly paychecks. As I recall, "payday" was on the first of the month. The Marine Detachment personnel picked up the checks for the Marines, and we were required to drop by the Detachment office and pick up our checks. My routine was to deposit my paycheck in the Bank of America branch in Oxnard, California where I had established a checking account.

Like most families, we would pay the mortgage, utility bill and other bills by checks drawn on this account. For cash, I would write a check and go to the local liquor store where I would generally buy an adult beverage and get some dollar bills for our "walking around" money.

On this occasion, on a Saturday about a couple of weeks after having gone through the "payday" ritual, our friend from the liquor store stopped his delivery truck in front of our house and walked up to the front door. This appeared to be a bit odd, since I never had "booze" delivered, but since we were friendly acquaintances, I greeted the fellow at the door. He then proceeded to tell me the check he had cashed for me just a few days before had "bounced". He showed me the check and it was marked "Returned Insufficient Funds". I assured him it was a bank mistake and he should resubmit the check for payment.

At my earliest opportunity, I went to the bank to find out why they had returned my check because of "Insufficient Funds". The clerk told me there were insufficient funds to cover that check, and two or three others that had just been returned to the respective payees. Upon examination of the account, it was apparent my account had not been credited with the amount of my last paycheck. At that time the Branch Manager was called in and he told me that the Federal Reserve Bank had returned the Government check because the Disbursing Officer had not signed it. The bank manager would not give me the check to take to the Disbursing Officer for signature and said the Disbursing Officer would have to come to the bank and sign the check before he could resubmit it and restore the funds to my checking account.

I immediately went to the office of the Disbursing Officer at NAMTC and expressed my displeasure with his performance of duty. It was obvious he was very embarrassed and he did not want me to make a "big stink" about it. He promised to go to the bank at once and sign the check.

In the next couple of days, more and more of our checks, written in the last couple of weeks, were "bouncing". Again, I contacted the Bank manager to find out why this was continuing to happen. His simple explanation was that the Disbursing Officer had not yet signed my paycheck. To put it mildly, I was very upset to learn he had not been to the bank and signed the check. Upon arriving at the Disbursing Office, it was obvious that it suddenly occurred to him he had forgotten to go to the bank and sign the check. He immediately left the office headed for the bank.

Once the check was signed and resubmitted, the funds were deposited into my account. All of the "bounced" checks were eventually made good. In spite of the Bank of America's branch manager being aware of what caused the overdraft problem, he refused to waive the "bad check" charges, which then amounted to about $100. Now, when your yearly taxable income is about $3,500, a charge of $100, especially for something that is not your fault, is difficult to tolerate. The fact the Bank of America would not waive the "bad check" fees was particularly disturbing. Needless to say, I moved my account out of the Bank of America to another bank.

*****

Is the Navy a "military" service?

When the Marines formed an unofficial group, which they entitled, the Marine Guided Missile Unit., Captain M. C. Dalby's rationale for forming the unit was, purportedly, for the purpose of directing their combined efforts in a project that would be more properly identified with the mission of the Marine Corps. Prior to forming this Marine unit, the individual Marine officers and enlisted men were scattered about the base, working on a variety of Navy projects. However, after having observed Captain Dalby over several years, I suspect his "real" purpose was to get the Marines away from the Navy personnel before they learned their "bad "habits.

While Captain Dalby was a Marine aviator, he was the most "military" Marine aviator with whom I ever had the privilege to serve. The Marines at NAMTC observed the regulations for the Uniform of the Day, which were common at all Marine bases during that time period. Greens, with or without the blouse, with long sleeve shirts and field scarves ("ties" for civilians!) was the Uniform of the Day. In summer, cotton khaki trousers, shirts with field scarves. The utility uniform was worn during work parties only. No Marine was authorized to go to the Post Exchange or travel off base unless he was wearing the Uniform of the Day or appropriate civilian clothing.

However, the Navy personnel were not required to conform to similar dress requirements. Most of the Navy persons were dressed in the blue utilities: Blue denim trousers and a lighter blue cotton long sleeve shirt. Generally the shirtsleeves were rolled up to suit the individuals taste. The white sailor's hat or a variety of "baseball caps" was worn as their headgear. The sailors' headgear was worn in a many ways; some cocked on the back of the head while others askew left or right off the head. Don't get me started about haircuts! Long oiled hair, usually with a huge pompadour, was the "fashion" item for the sailors of the time.

Years before, while stationed at the NAD, Charleston, SC, my commanding officer, Major James Ackerman, would not attend the movies on the base. As is the custom in the Navy, the officers were seated behind the enlisted personnel. Major Ackerman could not stand to look at the hairy necks of the sailors seated in front of him, so in order to preserve his demeanor he avoided the situation by not attending movies on the base.

The Naval officers at NAMTC were, for the most part, naval aviators. Of course, they wore the green or khaki uniforms for the most part. It was a rare sight to see a Navy aviator in the Navy blue uniform. Most of the aviators moved about the base wearing flight suits. Military discipline, as we know it in the Marine Corps, was none existent. Saluting was an occasional happening. One occasion involving saluting at NAMTC has remained in my memory.

On this occasion, I was accompanying Captain Dalby to the Navy installation on the beach. We were both wearing the winter green uniform, with blouses. As we approached the entrance to the building, Captain Packard, the Chief of Missile Operations at NAMTC emerged and was moving in our direction. Captain Dalby made a remark to the point, "Let's give him a real salute". At the proper time, we rendered two of the sharpest salutes in the history of the Marine Corps. It was obvious that Captain Packard was duly impressed; in fact he appeared to be surprised and confused. He did not return the salute, but said, in a mild, soft voice, "Thank you".

San Nicholas Island…a home away from home

The Naval Air Missile Test Center, Point Mugu didn't end at the water's edge. The island of San Nicholas lay about fifty miles off the coast and was an adjunct facility for the NAMTC. The Navy operated an airstrip on the island, which was essentially the only point of ingress and egress for the island. There was a small landing beach over which the major supplies for the facility were transported. There was the usual number of small buildings to support the airstrip operation and several other buildings which served as living quarters and messing facilities. A radar facility was available for support of the missile programs ongoing at the main base ashore.

The Marine guided missile program at NAMTC found the San Nicholas facility just what they needed to move their program ahead. The Marine guidance system was being designed to come ashore with a Marine landing force, set up in the beachhead and control missiles being launched at sea against targets facing the Marines ashore. The set-up at San Nicholas provided an excellent simulation. The Marine guidance equipment would be taken to the island and tied in with the existing Navy radar. The plan was for the LOON to be launched from a submarine off the coast of Point Mugu and guided toward the target near the island. The Marine guidance radar would acquire the LOON in mid-course, take control of the LOON and guide it into the target, Begg Rock, a large rock out-cropping near the island.

Running our operations from San Nicholas did incur some logistic problems for the Marines in the Guided Missile unit. The equipment was still in a "breadboard" stage, with components built into racks. After once moving the equipment to the island and tying in with the Navy radar, the Marines would fly out to San Nicholas to operate the system and conduct the testing. Those familiar with the coastal weather know that "fog" is the controlling element. It could be clear at San Nick and socked in at Point Mugu…or visa-versa.

This resulted in a lot of uncertainty, especially for the wives of the Marines going to San Nicholas. Normally, those selected would fly out to the island in the early morning, conduct the operations and return in the late afternoon. The aircraft was generally flown by one of our two Marine aviators, either Captain Dalby or Captain Johnston, but often by some Navy pilot who needed to get in his flight time.

The aircraft rarely remained at the airstrip, so with uncertain weather, our return depended on good weather at both Mugu and San Nick. You will not be surprised to learn there were many occasions when the Marines were "stuck" on San Nick for at least one night. Fortunately, the food was excellent and the sleeping accommodations acceptable. My wife, to this day, still remembers seeing Captain Dalby's automobile stopping in front of our house and seeing him approach the front door. She knew immediately what he was about to tell her, "Bob would not be home", he was "stuck" out on San Nick.

The airstrip on San Nick was relatively high above sea level. On several occasions, when flying to the island, below the fog bank, the pilot needed to gain altitude as he approached the island, in order to land. For a non-aviator, that always seemed a bit touchy.

The aircraft usually available for the flights to San Nick was the JRB, a two engine Beechcraft that accommodated the pilot, copilot and about six passengers. Most of the time, the right hand seat in the front of the aircraft was empty, so I would sit in the copilot's seat. On many occasions, the pilot, O.B. Johnston or Dalby would let me take over and "steer" the plane. I learned to keep the heading, altitude and attitude of the aircraft and generally enjoyed being an "aviator".

*****

There's the movie and then there is the real story…

During the summer of 1950 while Marie, the children and I were on leave in Michigan, a major movie studio came to Point Mugu to film scenes for the movie, *The Flying Missile.* This was one of Glen Ford's most unmemorable films. He played many roles and appeared in many excellent movies, but, in my opinion, *The Flying Missile* was not one of them.

In any case, while we were away, the people at the NAMTC had a ball. Some of the sailors and Marines had roles as extras in the movie. Later, when we saw the movie in a theatre, we recognized some of the people from the base, but other than the main gate and a few long shots of the headquarters building, the rest of the scenes didn't resemble the "real world" as it existed at Point Mugu.

For example, there were a couple scenes, which took place at the Officer's Club. In the movie the club looked like one of Hollywood's most exclusive nightclubs. In fact, the Officers Club at that time at NAMTC, was housed in a couple temporary huts on the south end of the beach area. The club had relatively low ceilings and there was nothing that looked very "fancy". It looked "Temporary".

The one scene that bothered me the most was of a visitor entering the Main Gate. A sharp "real" Marine was standing in the doorway of the Guard House. In the scene, the Marine was in the background, as a short, fat, sloppy, longhaired, unkempt "Naval" officer checked the credentials of the visitors. Some "real" Navy officers at Mugu didn't have the "sharpest" images, but there was absolutely no Navy officer at Mugu that looked as "scruffy" as this Hollywood actor.

The story line of the movie was about a Navy submarine officer who was sent to Point Mugu to work on the launching of a "flying missile" from a submarine. He had many difficulties, both personal and technical, before he successfully had the missiles "flying".

The fact we were working on a similar problem, and having some difficulties getting the support we needed, made the story line not as improbable as one may have thought. We only wished we had that wonderful Officer's Club, with the wonderful parties and all those glamorous women. But as usual, we couldn't have everything; we had to live in the "real" world.

*****

Flights to remember…

Other than our flights to and from San Nick, we took several trips to other places, such as the Naval station at Inyokern or NAS in San Diego. On one such flight to San Diego, I was "riding shotgun" in a JRB with Dalby as the pilot. As we approached the landing pattern, we suddenly found ourselves surrounded by Navy fighter planes. To me it seemed these fighters were above us, below us, and coming around us from all directions. It didn't seem to bother Dalby as he went through the procedure of landing at the air station. It turned out there were a couple carriers off the coast that were heading into port. I learned the procedure was for these carriers to fly their airplanes off the carriers into the air station as they approached the coast. The carriers were probably going to enter the San Diego harbor early the next day, but the squadrons were flown in the day before. In any event, it was quite an exciting few moments for this "ground pounder".

*****

I can always remember how O.B. Johnston's hands were shaking as he placed them on the controls of the aircraft. I can still see his right hand as he grasped the levers that controlled the power to the engines. His hand would be shaking as if he was in an advanced stage of Parkinson's. However, I learned that, shaky or not, O.B. was a very careful and safe pilot. Flying in and out of Pt. Mugu seemed to me to be more difficult than the take offs and landing I had experienced at other bases. The landing strip at Mugu ran north to south, and being on the coast the prevailing winds were either from the east or the west. On several occasions, as we approached the landing, with me in the second seat, it was necessary to "crab" the aircraft into the cross wind, and I have always marveled as to how we could touch down in that attitude and still make a good landing.

*****

When it comes to landings at Point Mugu, I can recall one made by a Marine Aviator who had been assigned to fly for our test program. This young Lieutenant, whose name I can not remember, was about to land and several of us in our office building along the east side of the strip were aware he was about to come in. Consequently, we were watching as he landed. The landing was spectacular! There was a lot of noise and sparks flying as he landed "wheels up". The aircraft was damaged but our Marine aviator was not injured. His pride was a bit bruised; however he was not worse for the wear.

  But there is more to the story of this young Lieutenant. Several years later, while I was stationed at the Marine Barracks, Naval Training Center, Great Lakes, Illinois, I had to pleasure to meet up with him again. It was evening of November 10, 1952. We were celebrating the Marine Corps Birthday at the Navy's Officer's Club and Brigadier General Lamson-Scribner, the CG for the Marine Aviation Reserve command at Glenview, Illinois was our Guest of Honor. Our Lieutenant was the General's Aide. We had a nice visit about our days together at Mugu and he told me he had just received orders to join the Navy's "Blue Angels". I congratulated him on his selection to fly with this distinguished unit, the "Crème de le crème". I also kidded him about his "wheels up" landing and urged him not to do that again! Unfortunately, about six months later, I read where while practicing with the Blue Angels, he had flown too low and crashed into a sand dune in Texas.

*****

One of my classmates at the Guided Missile course at Fort Bliss, Texas was a Navy Lieutenant Nick Evans. Nick had been assigned to NAMTC, Point Mugu following our graduation. I recall two incidents related to flying with Nick Evans. One of them occurred while we were visiting the Naval Ordnance Test Station, Inyokern while on a field trip with our Guided Missile school class. All of the aviators I have known had the same problem when they were in duty billets outside of a squadron. They were always scrounging "flight time". It seemed wherever they were; the aviators were working on scheduling an aircraft to get in their required monthly minimum hours of flight time.

Nick Evans was no exception and he had arranged to get an SNJ for an hour while we were visiting at Inyokern. Nick asked if I would like to go along for the ride and I thought it would be a nice experience, so I accepted. The SNJ was a single engine, low wing training aircraft, with a canopy that covered both the pilot's cockpit and the seat for the second passenger directly behind the pilot's position. The Air Force called this plane the "Texan" and it was used by all services as a training aircraft during World War II.

It was one of the scorching hot days in the desert, and I was promised it was a lot cooler a few thousand feet higher. We arrived at the aircraft, and with the assistance of a crewman, I settled into the rear seat. The crewman made certain that my parachute and my seat belt was properly "cinched up". We checked the intercom with the pilot and it wasn't long before we were taxiing out, getting ready for take-off. After Nick had done his "run up", we each closed our section of the canopy and Nick turned onto the runway for the take-off. It wasn't long before we were up several thousand feet and sailing through the clear cloudless sky with the scorching hot desert far below. About that time Nick suggested that we open the canopy and enjoy the crisp cool air. It was a new experience for me. I had never flown with only the sky above me. It was quite an adventure for one who had so little flying experience outside of commercial aviation.

So we were just cruising along, making holes in the sky, as some aviators say, when all of a sudden Nick decides to do a "roll over" to the left. As I understand it, a "roll over" is when the plane turns either left or right, dipping the wing and the aircraft rolls over on it's back. The maneuver is completed when the plane returns to the level attitude and is headed in the opposite direction. Well, however it is done it came as a complete surprise. I could feel the increased tension on the seat belt and harness and in the short time it took to compete the "roll over", thoughts of falling out of the plane raced through my mind. I can recall seeing the ground rapidly replace the blue sky "above" the canopy.

When everything was normal again, I called Nick on the intercom and asked "Why?" How certain was he that I had my seat belt and harness fastened? Did it occur to him that I might have been so relaxed that I had loosened the belt and harness? I asked him not to do it again. Once was enough!

A while later we made our landing approach to the airstrip. We had closed up the canopies and it became very hot inside the aircraft. It was not only hot, but it was extremely bumpy. I could feel myself becoming ill. I knew I was going to vomit. I held back as I looked for a receptacle and all I could find was my fore and aft cap. It had to do! It seemed like an eternity before we could taxi to the parking area where a couple crewmen met us. I can still remember the look on this fellow's face as he threw back the canopy and got a whiff of the mess I had created. All in all it was an exciting experience, but this time I didn't come up smelling like a rose!

*****

The next incident I will relate is one of those that you may have had to be there to see the humor, but the thought of it still causes me to chuckle. It was the second time I flew with Nick Evans and was after we had both been relocated to Point Mugu. I don't remember what occasioned this flight, but about four or five of us were flying from Mugu to someplace in the western United States. It was a short one-day trip or perhaps an overnighter. We had planned this trip for several days. Nick was the pilot so he checked out a JRB, the twin engine Beechcraft for the trip. One of the group was to bring along some sandwiches and coffee for us to snack on during the flight. The night before we left, I had the idea I would bring a cake for us to eat as a desert. For some reason, I baked the cake. If Marie had baked it for us, I would not have this story to tell. I didn't know it at the time, but it was probably one of the worst cakes I ever tasted. I don't know what I did wrong, I thought I followed the directions on the package, but this chocolate cake with chocolate frosting was a disaster. On second thought, the chocolate frosting, which was all ready prepared and came out of a can, was excellent. The cake was the disaster.

An hour or so after we were airborne, we broke out the sandwiches and coffee. Nick was in the pilot's chair and another aviator was sitting in the right hand seat. There were three of us riding in the passenger seats behind the open pilots' compartment. The noise of the engines was almost deafening. There was nothing fancy about this JRB, no insulation in the cabin fuselage to lessen the noise. Those of us in the back had to shout above the engine noise to communicate with one another. If you wanted to talk to Nick or the copilot, you would have to get up behind them and talk directly into their ear.

All of us enjoyed a sandwich or two along with the coffee. Then it came time for desert. I brought out the cake. It looked great in its nine- inch square pan. I cut it into several large pieces and those of us in the back had the first pieces. I took a piece to Nick and the copilot and returned to my seat. By then my fellow passengers had taken a bite or two and were laughing and saying bad things about my cake! After a bite or so, I had to agree with them. It was a terrible cake; even the frosting couldn't redeem it! About that time Nick turns in his seat and looking back at me, his face quite expressionless, he said, "Good frosting". We all just about died laughing. Nick was always a kind and gentle person and he was the last one who would say anything that would hurt another's feelings. Not being able to honestly say anything good about the cake, he chose to compliment me on the frosting. We decided that the cake had to go, so somewhere over the Arizona desert, some old prospector may have wondered what that brown stuff was that hit his mule!

*****

General Thomas comes to visit….

By mid-1950, some of the decision makers at the NAMTC and Headquarters, Marine Corps were beginning to learn about our guidance system and our successes. Our leader, Captain Dalby, was a very energetic, intense and persuasive officer. He carried the "political" load for the project and worked tirelessly at getting the "word" about our system to the people in the Marine Corps and the Navy who could provide us with the support we needed to develop and demonstrate the effectiveness of our system for All-Weather, Close Air Support.

One of the decision makers who came to see for himself was Brigadier General Gerald F. Thomas. I am not positive about General Thomas' position at the time of his visit. I think he was either the Head of the Marine Corps Equipment Board or in some Headquarters, Marine Corps job related to Research and Development. In any event, he had an interest in learning about our equipment and he was in a position to provide the support we hoped to receive.

As I recall, after inspecting the equipment and getting a briefing on the system from Captain Dalby, we all settled in at our small office in a building along the eastern edge of the runway at Point Mugu. In my mind's eye, I can still see General Thomas sitting, with a bit of a slouch, in one of the desk chairs. General Thomas didn't present the most military of appearances. He was an older man, although most senior officers looked old to me then! I remember, the uniform he wore, the service green elastique, was a bit wrinkled and not the best of fits. He was very soft spoken on this occasion and was very relaxed and friendly. It is my recollection only the four officers of our unit were with General Thomas during this informal meeting. I don't recall whether or not the General had any aide or any other officer with him at this time. Captain Dalby did most of the talking for us, but each of us had an opportunity to participate in the conversation.

One of our objectives was to get the Marine Corps approval of our plan to package our guidance system so as to make it serviceable in a combat situation. We envisioned, toughening our equipment and building it into a small trailer, developing related equipment and taking our system to Korea for a combat. evaluation. For this we would need the blessing and the money to rebuild the system. General Thomas was in support of our proposal, but he remarked at one time during our meeting, in words to this effect, "It is too bad you won't have the opportunity to try it out in Korea before it's over". At that time, the North Koreans were being pushed back to the Yalu River and the Chinese had not yet raised their ugly heads! As it turned out, about a year later, we were with the 1st Marine Division in Korea and Major General Thomas was its Commanding General.

*****

While stationed at NAMTC, we lived in a new house in Oxnard, California. It was a delightful two years for a young family. Bobby started school, Patty was anxious to do the same. There were many friends and "kids" in the neighborhood, which we all enjoyed. Pictured below is Bob and Marie, the "happy young couple" enjoying their backyard and the California sun!

Part IV   Post Korea

Do you remember how long it seemed before you became a teenager? For me, it seemed the time just dragged on and on. It was the same when I was looking forward to being 21 and old enough to legally buy a drink! Somehow or another as you grow older the years begin to just fly by. While it took forever to attain age 21, getting to 30 seemed to happen a lot quicker. Age 40? Age 50? With each decade the time seemed to pass more quickly.

I have a similar feeling about my Marine Corps career. Those early years seemed to be so much longer than those toward the end of my days on active duty. So many things happened in a period of only a few months in the early years. In my mind, the tempo increased following the Korean War. Post Korea experiences took place over years, not months. The only times we were ever stationed in one place for a full three years happened during the Post Korea period. We had three years in Monterey, California followed by another three years in El Paso, Texas and the time seemed to just fly by.

Before I was really ready it was time to make a decision about retiring or doing the full 30 years. It wasn't an easy decision, but having opted for a second career in education, I often think of what might have been, but in the end I have no regrets for having decided to retire in 1965.

In this part, I give you a rapid review of where we were, what we were doing and some of the people who made the trip interesting. So, you see, that is another story!

Major R.G. Harris, USMC in 1961

Chapter 24   In And Out…

A Quick Turnaround

I returned from Korea after a thirteen-month tour of duty and I was sent to the MCAS at El Toro for the purpose of setting up a training program for MASRT personnel. My seatmate on the flight home from Korea was a Marine Captain who owned a house in Santa Ana, near the MCAS, El Toro. However, he was being moved to a billet on the East coast. He didn't know what he was going to do about his house in California. Since my orders were to MCAS, El Toro, I was in need of quarters in the vicinity of the base, so we made a deal while enroute back to the States.

After a thirty-day leave, most of which was spent in Michigan, our little family moved from Oxnard to Santa Ana into the rented house. Fortunately, we were able to rent our Oxnard home to an Air Force officer and his family who were living in our neighborhood.

Probably the only eventful thing that happened during our short stay at El Toro was my promotion to Captain. Finally, after seven years as a Lieutenant the day finally arrived when I could pin on those "railroad tracks". It was a proud day in the Harris family.

Sam Dressin and I were the only "ground" officers in the "original" group who developed the AN/MPQ-14 and we had both been sent to this Marine Aviation base for the purpose of setting up a training program. However, what we found was part of the group we had left behind at Point Mugu, but no equipment. It was a disappointing time and very unsatisfactory duty. However, we were surprised when we received orders transferring us to "ground" officer duties after only four months on station. Sam was sent to the 2nd Marine Division at Camp Lejeune, North Carolina and I was moved just a few miles down the coast to Camp Pendleton where I was to join the 3rd Marine Division.

We had to notify our landlord about our sudden transfer and again search for a house in the vicinity of Camp Pendleton. We were lucky to find a nice two-bedroom ranch house just outside the Main Gate We moved to our new Oceanside home in early January 1953 and I began serving with the 3rd Battalion, 12th Marines. I was back in an artillery unit and I was quite pleased about that. Since I was now a Captain, I looked forward to becoming a Battery Commander.

The 3rd Marine Division was not up to authorized strength at the time of my arrival. At the time, the negotiations for ending the war in Korea were underway; however there had been one obstacle after another placed in the path of an agreement. The "word" was that in the event they could not come to an agreement at Panmunjon, the 3rd Marine Division was going to be sent to Korea. Consequently, the Division was receiving officers and men from the 2nd Marine Division and other posts and stations as it was being brought up to its authorized strength.

After a short stint as C.O. of the 3rd Battalion's Service Battery, I was assigned as C.O. of "G" Battery. At full strength, a firing battery such as "G" Battery would have about eight officers and 150-200 enlisted Marines. The Battery had four 105mm Howitzers and generally would provide the artillery support for an infantry Battalion.

With new personnel joining us almost daily it wasn't long before we had all the men we needed, but we were still short on officers. CWO Marvin G. Myers, who I had served with in 1947 while in the 10th Marines, was one of the officers in my Battery. Old Marvin was about as nimble as he was back then, but he was not up to serving as a Forward Observer and moving with the infantry troops. Fortunately, we joined eight brand new 2nd Lieutenants, fresh out of the Army's Artillery School at Fort Bliss and my concern about having "young" legs to move with the infantry was alleviated.

The pressure was on us to conduct intensive training in order to prepare for a possible overseas deployment. Our training schedule put us in the field on firing exercises several days each week. When we were not conducting live firing, we were maneuvering with units of the 4th Marines, the infantry regiment our 3rd Battalion supported.

Of the eight new officers, I selected Gene Shoults as my executive officer, the #2 in command of the Battery. Gene was not the senior Lieutenant of the group, but he was obviously the most intelligent and capable. I pride myself on having recognized his talent, since his career in the Marines and the job he did subsequent to his retirement more than verified my judgment of his capabilities.

Our paths crossed several years later, when Captain Shoults arrived at the U.S. Naval Postgraduate School to study Nuclear Engineering. It was my third and final year at USNPG, but we were able to renew our friendship during our year together at the school. Shoults retired as a Colonel and was soon engaged as a Super Grade civilian (equivalent in rank to an Admiral) to direct the Navy's program to develop the capability to preposition ships and supplies. The propositioning concept was a major factor in the successful execution of the Gulf War and the war in Iraq. Finally, Gene Shoults retired to his home in Annapolis, Maryland with his wife Marilynn. In 2009, at the age of 79, Gene Shoults passed away. He was laid to rest in Arlington Cemetery with former Commandant of the Marine Corps, General P. X. Kelly offering the eulogy

My Battalion CO was Lieutenant Colonel Lonnie D. McCurry from the great State of Texas. He was a wonderful fellow and an excellent Battalion CO. I came to know him well during the short time I was CO of the Service Battery and officed in the same area as the Colonel. After I had been transferred to "G" Battery, I received a call from the Sergeant Major informing me the Colonel would like me to drop in to see him at my convenience. Odd! It was nothing pressing, the Sergeant Major had added. However, if the CO wants to see you, urgent or not, you go! I decided to hurry on over to his office.

As we were visiting, Colonel McCurry tells me he has just received notice he had to sit for the Marine Corps GCT test. GCT meant "general classification test". Marines of all ranks were required to take the test and their scores were entered into their individual record books. It seems, however, there was a large group of junior officers who were not tested during WW II. These officers had been rushed to the Pacific Theatre and were never tested. Now the time had come for them to be tested. Lieutenant Colonel Lonnie McCurry was in that group. He had reviewed the records of the officers in the Battalion and found my score of 155 was the highest of the group. He wanted to talk to me about the best way for him to prepare to take this test. He was concerned about the test. He certainly didn't want to do poorly, not at this stage in his career.

I told him all I could remember about the test and generally told him to relax, because there was little he could do now, especially in such a short time, to prepare for the test. Just relax; take the test and all will be OK. I really never learned how well he did on the test, but he seemed relaxed and at ease subsequent to the examination.

As the units of the Division were training to achieve the desired level of combat readiness, the rumors kept flying about our probable deployment to Korea. The peace talks were stalled and the likelihood of a cessation to the war was considered very unlikely. The "scuttlebutt" (Marine/Navy talk for rumors) was that all veterans of Korea were to be replaced by those who had not yet served in that conflict. The "scuttlebutt" seemed to be true as the Korean veterans were being transferred out and new "blood" arrived to serve in their place.

There weren't many social activities during this period, however, on one occasion the regimental officers and their ladies were invited to a Barbeque at the Vista home of Colonel Leonard F. Chapman and his lady. It was a very casual affair and Chapman's were excellent hosts. Colonel Chapman was our Regimental commander and years later he was the Commandant of the Marine Corps

About this time a bigger ranch home on our street became available to rent when the owner, a Lieutenant Colonel and his family were transferred to another station. We had the opportunity to rent this larger house and move in immediately. It was a difficult decision since there was the possibility I would be moving out with the Division if and when they were sent to Korea.

However, since I had only been back in the States for about seven months and Korean veterans were being transferred out of the Division daily, I figured I would be left behind if the Division did receive movement orders. So, we decided to rent the bigger home and we moved up the street.

It may have been only a week or so after we had moved into the new home when the Marines announced that all Korean veterans would be relieved of duty with the Division **EXCEPT** Company and Battery Commanders and First Sergeants. Furthermore, the Division was going to leave in about a month for Korea.

In spite of this pronouncement I felt certain that any day I would find my replacement joining the Battalion and I would be reassigned to a post outside the Division. I even heard rumors that a Guided

Missile trained officer was on his way to Pendleton and I would be transferred to NOTS, China Lake, California upon his arrival.

The embarkation date was rapidly approaching and there was no sign of a replacement, so I made plans to leave with the Division. Marie said she would prefer living in our Oxnard home rather than remaining in Oceanside if I was going back overseas. So, we contacted the Air Force officer who was renting our house in Oxnard and he agreed to vacate the house so Marie and the children could return to their home. There was not enough time to move Marie and the children to Oxnard before I boarded the ship for Korea. Consequently, we had to make arrangements for the move to be made after my departure. This meant Marie would have to work with the movers and then drive to Oxnard and reoccupy the house without me.

While all this was going on at home, I was working to make sure that my Battery was ready to ship out for combat in Korea. Thankfully I had two excellent Sergeants in 1st Sergeant Price and Gunnery Sergeant Daniluk. Also with Gene Shoults and Marvin Myers we had a powerful duo: brains and experience. The other Lieutenants were hard workers and were primed and ready to go. Even with such good people helping, the job was demanding and, after all, I was the one who had the responsibility for the readiness of the Battery. I was torn between my duty to the Marines and my duty to my wife and family, it was a very stressful period. However, the most strain was placed on Marie. She had managed the household and cared for two young children for the thirteen months while I was in Korea. She had been through three moves since my return in less than a year and she was facing another move alone.

Finally, the day came and our unit went aboard the USNS *General Patrick* and we headed out to sea for Japan. Yes, we were going to deploy to Japan. In the final weeks just before our deployment, a Cease Fire Agreement was signed in Panmunjon. One might have expected the movement would have been cancelled and we would have stayed in Pendleton. However, the decision was made to move our Division to Japan, so we found ourselves at sea heading for the "Land of the Rising Sun".

A day or so after I had left, the movers arrived, loaded our furniture and promised delivery the next day. When they finished the loading it was after dark and Marie decided to stay overnight at a Travel Lodge in Oceanside and make the trip north through Los Angeles to

Oxnard the next morning. She made her way through the streets in Los Angeles and up the coast to Oxnard. She arrived before the furniture van and was there to direct the unloading. Once she was settled in her home, she enrolled the children in school and for the second time in less than a year began the whole process of living without a husband for another thirteen months.

Meanwhile, I was on another two-week voyage across the Pacific Ocean. Once I was settled, I met with two "Guided Missile" Captains who had been transferred to the Division from the Terrier Missile program at NOTS, China Lake. One of the officers was Jack Miles. Jack told me he was to replace me in the Division and I was to be transferred to China Lake as his replacement. I was not surprised to hear this, since I had been told several weeks before that someone was coming to replace me. Several years later, I visited the Officer Personnel section at HQMC and was able to review my file. I found a copy of these dispatches:

From: CMC To: CG, 3rd Marine Division Request disposition of Captain Robert G. Harris 045803. It is the intention of this Headquarters to transfer Captain Harris to NOTS, China Lake for duty with Terrier Missile Program.

From: CG, 3rd Marine Division To: CMC Captain Robert G. Harris 045803 is deployed with the 3rd Marine Division at sea.

The "scuttlebutt" was true, but the bureaucratic wheels moved too slowly and I was required to make an unintended trip to Japan. How would my Marine career have differed if I had been transferred to China Lake?

Marie suffered the most from this rapid turn around. The strain of caring for two small children and maintaining a house without any assistance for another year was just too much to expect of her. But, that's another story!

Chapter 25   Camp Fuji

The 12th Marines occupied an old Japanese Army camp on the southern slopes of Mount Fujiyama. It was quite a sight to wake up in the morning and look up to the old snow-capped volcano. Just like a National Geographic picture or a tourist's post card. It was real and it was in our backyard. There were many wooden buildings to house our Regimental and Battalion offices, supply stores and maintenance activities. The accommodations for the Battery offices and the billeting for the Marines and their officers were in pyramidal tents. The floor and sides upon which these tents were erected were of wood. So, the tents were semi-permanent, so to speak! The three firing battery commanders, Bob Harris of "George" Battery'; Jim Leon of "How" Battery; and Ed Koster of "Item" Battery were bunked together. We all got along very well, even though Ed was the "Prussian" type officer. His style of leadership was entirely different than that of either Jim Leon or me. He was very boastful about "his battery". According to Koster, "Item" Battery could out-drill, out-shoot, out-play or out-do any of the other Batteries. "Item" was a good outfit, however when it came right down to it, our Batteries did just as well and we didn't have the men shaking in their boots when we came through the Battery area. Ed was a former enlisted man and both Jim and I were from the college programs. In spite of that, he was a good fellow to have in the tent with us and he did his share of the work keeping it neat and tidy!

With the signing of the truce agreement at Panmunjon, the Korean War hostilities came to an end. Instead of keeping us at Camp Pendleton we were moved to Japan. Because of the artillery ranges at Camp Fuji, our regiment had been assigned to the camp. Camp Fuji was in the country. The towns surrounding the Camp were rural villages. It was not unusual to see the "peasants" thrashing the rice with the disjointed pole. On festival days, you would see young girls wearing kimonos with their faces heavily rouged. What that was all about we didn't know. But the mothers enjoyed having the girls pose for our cameras.

As we already knew, the Japanese beer was "itchiban" and the large peanuts served in Japanese taverns were enough to make a meal by themselves. Life in the country was stress free and quite enjoyable for a "round-eye". One early evening, Lieutenant Gene Shoults and I were returning to catch our ride to the camp and we were walking down a residential street in this small village. We suddenly realized that most of the families were taking baths. The room with the communal tub was on the street side of the house and as we passed each house we could hear the people bathing. I suppose we could have looked in too, but that may have been a breach of etiquette.

However, it was not all fun and games. I found out the hard way after I went to the Sick Bay with a very bad cold.

During WW II and for some time thereafter, the Navy Doctors and their Corpsman were very liberal in the dispensing of Penicillin. It was the "cure-all" and on many occasions, I., like many others, was given Penicillin for minor ailments, colds, sore throats, coughing, what ever! However, this time was one time too many and I had a violent reaction.

After a day or so of lying in my bunk, and breaking out with large red welts, our Navy Doctor had me transferred to the Naval Hospital at the Yokosuka Naval Base. I rode in the front seat of a 2 ½ Ton Truck over the country roads and I felt every bump in the road. With my body covered with welts the pain was amplified every time we hit a bump. I was so happy when we finally arrived at the hospital.

After I was examined, I was given some baths to relieve the itching and pain of the welts. I was also put on a regimen of cortisone, which in a couple days got me back to normal. As I lay in the bed, I had to be careful not to strike my feet on the iron footboard of the bed. When I accidentally bumped the foot, the pain would radiate up through my entire leg. Before the cortisone took effect, the opening in my throat had begun to narrow and it made swallowing very difficult and painful. Ever since this episode I have been very careful to avoid another Penicillin reaction.

The day I returned to duty from the hospital I arrived a short time before my Battery was about to march into the field and join the Regiment in a live firing exercise. The exercise was unusual since all the Battalions of the Regiment were involved. Lieutenant Shoults and our Gunnery Sergeant Daniluk briefed me on the exercise.

Daniluk had been on a road reconnaissance the day before and he knew the route our Battery was to follow to get into position. Since I had no idea how to get to where we were supposed to go, I had Daniluk ride with me in the lead jeep.

So, when it came our turn to move out, we started down the trail that Daniluk had been shown by the Regiment the previous day. Things were going quite smoothly, since we were following the tail end vehicle of the Battalion ahead of us for some time. There was no way we could get lost or get off the prescribed route as long as we had that vehicle in sight and after all, Gunny Daniluk had been over the route only yesterday.

We came up over a hill and the vehicle ahead of us was not in sight. We continued down the road, still no vehicle in sight. We finally came to a fork in the road and we needed to make a decision…left or right? Daniluk was not certain, but he thought it was the one to the left. What to do? I had our whole Battalion behind our Battery and I think there may have been another unit following our Battalion. In any case, I went with Daniluk's best guess and for a while it looked like it was working out OK.

However, we soon found ourselves moving through another Battery's position…right between their guns. This was not the way to do things. The Battery CO was very upset. However, it was a single path, it was impossible to leave the path and turn around. Besides there were up to a hundred vehicles, many towing howitzers on the single lane road behind us. We had led half of the Regiment on the wrong road! There was nothing to do but keep moving and lead everyone through this Battery position. The whole mess delayed the firing exercise for over an hour. I was not looking forward to facing up to Lieutenant Colonel McCurry or Colonel Chapman You just take the responsibility for the foul-up. That is how it has to be, if you have the authority you also have the responsibility.

Not long after this episode, I received a message from the American Red Cross informing me that Marie was ill and they recommended I be returned to the United States on Emergency Leave. The Navy Doctors at the Seabee base at Port Hueneme, very close to Point Mugu, had been treating Marie for several weeks. It seemed the pressure of all that had happened in the past couple of months had finally taken its toll. I met with Colonel Chapman and he granted a 30-day Emergency leave. I was able to find space on a Navy transport aircraft for a trip to Midway Island, from there I flew in an Air Force cargo plane to Hickham AFB in Hawaii.

The Air Force cargo plane was the biggest plane I have ever seen. There was literally a hanger inside that aircraft. I was the only passenger aboard, so I had an opportunity to "tour" the plane during our flight to Hawaii. I could picture the crew having a basketball game in the "hanger", there was plenty of room and the height of the "ceiling" would allow one to shoot a basketball! It was a multi-engine propeller plane, which has undoubtedly been replaced many times since then.

With the priority given to those on Emergency leave, I was able to catch the first plane out of Hickham heading for Travis AFB in California. It was a four-engine prop job, same as the Douglas airliner of the day. It was a very long and boring flight to California. They told us we were facing headwinds all the way. Finally, we arrived at Travis and we noticed that the plane scheduled to depart several hours after our flight was already unloading as we came to the gate. So much for priorities!

I took a train from San Francisco to Oxnard arriving in the middle of the night. I was fortunate to find a taxi available and soon I was knocking on the front door of our house on McMillan Street. Marie came to the door and she was very surprised even though she knew I would be coming home very soon. She had lost weight and was obviously in need of companionship. She had done a wonderful job maintaining a home for our children during my thirteen-month tour in Korea but to have to do it all over again was too much to ask. She was "pooped out".

After I talked with Marie and with her Doctors, I wrote to the Commandant of the Marine Corps requesting permanent change of station orders to either Point Mugu or somewhere in the Midwest where Marie could be close to her parents and relatives.

Within a few days, I received orders to report to the Marine Barracks, US Naval Training Center, Great Lakes, Illinois. But, that's another story!

Chapter 26   Good Heavens, Great Lakes!

Who would have ever thought we would be at Great Lakes, Illinois for duty? However, here we were living in a comfortable ranch house in the government housing area called Forrestal Village. There must have been a bargain sale on concrete when they decided to build the houses in Forrestal Village since they were made with poured concrete walls on a concrete pad. The interior walls had the markings from the forms used in the pouring of the concrete. Nevertheless, the buildings were relatively attractive and provided a nice home for our small family.

At the time, the Naval Training Center at Great Lakes had a Marine

Barracks, commanded by Colonel William K. Enright. The command was composed of three Platoons: Headquarters, Guard and Schools Platoons. The Guard Platoon operated the Navy Brig for the USNTC and the Ninth Naval District.

Marie and me at the Marine Corps Birthday Ball, Gt. Lakes, 1953

The Schools Platoon was composed of all the instructors and students attending one of the Navy's schools at the Naval Training Center, Great Lakes. I was assigned as Officer-in-Charge of the Schools Platoon.

At the time, there were about 20 Marine Instructors in the Navy's Electronics School and one or two in the Journalism School at the

Center. The Marines under instruction totaled about 200 and they were coming and going as the classes began and ended.

Upon reporting, I was pleased to find Sergeant Major Sheppard who had been our First Sergeant at the V-12 Unit at the U of M. I didn't ask him if he recalled my "near miss" at being banished from the program. I decided it was better to let sleeping dogs lie!

The lead NCO of the Electronics instructors was Master Sergeant Antonio Dindio. Many years later I met up with Dindio again when I joined the 1st Battalion, 12th Marines in Okinawa and found him as our Battalion Sergeant Major.

The Marines Corps numbered several hundred thousand, however on occasion you would meet some of your former comrades in a new and different environment. These reunions were generally very pleasant and provided an opportunity to reminiscence about "the good ol' days".

My military duties were rather routine once I had the opportunity to improve the barracks and the office facilities. It was obvious my predecessors had not viewed this command with much interest. My predecessor had been operating out of an office the size of a closet. So, I commandeered an unused squad bay and had our Marines build two large offices at one end, one for the 1st Sergeant and one for me. At the other end of the squad bay, we constructed a amateur radio facility. We began operating one of the most powerful amateur stations in the Midwest. Many of our instructors were "ham" operators and the Marine students were very interested in learning and it became a very active off-duty activity. Once the upgrading was accomplished my First Sergeant "ran' the day to day operations and I was allowed to direct my efforts in other areas.

Each year the Ninth Naval District command at USNTC, conducted a fund-raising activity for the Navy Relief Socirty. I was assigned to represent the Marine Barracks on the District's committee to organize and conduct the event, the Navy Relief Carnival. After being nothing more than a representative the first year, I was appointed Chairman of the event for the following year. I threw myself into the enterprise and the results were fabulous! I literally worked full time on the Carnival for a couple of months. We organized each of the commands and outlined their specific missions and were fortunate to have leaders in each command who were capable and enthusiastic. I visited with Schlitz Brewing Company in Milwaukee, Curtis Candy in Chicago and others, each of whom contributed product and money to support the event. For example, Schlitz donated a truckload of bottled beer. Our entertainment committee signed Count Basie to play at our evening dances. It was a marvelous extravaganza, which made a record amount of money for our charity, the Navy Relief Society.

Bobby was just eight years old and anxious to play baseball in the Little League. Unfortunately, the Little League organization in our area was very weak and without a playing field. Together with my neighbor across the street, Lieutenant Commander Pape, DC, USNR, we essentially "took over" the Little League in Forrestal Village. The Navy provided an area for a ballpark and also provided the labor and funds to construct a very professional backstop and fences. They graded the area for the ballpark, but it was bare of grasses. That's when I marshaled the 200 Marines of the Schools Platoon. With the Navy providing the sod, the Marines came out every night and laid sod until we had a first-class ball field. The Marines led the Opening Day Parade. See Photo below.

In 1978, Marie and I were traveling in the southern part of Illinois, as I was visiting a community college in the area. We went into a restaurant in Carbondale and as we were eating lunch, Marie said, "Isn't that Dr. Pape?" And it was! We visited for just a few minutes but long enough to learn he had established a dental practice in a town near Carbondale. Small world, isn't it?

Bobby was quite an active fellow while in Forrestal Village. One day a car full of Naval officers came driving up to our house and reported that some young fellows in the vicinity of our back yard were shooting a BB gun at the cars coming down the road bordering our community. It seems that one BB struck the window on the driver's side of their vehicle. Fortunately, the window was up and no damage was incurred. It didn't take us long to find out that Bobby and a friend of his were the culprits. To my knowledge, that was the end to their "sniping" days.

On one occasion, our niece Diane Loucks came back with us after our visit to Michigan. Diane was to stay with us for a week or so and then we would return her home for the rest of her summer vacation. Each day we would try to figure out something new and exciting to show the young 12-year-old. We frequently went to the movies at the USNTC main theatre. Prior to the showing of the movie, the Navy orchestra would play several numbers. One of my favorites, which they seemed to play every time we attended, was Leroy Anderson's "Seranada". Diane had been with us for about a week and she seemed to be enjoying her visit as much as we were enjoying having her with us. On this day, her mother Jean called to see how things were going. Marie talked with her sister for a few minutes and then turned the phone over to Diane. As soon as she put the phone to her ear, she broke down in tears and blurted out "I want to come home"! She was all right up until she heard her mother's voice and then she was overcome with homesickness.

We attended several social events on the base during our time at USNTC. There was the Marine Corps Birthday Ball where Brigadier General Lamson-Scribner was the guest of honor and used my sword to cut the cake. However, the most memorable party was the one held by the Electronics School. It was a costume party and Marie and I decided to go as the Old Gold Dancing Cigarette Packs, which were so popular on the television advertising for the tobacco company. We constructed a couple of wood frames, similar to a large box kite, and covered the four sides with a light brown wrapping paper. In lieu of the Old Gold logo, we substituted the Globe and Anchor of the Marine Corps. Using the Old Gold style of lettering we added slogans like "Semper Fidelis" and the "First to Fight". All in all, it was a very good job. Marie's pack was smaller than mine but both of us had to wear shorts and show our legs below the "box".

 Marie always had very shapely legs and with the nylon hose they looked terrific. On Marie's legs alone I was certain we would win the prize for the best costume. During the ball, we would make our appearance on the floor, then retire to a room and put our "packs" away and put on some other more traditional garb, return to the party and dance a few times then return in our costumed state. When they announced the winners for the best costume we came in second to the Navy Captain and his wife who came as a pair of Raggedy Ann dolls. Our friends told us we were robbed, and they may have been right. There is no doubt the commanding officer of the Electronics school had more clout than a Marine Captain.

Besides the Little League, Bobby became a Cub Scout and Marie became a Den Mother. It was a new experience for both of them and after a couple years both were exhausted. I am convinced that Cub Scouting was all Bobby could handle, he was "burned out" He never had an interest in the Boy Scouts.

Marie and I became caught up in the "painting by numbers" craze while in North Chicago. (Forrestal Village was actually in the city of North Chicago, Illinois). We spent hours working on a French street scene and honestly, when it was completed it didn't look bad at all!

Being so close to Hammond, Indiana gave us the opportunity to visit with my Aunt Olive and her husband Bill Haman. By then, my grandmother had sold her home and moved in with them. It was a nice way to spend a Sunday by having dinner with my relatives. Bobby and Patty were completely bored with the whole thing, but they had no choice but to go along.

My "second" mother, my
Aunt Olive and her husband
Bill Haman

My Grandmother Johnson,
the only Grandmother
I ever knew!

Undoubtedly the most interesting and unusual experience during my two years at Great Lakes occurred one day in the early spring of 1955. Colonel R.R. Van Stockum had relieved Colonel Enright as the Commanding Officer and he requested my presence in his office. Upon reporting I found that he had "volunteered" me for a special assignment. It seemed the Navy planned to transport a nuclear warhead for their Regulus missile from their Clarksville Base in Tennessee to the Naval Station in Alameda, California. As I understood it, the Navy had been transporting these nuclear devices by air in the past and they were interested in a trial run using rail transport.

I eventually learned while the Clarksville Base was under Navy Administration, the personnel at this nuclear weapons facility was made up of civilians and representatives of all the services. While it was located in the State of Tennessee, it was surrounded by the Army's Fort Campbell, which is considered to be located in Kentucky.

I was assigned a detail of ten enlisted Marines from our barracks and one Navy cook. We traveled from Great Lakes by bus to the Clarksville Base. Upon arrival, I was given the orders for our mission. Our group was to serve as an armed guard for the nuclear weapon during the trip. The nuclear device was loaded inside a regular boxcar and I was required to examine the seals on the car and sign for the cargo.

A "drover" car was provided for our travel and it was attached to the boxcar. One half of the drover car was a galley, with built in coal cooking ranges on one side and "ice boxes" on the other. Our cook drew rations for the trip and they were loaded in the "ice boxes" and the cabinets. The coal bin was loaded with coal and several hundred pounds of ice were packed into the "ice boxes".

The other half of the drover car was where the bunks were located. There were three sets of double bunks on each side of the car. The toilet facilities were at the extreme end of the car. On the top and in the center of the car was a cupola. It was about six feet square and each side had a padded seat about three feet wide. There were glass windows on each of the four sides of the cupola, which provided an excellent spot to observe the passing terrain. I spent many hours sitting in the cupola reading books.

Soon after our arrival, we moved into the drover car and the next morning our two cars were moved to a nearby rail yard where we were eventually added to a freight train being made up in the yard. Whenever the train was stopped, we would place two armed Marines outside and alongside the sealed boxcar. If we were ever asked as to what was in the sealed boxcar, our cover story was that we were transporting some new type of rocket. Later as we were in the rail yards of El Paso, Texas, we were having some ice loaded on the drover car and one of the workers asked me what we had in the boxcar. I told him our cover story and he laughed and said, "I bet you got an atom bomb in there"!

Our journey took us through Memphis, across Arkansas and through Texas all the way to Los Angles, California. There were signs on each of our cars that said "NO HUMPING". This meant that the railroad yardmaster was not supposed to push us over a "hump" when making up the trains. He was not to let our cars roll freely and collide with other cars. It was against regulations to "hump" cars with personnel or ammunition, however none of the yardmasters obeyed the rules and we were humped over and over again.

It was early evening when we were dropped off in the Los Angles rail yards. I was instructed to contact the yardmaster in each of the yards upon arrival and attempt to get our cars on the next train leaving along our route. In Los Angeles, I was able to get us on a fast freight heading north along the California coast. In making up the train, we had a wild frightening ride as we were "humped" and ran free for a couple of miles, picking up speed as we rolled along. We were becoming quite fearful of the impact we would experience once we met up with the train. Fortunately, there was a braking mechanism in the tracks that slowed us down and the feared "collision" was nothing more than a good jolt.

After about seven days, we arrived at the Naval Station in Alameda, where I was relieved of the sealed boxcar. The Navy transportation office in Alameda arranged to have our drover car attached to a fast passenger train, the California Limited, for the trip back to Chicago. For the next couple days, our Marines had a ball. Several of them made acquaintances with some young ladies in the other cars and they enjoyed the trip back across the continent.

Our Navy cook did a wonderful job during the trip. The "rocking and rolling" of the train didn't present any problems for him. He said that he had cooked on Destroyers and if anyone can do that, the train is a cakewalk. We ate beef roasts with all the trimmings, chicken and dumplings, food as good as one could "hope to die for". It was a very interesting and unique experience.

Ever since I had completed the Guided Missile course at Fort Bliss, I had wanted to attend the Naval Postgraduate School and earn a Masters Degree. While at Great Lakes, I submitted my request, pointed out that while I had not yet received my Bachelors degree, I had completed four years of college, graduated from the Army's Guided Missile School and participated in the development and combat evaluation of the Close Air Support Radar team. The basic requirements for PG School were completion of mathematics through Calculus and one year of Engineering Physics. My course work at Michigan State and Michigan was in excess of these requirements.

Finally, on June 6, 1955, exactly ten years from the day of my commissioning as a Second Lieutenant, I received orders to report to the U.S. Naval Postgraduate School, Monterey, California for duty under instruction in the Ordnance Engineering (Guided Missile) course. So, after a 30-day leave in Michigan, it was "California, Here We Come" for the Harris family. But, that's another story.

Chapter 27   PG Stands for Postgraduate

In the beginning the U.S. Naval Postgraduate School was located on the Academy grounds in Annapolis, Maryland. In 1951, the whole school, faculty and students, moved to Monterey, California. The Navy had purchased the old Del Monte hotel and its spacious grounds earlier and it made an ideal setting for an educational institution. The USNPGS offered courses in several engineering disciplines as well as other sciences and applied sciences. It was staffed by a civilian faculty and was accredited by the Western States Association, the same accrediting organization that examines other institutions such as Stanford in the western part of the nation.

When we arrived in the fall of 1954 we found a very nice three-bedroom home in a residential community nestled in between the cities of Monterey and Seaside. It was the "city" of Del Rey Oaks. Many of our neighbors were also the families of students at the school. Our old friends Sam and Sue Dressin lived very close to our new residence and they were the ones who found the house and arranged for us to rent it. Sam, now a Major, was one year ahead of me at the school and he was pursuing a program in Electronics Engineering.

I had been assigned to the Ordnance Engineering program, which allowed the individual student some latitude during the three-year program. The Masters Degree in Electrical Engineering was the primary degree for the students completing the Ordnance Engineering program. In my case, since I had selected optional courses in applied mathematics and operation analysis, I could have had my Masters degree in either Mathematics or Electrical Engineering. Since my Bachelors was in Mathematics, I chose Electrical Engineering.

While earning a Masters Degree was the primary incentive for the students, the Navy's purpose was slightly different. In the three-year program, we studied the various disciplines related to Guided Missiles: chemistry, chemical engineering and propulsion systems: metallurgy: aerodynamics; electronics, servomechanisms and control systems; advanced mathematics such as vector analysis and Differential Equations, Laplace transforms; Static and Dynamic Mechanics; and the list goes on! Even though my major emphasis was in control systems, I accumulated about 40 credit hours in Chemistry and Chemical Engineering during the three years of study.

Our class was composed of Navy and Marine officers all of the same rank. They were Lieutenants in the Navy and Captains in the Marines. We also had Lieutenants from the Greek and the Chilean Navy in our class. Robert C. Morrow, William J. Trisler and I were the three Marine Captains. The Ordnance Engineering Department Head assigned Bill Trisler as our Section Chief and he served in that capacity until I was promoted to Major in our second year at the school. When they decided that Trisler was the senior officer in our class, I just assumed he was senior to me. (I wasn't one to "keep my

finger on my number"). It came as a surprise to everyone when my promotion came through and everyone realized that I had been the senior officer all along. To tell the truth, I was pleased they had made the error. The Section Chief had a lot of extra work to do and especially during that first year, I am pleased that Bill Trisler had the burden and not me!

The Ordnance Guided Missile students upon arrival in 1955
1ˢᵗ Row L-R: Capt. Wm Trisler, Lt. Bobby Potts,
Captain R."Red" Morrow
2d Row L-R: Lt R. Hodnett, Lt. M."Mo" Paul, Capt. R G. Harris.

"Red" Morrow and Bill Trisler were both aviators and they were both of small stature. They went everywhere together and had that "devil may care" attitude that many aviators seem to possess. We referred to them as "the Gold Dust Twins". Bill and his wife Jackie had purchased a much larger house than most of us occupied and since they had more room, their place became "the" place for a lot of our parties.

The course load was heavy and demanding. Every one of us had to set up a special place in our home where almost every night you would find us...studying. Since our bedroom was the largest room in our house and since we didn't have a "dining" room, I placed our drop leaf dining table against the wall in our bedroom. It became my study table. Each night after dinner, I would make my way to the bedroom, close the door and "hit the books". I didn't realize until recently, when Marie told me, that when I left to begin studying, Marie and the children turned the TV volume down low and maintained the quiet. I didn't realize they were being that considerate. As I remember, I never had any problems with noise while studying. I never had to ask for them to "be quiet"; they just took it upon themselves to "keep the noise down". When I learned of their efforts to help me, even after some sixty years, it made me feel warm and appreciative of their support so many years ago.

It was a grueling routine. Study every night. Problems to solve. Papers to write. "Cramming" for the Exams. But when Friday night arrived it was time to put the books aside and have a party!

Most of our parties were made up of about five or six couples and the favorite drink, largely because it was inexpensive, was a wine punch. Red Morrow or Bill Trisler would drive up to some nearby California winery in Red's open cockpit MGB, wire wheels and all, and buy a couple gallons of some red wine. Often each of the quests would bring along a bottle, or a part of a bottle, of what ever they had at home. It would all go into the wine punch, along with some orange slices and whatever else seemed appropriate. On occasion Bill Trisler would prepare his special "Captain Morgan's Blood" or the notorious "Artillery Punch". It was fun to drink these concoctions during the evening, but the mornings that followed were "migraine" miseries. I recall one New Year's Eve party caused me to watch the New Year's Day football games, lying on the couch with a cold washcloth covering my eyes. I would risk a peek at the TV every once in a while, and hastily cover up again. Now that I am very much older, I can't imagine why I thought an evening of "fun" was worth all the suffering that followed.

When we were in our third year Marie and I recognized that we had never hosted a party. We had been to many gatherings at the homes of most of our classmates, but we had never entertained at our house. We needed to "pay back" all our friends for their hospitality. Our home was too small for a "cocktail" party but our back yard was relatively large. We also noted that all of the parties had been the typical indoor cocktail party with some chips and dips. We decided to hold a "beer bust" in our back yard and invite everyone from our class and then some!

I borrowed a squad tent from the Quartermaster at nearby Fort Ord. The tent was 60 feet long and 20 feet wide. It filled over half of our back yard. Our friend, Marine Captain Richard I. Sudhoff, better known as "Suds" showed up with his electrician's belt and installed Chinese lanterns throughout the tent. He also hooked up a sound system that provided the music for the affair. Navy Lieutenant Les Etchison and Marine Captain Joe Holicky operated two charcoal grills and did the hamburgers and hot dogs. Les was a member of our Ordnance Engineering section, but Joe was just in town to attend the Army's Foreign Language School in Monterey and volunteered to help at the party.

Joe Holicky and I went back to our days together in the V-12 at Michigan. We played football together on the UM Junior Varsity. One day Joe and another friend, "Whitey" Adams came with me to a practice session of the Fenton High School football team where my former High School Coach Ivan Williams allowed us to show some of the techniques we had learned from the coaching staff at the UM.

We went through several ½ barrels of beer that afternoon and evening, and thanks to our neighbors, our guests were able to find adequate toilet facilities. We had invited all of our neighbors to the party and most of them were in attendance. That was a good thing, because the guests had parked their cars along both sides of our street for several blocks in each direction. It was a really big "Beer Bust". It was such a success that for several years later when I would accidentally run into someone who had been at the party, perhaps in the corridors of the Pentagon, one of the first items of conversation was about the great time they had a our "beer bust".

Our days on the Monterey Peninsula were not all studying and partying. We had two children who were very full of life and they had their friends and their activities.

Little League Baseball took most of Bobby's time during the summer months. He was a member of the "Whiskerinos" team in the Seaside Little League. Bobby was one of their "stars" as a pitcher, a shortstop and at bat. He had a wicked fastball and had most of the batters quaking in their sneakers as it came their turn to bat. Along with the fastball came streaks of wildness and that added to the batter's fear factor. On one occasion, a young man of Chinese descent came to bat and unfortunately didn't step back far enough on one of Bobby's high inside fast balls and he caught it in the left cheek bone. We all rushed to his aid, hoping he wasn't seriously hurt. The batting helmet was no protection for a fastball in the face. Fortunately, the young man was a bit dazed but otherwise undamaged.

Bobby's form at the bat or in the field was exceptional. He played the shortstop position flawlessly and his throws across the diamond after backhanding a hit in the hole were professional in appearance. His batting form was outstanding. I used to say he even looked good striking out! I was thinking he might have the stuff to go all the way. But, that's another story.

Bobby's success in baseball continued through Babe Ruth league, American Legion ball, Varsity Baseball in High school and on into college at Michigan State, where he earned his Freshman numerals. In his sophomore year, Bob participated in the Varsity vs. Alumni game at MSU. The alumni had three pitchers return for the game: Robin Roberts, Hall of Famer of Philadelphia Phillies; Ron Perranoski, All Star relief pitcher of the Los Angles Dodgers; and Dick Radatz, All Star reliever for the Boston Red Sox.

When it came time for Bob to bat, he found that he could get the bat around on Roberts, but against Perranoski or Radatz, he not only couldn't get the bat on the ball, he couldn't see their fastballs. He realized he had come as far as he would go, so he gave up baseball.

Patty's big things for a while were ballet, tutoring and dodge ball. Along with the Dressin's daughter, Debbie, Patty took ballet lessons and the old movies we have of the two young ladies demonstrate there were no career opportunities in dance for either of them.

Patty was always excited about playing dodge ball at school. She was evidently fairly skilled at the game and seemed to enjoy pummeling her classmates with the ball. But the activity she probably enjoyed the most was helping our little neighbor "Toodie" Carter in her "play school". I believe Patty was a natural born teacher. At this early age she had the patience and the skill to teach young people. Joan Carter stated her belief that Patty's "tutoring" of her daughter better prepared her for reading than the formal schooling. It is interesting that in recent years; Pat worked for the school systems in Orange County, California with the remedial reading classes and tutored children of Taiwanese immigrants in the English language.

Marie and I can remember how excited Patty was when at an evening meal we broke the news to Bobby and Patty that Marie was pregnant. The thought of having a baby in the house was just too thrilling for her to contemplate. Bobby was very pleased, but it wasn't his makeup to display a lot of emotion.

Unfortunately, a new baby for our family never happened. One evening we all attended the showing of "Bridge over the River Kwai" at a theatre in the town of Carmel. During the movie, Marie indicated something unusual was happening and we had to leave the theatre and return home. Shortly after we arrived home, Marie suffered a miscarriage. I had contacted the hospital at Fort Ord and they instructed me to bring Marie to the hospital and if possible the products of the miscarriage. Marie was about four months into her pregnancy and the fetus was small, but distinguishable. We believe we lost another son that evening. We often think about how our lives would have been different if we would have had another child. Hearing the music from the movie, the "Colonel Bogies March ", or mention of the movie itself, always brings back the memory of a sad time in our life.

Marie and the children were frequently pestering me about going camping. The Big Sur country was not far from us and it was probably one of the best camping areas in the world. I always had to remind them that being a Marine, I had done my share of camping. There was nothing new to me about sleeping in a tent or on the ground. I had experienced meeting nature's call while in the "wild" with no modern convenience. Camping to me was not something I wanted to do in my spare time. However, they finally got to me and I agreed to a camping weekend in the company of our neighbors and good friends, the Frank Carters, who lived across the street from us.

Lieutenant Frank Carter, USN and his wife Joanne and two small children, "Toodie" and toddler Robby were going to do their camping in a small trailer. I went to the Quartermaster at Fort Ord and checked out a couple of "pup" tents and four rubber mattresses.

Upon our arrival in the "woods" of the Big Sur, we found a wonderful campsite, on the high ground overlooking a nice mountain stream. I set up the two pup tents near the Carter's trailer. As a Marine should do, I ditched the tents on both sides, just in case of rain, and set up the air mattresses, two to a tent.

I must admit we had a very nice time frolicking around in the woods and fauna for most of the day. Returning to camp to enjoy a nice meal and an open fire. It became dark and we all retired to our separate abodes. It wasn't long after we were ensconced in our beds that the heavens opened up and we were experiencing a torrential rainfall. The amount of rain falling was more than I had anticipated and the shallow trenches were not adequate to handle the water coming down the hillside into and past our tents. We were floating on our mattresses and barely keeping dry for the remainder of the night.

At morning light, the rain had long stopped and we were "up and at 'em" looking for breakfast. What we found is that both Frank Carter and our Bobby had an ugly case of poison oak or poison sumac. And, worst of all little "Toodie" had the mumps! It was time to pack up and go home!

To make matters worse, the pictorial record of our fun day in the woods was ruined when I learned that I had double exposed the movie film. Now, if we want to revisit our trip to Big Sur we have to mentally block out the images of a Whiskerinos baseball game!

My major professor at the PG school was Dr. George Thaler. Professor Thaler had distinguished himself in the field of Servomechanisms. The text he had written on the subject was used in most of the nation's engineering schools. George Thaler became a personal friend. This came about primarily through Little League baseball. George was the coach of the "Whiskerinos" and a neighbor as well. His son, George Jr., played on the team and George asked me to assist him with the team after he had "drafted" Bobby for the Whiskerinos. So, for two seasons, George and I were the team's coaches. George Thaler was a very odd duck in many ways. He was kind of a friendly "nerd". He was obviously very intelligent but he appeared to a bit awkward in social situations with his students, all of whom were about his age, but who had followed a different career path. I remember visiting Professor Thaler in his office and having him offer me a cup of tea. He loved his tea! He would boil up some water on a hot plate and then pull out the upper right-hand desk drawer. In an glass ashtray, he would have the "duty" teabag. Since he generally made only one cup of tea at a time for his personal consumption, he would place the partially used tea bag in this glass receptacle for future use. I don't know how many cups of tea he got from one teabag, but I suspect it was more than one should expect.

Our back yard backed up to the property of the Monterey Airport. We couldn't see or hear the planes at the airport, so the location was not detrimental. On one occasion, President Eisenhower visited the Monterey area, and we drove over to the airport and had an opportunity to see his airplane, the *Columbine*. It was not known as *Air Force One* in those days. It was a four-engine propeller aircraft as I recall and not that much different from the commercial airliners of that day.

In addition to the big "Beer Bust", I best remember our backyard as the spot for our "Crab Feasts". We would go down to the Monterey wharf area and buy cooked crabs, bring them home and on the picnic table spread with newspapers, tear them apart, dip them in melted butter and eat as much as we could handle. It was a real feast!

In the final part of the third year, the students were sent out to industry to learn what was happening in the "real world' of guided missiles. I was assigned to spend my term at the Lockheed Missile Systems facility in Sunnyvale, California. I was assigned to the Reliability Engineering Department because of my interest in this area.

At the time, this Lockheed facility was developing the Polaris missile. The Polaris was to be the first underwater launched missile. I remember the celebration that occurred in the plant the day it was announced that they had experienced their first successful underwater launch with a test vehicle. This was a major breakthrough in the development of this submarine launched missile.

My mentor at Lockheed was the Department Head, John Yueh. John was of Chinese descent and on one occasion, Marie and I joined

John and his family for an authentic home-cooked Chinese dinner. We sat at their large round dining table complete with a Lazy Susan filled with delightfully tasty condiments and foods. We really enjoyed being part of his family at dinnertime.

The government contracts with the various missile contractors generally included provisions for the contractor to demonstrate the reliability of the missile or component being produced. Demonstrating the reliability of a missile as large and as complex as the Polaris was a daunting task. I learned of a theory being presented by one of the mathematicians at the Stanford Research Institute in nearby Mountain View, California. The fellows name was John Bateman. I arranged to meet with John and after he briefed me on his idea, he welcomed my suggestion that I work with the theory in developing my master's thesis. In one of our many subsequent meetings I had the opportunity to ride in John's automobile. It was a Citroen sedan. It was one of the most unusual rides I have ever experienced, before or since. It was as if we were floating on four different springs.

John Bateman's concept of predicting the reliability of a complex system was to mathematically combine the reliability of its component parts. When the product is something inexpensive, such a light bulb, one can set up a test with thousands of light bulbs and burn them until all of them fail. By recording the length of life of each of the bulbs before they fail, the reliability can be determined. However, when you are working with a complex and very expensive system such as the Polaris missile, you can not afford to launch thousands or even one of these missiles just for the purpose of determining the system reliability. Consequently, Bateman was proposing the testing of each individual component for its reliability and then mathematically combining the computed reliabilities into a system reliability. I used this proposition for preparing my thesis. John Yueh thought the thesis was good enough to submit to a professional organization for publication. He submitted it to the Institute for Radio Engineers, a long-standing professional organization in the field. The IRE was so named in the early days of radio, and had long since encompassed many areas in communications and weaponry.

The paper was accepted by the IRE and we were invited to present the paper at the Institute's annual convention in Washington, D.C.

You may have noticed that "my" paper had become "our" paper. This happened because John Yueh made himself the co-author when he submitted the paper to the IRE for consideration. He thought that with his name on the paper, we would receive more consideration. I think he was correct; but I did resent having his name on MY paper.

Living in the "real world" of a missile program was very enlightening in many respects. It helped develop my self-confidence in my ability to understand and perform some of the tasks for which many other engineers were being paid "big bucks" to perform.

For example, one day during a coffee break one of the Lockheed engineers was talking about a problem he was having in determining the performance of a pump in one of the internal systems on which he was working. I really didn't know anything about pumps, but I did understand how to use Eshbach, an engineer's handbook. I opened up my Eshbach and turned to the section on pumps. Within a few minutes I was able to go to that engineer with the problem and show him the formulas needed to calculate the performance of his pump. A few days later, it got back to me that the word in the shop was "if you needed help on pumps go see the Harris fellow!" Man, if it was that easy, they should be backing up to the pay table!

In order to not leave Marie and the children without transportation while I was in Sunnyvale, I purchased an old Dodge coupe for $50. It was a remarkable price for a remarkable old car. It ran very well, even though when you looked down below your seat you could see the pavement going by through a couple of rather large holes in the floor. It all held together for the three months I spent at Lockheed, and best of all I sold it for $50 when I no longer needed it!

On Patty's birthday in March of 1956, the four of us traveled to San Francisco to have lunch on Fisherman's Wharf and see the movie "Around the World in 80 Days" which was showing on the big screen at one of the city's finest theatres. When it came time to order our food, Marie, Bobby and I ordered the Lobster dinner. When it was her turn, little Patty said, "I'll have a grilled cheese sandwich, please". She was a polite little girl, but a "grilled cheese" sandwich on her birthday? We have never let Pat forget it!

Years later in about 1965, while Marie, Pat and I were dining at the Officer's Club of the Naval Ordnance Plant in Washington. D. C., we each ordered a whole boiled lobster for dinner. The club was quite crowded with many Navy officers and their guests at the time. After the dinner was served each of us started dealing with the hard-shelled crustaceans in our own way, when all of a sudden, Pat's knife slipped and her lobster leaped from her plate and fell onto the nearby dance floor. Our seventeen-year old daughter was very embarrassed, but the waiter promptly cleaned up the mess with no extra fanfare. And as far as the lobster meal was concerned, the Club graciously served another at no extra charge. Real class, much appreciated by all!

When we reminisce about our days on the Monterey Peninsula, we recall driving over to nearby Castorville, the "Artichoke Capitol of the World" and buying a large bag of prime artichokes for only a $1. With our roots in the Midwest, we were becoming "gourmet" diners in Monterey. We ate our share of artichokes, avocados, crab, clams and oysters…and developed a graving for sour dough bread!

Our family had one experience during our three years in Monterey, which we would not want to repeat.

One of the large Cruisers in the U.S. Navy made a port call to Monterey and the Captain extended an invitation to all USNPGS officers and their families to "come aboard" for a tour of the ship. On the day of the visit, we went to the wharf in Monterey, where the ships launch was loading the invited guests for the movement to the ship, which was anchored further out in the bay. The water appeared to be a bit choppy, even in the wharf area, but we went along with the others and loaded aboard the boat. Within a few minutes we were clear of the breakwater and into some fairly boisterous sea. The waves were tossing us about and I was concerned it might be very difficult transferring from the launch to the ships gangway.

Soon we arrived alongside the cruiser, which loomed as a huge vessel as we approached the platform at the bottom of the gangway. The platform was wet and with each crest in the wave, it would be doused again. There were a couple of sailors on the platform waiting to assist the newcomers from the launch onto the platform. However, the seas were moving the launch up and down a good three or four feet every few seconds. When one made the move from the boat to the platform, it had better be as the boat reached the zenith in it's up and down motion. I had boarded other ships in rolling seas in the past and from that experience, I knew how to make the transfer. However, I was fearful for Marie, Patty and Bobby. When it came time for them to leave the bouncing boat, I was very relieved when the sailors had them safely on the platform and they began their climb up the ladder to the main deck. We enjoyed the tour of the ship, but all the time, we were apprehensive about stepping off into the bouncing boat while leaving. Of course, all went well, but it was something we were not anxious to repeat. It was too dangerous!

Graduation day 1958 finally arrived and we were all proud to have survived three interesting but difficult years. When I was selected to attend the Postgraduate School, I had not completed the requirements for my Bachelors degree. My friend and mentor at Michigan State, Dr. Paul Dressel, had gathered all of my academic credits earned at Michigan State University and the University of Michigan, and had petitioned the Faculty Board on my behalf. The Board had agreed to award the degree upon my completion of nine credits in the Humanities. While I was stationed at Great Lakes, I attended nearby Lake Forest College and completed the required courses and transferred them to MSU. Finally, in 1956, while I was attending the PG School, Michigan State awarded me a B.A. in Mathematics in absentia. Consequently, I received my Bachelors in 1956 and my Masters in 1958. Now all I needed was the Doctorate to complete the Trifecta, but that's another story!

"The Whiskerinos", 1957 Champions of the Seaside Little League. Bobby Harris is the 2nd player from left on the top row. The Coach is George Thaler, Professor USNPGS. It's me at far right, top row.

Chapter 28   Fort Bliss Revisited

We were pleasantly surprised to receive orders to Fort Bliss upon graduation from the U.S. Naval Postgraduate School. I was to report to the Army's Air Defense School for duty with their Missile Science Division as an instructor in the Guided Missile Staff Officers course. This course, which the Army generally referred to, as the "1181 Course" was one of the most prestigious ones offered in the Army's school system at that time. The Army called it the "1181" course because with completion of the course the Army officers received the additional MOS of 1181. (For those unfamiliar with the term MOS, it is the Military Occupational Specialty number which identifies the

qualifications of each member of the Army). This was the same course I had completed in 1949. The Marine officer assigned to the Missile Science Division when I was a student was 1st Lieutenant Cornelius "Corky" Sheffer. Subsequent to our first meeting at Fort Bliss, "Corky" and his family became good friends of ours. We served together on a couple other occasions and after retirement, we would visit them in their Cleveland home. Lt. Colonel Sheffer died in the late 1990s.

The Missile Science Division was organized into two branches: Engineering and Advanced Missile Techniques (AMT). All of the electronics instruction, including guidance systems, was conducted by the AMT branch. Since my program at the U.S.N. Postgraduate School was not "heavy" on Electronics, I was pleased to be assigned to head the Engineering Branch.

An Army Major William H. Holcombe Jr. was the Head, AMT Branch. Holcombe and I had been classmates in the GM course in 1948-49. He was a West Pointer and the son of an Army General.

The Chief, Missile Science Division was Army Lieutenant Colonel Burns. Colonel Burns was "old Army" in his actions and appearance. He certainly was not an "academic". I have no idea of his background in guided missiles or his formal education. I found him to be a very good administrator and he ran a "good ship". What I liked about him was he gave me my assignment and stood back and let me do my job. He was an older fellow and I can't remember him doing any socializing with the staff members

The Engineering branch was responsible for the instruction in several areas: a review of mathematics through Calculus and Engineering physics and engineering applications such as propulsion, servomechanisms, and aerodynamics. In addition to the administration of the branch, I was responsible for teaching several courses: Servomechanisms, Vector Analysis; and Mechanics.

After being at Fort Bliss about six months, a Brigadier General Stephen M. Mellnik (pictured on left) arrived at the school. For the next several months the officers in command positions were "quivering in their boots". The General was a survivor of the Bataan Death March and he was a tough bird! He had bought into some new management theories and he was applying them to all units of his command. His office wall was plastered with all kinds of charts of the performance measurements he was using to evaluate the effectiveness of the various units and their commanders. His motto was "The only job that is done well is the one the boss checks".

General Mellnik had scheduled inspections for each of the instructional units in the school. Already the word was out that he was not only difficult to please, but if the officer being inspected was not up to par, he was being relieved on the spot. As they said, the General was "kicking ass and taking numbers"! The day that our division was to be inspected was rapidly approaching.

In preparation for our inspection, we were all working to assist Colonel Burns with his presentation. We were making the necessary charts and briefing him on all aspects of the operation. Finally, the day arrived and the General and two officers from his staff arrived at our offices.

The General, a small bald-headed man, moved quickly through our office space directly to the Colonels office, where our leader was there to greet him. They all went into the office, closed the office door and we all settled back at our desks and tried to do some work, but all the time wondering how things were going in the office.

It was not very long before the Colonel's office door burst open and the General and his henchmen, moved through our space at a fairly rapid pace. The General, who didn't smile much in any case, didn't look very happy. Colonel Burns then motioned for Major Holcombe and me to come into his office.

The General had not been pleased with what he was hearing from Colonel Burns and he terminated the presentation, got up and left the office. It wasn't until the next day that we learned Colonel Burns had been relieved of his duties as Chief, Missile Science Division. I don't recall seeing Colonel Burns again. I believe he cleaned out his desk that night and was transferred to some other post. If he was still at Fort Bliss, we failed to see him on the base. He was gone!

Colonel Stevens, the officer in charge of the Electronics Department of the school, of which our Division was one of his units, called me in that next day and informed me I was to be the new Chief of the Division.

It seems that even though Holcombe and I were both Majors, I was the senior Major. It didn't make any difference that I was a Marine, I was senior and I was to take over the Division. That was the good news. The bad news was that General Mellnik was coming back in one week for a re-inspection and I had better be ready!

The General arrived right on time and I was in my new office awaiting his arrival. I had the charts all set up and I was ready to give him all the information he could possibly want, or need, to know about "my" division.

When he entered the office he came to a sudden halt, looked me over and exclaimed, "What, we have a Marine in charge of this division"? I replied, "Yes sir, General. You know that if you leave a crack in the door, we'll sneak in and take it over". He laughed and from then on I was "in like Flint". He made the comment that there were two "prestige" programs of instruction at this artillery school: the 1181 Course and the Atomic Weapons Orientation Course

(AWOC).   He laughed as he pointed out that one has a Marine in charge and the other a Medical Service branch officer. The rest of the inspection went handsomely and he shook my hand as he left and he was smiling.

From then on, the General had nothing but good things to say about the Division and me. However, it did bother me when he would phone me directly and ask for certain things to be done. After one or two direct communications with the General, I went to Colonel Stevens, my immediate superior.

I told him I felt very uncomfortable with the General dealing with me on a direct basis. I wanted him to know I was not one to go over the head of my superiors.

Colonel Stevens said, "Bob, you go right ahead and deal directly with the General. Just keep me informed as to what is happening, so I won't get blindsided." He was very pleased with the fact that the General was happy with our Division since it also helped keep the General off of his back.

Our division, the Missile Science Division was the "think tank" for guided missiles in the Air Defense School. In addition to providing instruction, our staff became involved in doing studies and providing research for others. It was not uncommon for General Mellnik to phone and say something like, "Bob, I am going to speak to a group next week and I need some information about…" We would do the research and provide him the information, which he could include in his remarks.

General Mellnik was also concerned about what he perceived to be a decline in the support for the 1181 course from the Army as well as the other services. He viewed it as the "feather in the cap" of the Air Defense School and he wanted to see the course receive the proper recognition.

He sent me to Washington on one occasion for the purpose of visiting the Army personnel group who were responsible for selecting officers for advanced courses of study, such as our 1181 course. My mission was to ensure that those people making school assignments understood the program and to provide this information to those officers who had an interest and would qualify for the program.

In order to draw attention to the course, he promoted a "reunion" banquet for all former 1181 graduates. Mailings were made to all former graduates inviting them to return for the affair. As guest speaker, he obtained the President of Texas Western College, now the University of Texas El Paso

Left: Me speaking to those attending the "Reunion" Banquet, June 1961 at Fort Bliss Officers Club.

The incoming students for the next classes came from the U.S. Army along with several from the Canadian Army. The Navy and Marines were no longer using the program

I was blessed to have an exceptionally well-qualified group of instructors. Norm Owens, a civilian mathematician, was our "leading light". He was an exceptionally intelligent individual with a very dry sense of humor. By a strange coincidence, Norm's mother was a graduate of Fenton High School in the early 1930s. When we left El Paso three years later we sold our house to Norm Owens. Later in my journeys, I visited with Norm who was still working as a Civilian employee of the Army but in the Washington DC area. It was also interesting to learn that another civilian instructor, Don Vance, came from Holly, Michigan and that his family still lived there.

Others I remember with fondness were: Captain Ed Williams, Captain Fred Haberman, 1st Lieutenant Jerrold Wolterstorff, 1st Lieutenant Woiton, 1st Lieutenant Joe Divis and Major Poage. Civilians Don Vance and Mr. Stafford were also on this staff. Stafford had been an instructor in the course when I was a student in 1949. One often hears about professor's who have taught the same course for so many years that they have "yellow" class notes. Stafford's notes had disappeared since he had it all memorized! I wasn't surprised to find him still presenting the same material as he did in my 1949 class! After I took over the Division, we finally got him to re-think and update his material.

In about 1970, when I was President of Johnson County Community College, I hired Ed Williams who had retired as a Lieutenant Colonel. Ed's work at the college was in institutional research. He did an excellent job for the college and retired for a second time. It is my understanding that both Poage and Holcombe acquired General officer rank before their retirements.

Of all the students who passed through the course in the three years I was with the Division, there is one who merits special notice. As a student, he was Captain Raul Garibay. Most of the people pronounced his last name as GAR-A-BAY...but in Spanish it was GA-REE-BAY. But to his fellow students he was Gabby. Garibay was an intelligent, humorous person and a delight to have around. He told of his ancestors escaping to the United States across the Rio Grande just ahead of Pancho Villa in a very hilarious manner. On one occasion, during a break between classes, a group of the officer students were standing in the hallway outside the classroom discussing the news of the day. They happened to be discussing the situation in the Far East where Communist China was threatening the Taiwan controlled islands of Matsu and Quemoy off the China coast. Captain Garibay belatedly entered the discussion with the provocative statement "We ought to let those Chinese sink or swim". One of the officers in the group took immediate exception to the remark and stated, "I'll have you know that my wife is Chinese". Without an instant of hesitation Garibay responded with "Don't tell me your problems, I married a Mexican". Not even the offended one could handle that...everyone broke down in laughter.

Gabby and his wife were indeed "Mexicans" and we enjoyed visiting with them when Rita would prepare some Mexican food, especially her Chile Rellanos. On one occasion, when my mother and father were visiting us, Gabby went with us as we toured Juarez. They asked about seeing the Bull Ring, and he took us there, "sweet talked" the custodian, who allowed us to enter the "ring" itself. This really impressed my parents. He was such a "fun" fellow, my folks talked about him for years.

It was the Fall of 1979 while serving as the President of McHenry County Community College in Crystal Lake, Illinois, when I received a letter from Colonel Raul Garibay, USA, the Defense Attaché with our Embassy in Mexico City. Gabby and Rita were inviting us to spend the Christmas Holidays with them in Mexico City. From the moment, we arrived in Mexico City, it was a wonderful experience. Our Defense Attaché was provided with a very large home, with at least two- bedroom suites to accommodate guests. The Garibays had also invited old friends, a retired Army officer and his wife, to be with them during the holidays. Each party had their own suite. The Garibays had two Mexican women who did the cooking and took care of the large house.

We did the usual "tourist" things, visited the historic points of interest in the city, attended a performance of the "Folklorica" and punted through the Xochimilco's Floating Gardens. One day, we traveled about 30 miles out of the city and visited the Pyramids of Teotihuacan. Gabby had a close relationship with Mexico's Secretary of Defense and on this occasion the Secretary provided a bus with a driver and guard to take the six of us to the Pyramids. It was a large "Greyhound" type bus, both the driver and the guard were carrying sidearms and the lunch aboard the bus was extravagantly delicious…as were the pyramids!

President Carter had appointed a man from Wisconsin as his Ambassador. Garibay told me the Ambassador could not speak Spanish and had no interest in learning the language. Garibay had the facility to immediately translate Spanish to English and via versa. He would accompany the Ambassador and stand at his side providing this instant translation. I had the occasion to witness this talent later during our visit.

Our evenings were occupied by accompanying the Garibays as they made calls on the Christmas parties and "open house" affairs. the various foreign Embassies and Mexican government officials were holding On our last day, it was the Garibays' turn to host a Christmas Party. The Defense Secretary provided his own private Mariachi band for the party which was well attended. During the evening, I met the Soviet Military Attaché. He was a Ukrainian and an Artillery Officer. The Soviet officer spoke no English and had learned his Spanish in Cuba. Garibay stood between us as we conversed, doing his "instant relay" act. This conversation and the pleasure of requesting my favorite Mexican songs from the Mariachis made the evening very enjoyable.

I know the Garibays retired in the El Paso area because in the late 1980s I received a form letter from the El Paso Schools to provide a reference for Raul Garibay who had applied for a position as a teacher in their district. Unfortunately, as it does too often, especially as one ages, we have lost contact with this very interesting man and his wife. Now let us return to 1958 and El Paso, Texas

It was a very unusual way in which we purchased our home in El Paso. While at the USNPG School, I became acquainted with an Army officer who had received orders to Fort Bliss. He told me of this new subdivision in the northwest section of El Paso where he had purchased a new home for $16,000. He had some literature and floor plans of the models the developer was building. I contacted the developer and Marie and I selected our lot and the model from material he provided. The house was finished and waiting for us when we arrived in El Paso.

The day we arrived at our new house must have been one of the hottest days we have ever experienced. As we were walking around the house just entering the back yard, Patty leaned heavily against her mother's leg. At first Marie thought she was pulling on her, wanting attention. However, she had passed out from the heat. We took her to our new neighbor's house next door to revive her. It was a memorable introduction to some high desert heat!

After the first year, both Bob and Pat went to new schools. Bob was in the first group of students at the new Irvin High School. He had suffered through a terrible year at Magoffin Junior High School where the atmosphere around the school was polluted by a group of delinquents who harassed the students at the school. He hated to go to school under those conditions. However, at Irvin he found a great deal of success and enjoyment. He was a pitcher and the starting shortstop on the varsity baseball team and was on the varsity basketball squad his two years in the school.

During basketball practice his second year he broke a metacarpal bone in his right hand. I took him to Army's Beaumont Hospital where they placed a pin through his knuckle into the bone. I recall telling him to "act like a Marine" during the procedure and I am pleased to say he did us proud.

Pat had three years in elementary school, all of which I believe she enjoyed very much. She made friends easily and has maintained contact with one neighbor girl throughout the following years.

While in El Paso we added an English Springer spaniel to our family. The young dog experienced his first snowfall and reacted much like the children in the neighborhood as he rollicked running through the snow.

Marie and I had many friends, mostly military families; however, our best friends were probably Tommy and Ken Walker. Tommy was the owner/operator of a service station in our area. I first met Tommy through the Little League where he coached the team on which Bob played. Tommy was a cigar chewing, tobacco spitting fellow originally from Tennessee. He was a sports enthusiast and we soon found ourselves rooting for Texas Western football and

basketball teams along with Tommy and his wife. Their son David was the same age as Bob and they played baseball together.

In the summer, Bob had a job working for Tommy in his gas station. Tommy was a hard task master and Bob learned how to work those summers. Anyone pumping gas, washing car windows in the heat of the summer in El Paso earns his money.

We were also delighted to find Major Jim Hitchcock and Maribelle living on the same street. We had lived in the same apartment house in Ysleta in 1949-50. Marie and Maribelle did a lot of the shopping together, traveling in a three-wheel Italian car the Hitchcocks had brought home with them from their last tour in Europe.

One day as Marie was returning from one of these shopping tours and they were approaching our house, Marie was surprised to see Bob driving our large 1955 Buick Roadmaster down the street. It seems Bob had decided to take the car for a ride around the neighborhood while his mother was away. When he saw her coming home, he knew he was in for a bit of trouble and he was right.

I had my first taste of being a member of a service club when I joined the Sunrise Optimist Club in our area. Tommy Walker was a member there and the Optimists were the sponsors of the Little League baseball league in El Paso. The club met for breakfast, which made it convenient to eat breakfast and then go directly to my office at Fort Bliss. I was the only Marine in the club and the others were civilian business men in our community. It was a very rewarding experience and for the first time I felt like a member of the community.

I enjoyed my duty with the Army at Fort Bliss. I believe most of the Marines who are assigned duty with the Army have similar experiences. The Army generally treats the Marines who serve with them better than they do their own troops. I have often thought about why this happens and I have come up with a couple ideas on the subject. First, the Army knows the Marine Corps only send their best representatives. Second, the Marines know, as a representative of the Corps, they have to be at their best. Third, because they are, in fact, really better and Fourth, when it comes to Marines, the Army has an inferiority complex!

In any event, after I had left Fort Bliss and joined the 12th Marines in Okinawa, I was pleased to receive the Army's Commendation Medal for "Outstanding" service as Chief, Missile Science Division. The Commanding General of the 3rd Marine Division, Major General Robert Cushman, presented it to me. General Cushman later served as the 25th Commandant of the Marine Corps. Thus, began my service on Okinawa, but, that's another story!

MG Robert Cushman, Major Robert Harris and LtCol Ormand Simpson

Chapter 29   Okinawa

I had been serving outside of the Fleet Marine Force for almost nine years, so when my orders detaching me from duties at Fort Bliss arrived, I was not surprised to find I was on my way to join the 3rd Marine Division on Okinawa. All Marine officers, regardless of their specialty, should expect to serve about every third tour "with troops" in a tactical unit of the Fleet Marine Force. Unlike the Army and the Air Force, duty with the Fleet Marine Force outside of the United States meant serving without the accompanying dependents.

FMF units such as the 3rd Marine Division were like naval ships at sea: Ready for immediate deployment to the scene of the action. This concept dictated that the Marine's dependents could not accompany them on an FMF tour of duty.

Consequently, Marie and the children returned to Fenton, Michigan where we rented a house on Appletree Lane for the "duration" of the tour in Okinawa. Bob and Pat were able to attend Fenton Schools. Bob began his junior year while Pat was in the 8th grade.

Bob attended Irvin High School in El Paso for his first two years and as a freshman he made the varsity basketball and baseball teams and was a "starter" on the baseball team at shortstop. He was able to continue his high school sports at Fenton High School.

The initial idea was to have Marie, Bob and Pat join me at our next duty station upon my return to the States after an anticipated 13-month tour with the 3rd Marine Division. However, when I returned both Bob and Pat had begun their school year, both had made new friends and Bob was playing varsity sports and wanted to stay in Fenton for his senior year. Consequently, we decided to have the family stay in Fenton until Bob graduated and I would continue on to my next duty station without them. But, that's another story.

I spent about three weeks on leave in Fenton, where we were able to get the family settled in a nice three-bedroom home in a subdivision close to Lake Fenton and my parent's home on the lake.   When it came time to leave, the whole "Royal" family was at Willow Run Airport near Detroit to see me off on my way overseas. Jean and Cam Loucks and their two girls, Marie's parents, my parents and Marie and our children were all there to wave "goodbye". The home movie shows me walking across the tarmac to the movable stairs, climbing the stairs and then turning and waving "good-bye" ala President Nixon. As I was walking to the plane, I placed something in my right trouser pocket. I didn't discover what it was until I was flying somewhere near Denver, Colorado.

Minutes after my plane had departed, the family moved back to their cars in the parking lot. My father prepared to drive my mother and my family back to Fenton in our car. When he asked Marie for the car keys, she suddenly realized I had failed to give them to her and probably had them with me. A couple hours later, I happened to reach into my right trouser pocket and made a startling discovery. I had the car keys! After some heroic effort, they got the car started and made the trip to Fenton.

My plane trip to Okinawa took me from the Travis Air Force base near San Francisco to Japan via Anchorage. Alaska. Riddle Airlines was the operator of our four-engine propeller airliner. Riddle was one of the airline contractors that moved troops back and forth across the Pacific. It was a long and tiring flight and some of us guessed the reason we were flying so slowly was because Riddle, who allegedly also made model airplanes, had forgotten to use the big rubber bands in our plane.

From Japan, it was a short hop into Kadena, the largest Air Force installation on Okinawa. After reporting in to the Division Headquarters, I was assigned to the 12th Marines as I expected. So here I was back in my old Regiment, only this time I was a Major and too senior to return to my old job as a Battery Commander. I was assigned as S-3 of the 1st Battalion, which was commanded by Lieutenant Colonel John Sullivan.

I knew John Sullivan. We had served together as Lieutenants in 1947-48 with the 10th Marines at Camp Lejeune. John was a First Lieutenant while I was still wearing the Gold bars. Even then, John would let me know that he was my senior. John was a graduate of VMI and a bachelor. John was a closet drinker. You wouldn't find him at the club having a few drinks with his colleagues, but you knew he was a drinker. He was also very prim and proper. I remember how two of our Warrant Officers at the time, Henry and Holman, would kid him about his swagger stick. They accused him of having a different swagger stick for each day. You could tell their remarks bothered him, but they didn't care and they gave him a bad time, most of the time. John was one of those officers who we classified as "having his finger on his number". This meant that he was overly concerned about his number in his rank. As a Lieutenant, you had the feeling he thought someday he would be the Commandant.

I knew I was going to be in for a bad time with John Sullivan, but I had no choice, so I reported as ordered. I was woefully out of touch with Battalion fire direction procedures and had to learn on the job as rapidly as possible. I was pleased to find an old friend in the Battalion Sergeant Major. He was Antonio Dindio from the Electronics school at Great Lakes.

It was difficult to please John Sullivan and after about a month, I believe the Regimental Commanding Officer, Colonel Clifford B. Drake rescued me before Sullivan could do me real damage. I first met Colonel Drake, then a Major, back at Camp Lejeune also. He made me his S-4, Regimental Logistics officer. I had never served in the "4" position on any staff previously, instead, I had always been in the "3", or Operations part of a unit. However, I learned to enjoy the new responsibilities and being out of the "line of fire" in Sullivan's Battalion. As it turned out, it could not have been a better "career" move even if I had planned it.

My areas of responsibility as the Regimental S-4 encompassed supply, motor transport, ordnance, embarkation and other logistical matters. Almost immediately after assuming the position, we were faced with some terrible maintenance problems. It seems that the "cupboard was bare" when it came to replacement parts. The story was that when General Shoup commanded the Division, before he was selected to be the Commandant, he slashed the expenditures for the Division, returned unused funds in order to make himself look good. As a result, the Division suffered and the shortage of replacement parts was severe. This became even more evident as we began preparations for a Regimental motorized parade. More than half of the vehicles could not run! The Colonel was quite concerned on how the Regiment would be judged if we were unable to field enough trucks and other vehicles to conduct the review. The Commanding General and other General officers from HQMC were scheduled to be at the Parade and watch the artillery regiment pass in review.

As the date of the review approached most of the Battalions were busily repainting old jeeps and trucks attempting to make them as presentable as possible. The mechanics throughout the regiment were busy scrounging needed parts for their dead lined vehicles. There was a lot of dealing going on among the NCOs of the Division. I suspect that some vehicles in the infantry regiments were being dead lined for parts as their maintenance people "loaned" some essential part to some friend in our regiment.

The Marine Corps always points with pride as to how much less it costs to field the Marine units compared to the cost of a similar Army unit. It is true, we are a much more frugal lot and we do get along with less than our Army counterparts. Perhaps because they always had more of everything helped us in this instance.

At this time of shortages, we did find one source, which became a cornucopia for parts and other scarce supply items. The Army Salvage facility at Machinato was where the Army units turned in obsolete or damaged property. Their junk became our treasure. Everyday we would have maintenance personnel from our regiment down at Machinato rummaging through the surplus and scrapped Army materiel. We had our own "junk yard" and it was amazing how many trucks we were able to fix up and get running because of the parts we picked up at the salvage yard. And best of all, it was free!

The day of the Regimental Motorized Review arrived and it was amazing how good we looked as we passed in review. Colonel Drake was beaming as he received many kudos from the Generals present at the review. He personally thanked me for "a job well done" and the "well done" was passed along throughout the organization.

The Officer's Mess of the 12th Marines was a scene of celebration that evening. Colonel Drake hoisted several of his "deep dish" Martinis and "rang the ship's bell" several times to the cheers of his officers. Colonel Drake had procured a very large Martini glass and it was kept for him behind the bar at the club. When the Colonel entered the club, the bartender reached for this oversized glass and mixed him a Martini. We all referred to his drink as the "deep dish Martini". It was the custom in the 12th Marines that whoever rang the ships bell in the barroom would buy a round of drinks for everyone present. On the occasion of some especially good news it was customary for the recipient of the good news to come to the bar and ring the bell. So, when a new baby was born or someone was promoted, the bell rang and everyone drank to the happy occasion. The only one who could ring the bell without retribution was the Commanding Officer. Colonel Drake liked to ring the bell and we shared his enthusiasm for bell ringing! Before you wonder how anyone could afford to buy drinks for everyone, you should know that the price of a drink in our club was only ten cents!

Even though the drink price was only ten cents, our club, like most of the other clubs, made a handsome profit. It wasn't because we were serving "cheap" liquor at the bar. Our "bar" gin was Beefeaters for example. Only the best brands were stocked. It was because we purchased the liquor free of taxes.

The regulations governing the clubs set a limit on the amount of funds any club could accumulate. Any monies over and above this specified amount were required to be surrendered to a Division fund. As you might expect, no one was interested in sending "our" money to the Division! So, the problem became how we ensure that we don't make so much profit that we have to send "them" our excess funds.

One of my collateral duties was to serve as a member of the Officer's Club governing board. In addressing the problem, we recognized having more free drink "happy hours" would only exasperate the problem. We learned when we had an extended "happy hour" with free drinks; we drew a larger number of officers to the club. They would get a good start on drinking during the "happy hour" and were more likely to stay in the club and continue drinking. (Even though the cost went back to ten cents a drink).

The result was more drinks were sold following "happy hours" and we made more profit! We decided to place several free bottles of wine on each of the mess tables at each evening meal. Most of the very best wines cost about a dollar a bottle, so this "giveaway" didn't do much to reduce our surplus. There didn't seem to be any solution to the problem, and we eventually, albeit reluctantly, surrendered our excess profits to the Division.

When I first arrived on Okinawa, the 12th Marines were located at Camp Hague, which was located in more rural section in the central area of the island. Camp Hague was made up of "temporary"

buildings that had been there for perhaps twenty years. It was mostly Quonset huts, of different sizes, or other building with corrugated metal siding. It was in a semi-tropical setting and the weather those first few months was hot and humid. Very hot and very humid! My home away from home was a small metal hut in "officer's country", just up the hill from the Battalion areas. We were surrounded by all kinds of tropical vegetation. Our hut had a couple small banana trees just outside our door. The bananas were exceptionally small so we didn't bother trying to eat them.

I shared the hut with a representative of the American Red Cross. He was in his mid forties, bald and he sweat profusely. I would generally be "home" when he arrived, with his khaki uniform soaked

through. The first thing he did after tearing off his outer clothing was to head for our refrigerator and pour himself several "fingers" of purple label rum. He would then fill the remainder of the water glass with Coca Cola. 150 Proof Rum and Coke! When that disappeared in short order, he had another one just like it! That was his drink and he never varied from it for the month or so we lived in the same hut. Each room was equipped with a single bed, desk and chair, an easy chair, lamps and a large sized closet. During that summer, you would usually find me sitting in my skivvies (underwear shorts for civilians) with my stereo phones attached to my head, writing a letter home.

I had purchased a reel-to-reel Akai tape recorder, of near professional quality, and I would listen to my favorite music on my stereo headsets. The Army ran a recreational facility with thousands of LP albums which they allowed you to copy onto tape. Some of us spent hours recording large reels of some of the very best music. I often think if it hadn't been for my tape recorder and those tapes of wonderful music, my tour of duty would have been a lot more difficult. As it was, the music filled many of my hours and tempered the feeling of loss one has when separated from the ones they love.

I learned the Majors in the 12th Marines had come up with another fun thing to do while serving on Okinawa. Years before the officers of that rank formed a "society" and named it the "YMCA". There was nothing Christian about this group. The letters stood for "Young Majors Carousing Association". They had designed a white sports shirt with a bright red collar and with the Marine Corps emblem embroidered on the breast pocket. Above the pocket your name and the letters "YMCA" were also embroidered. The Major who had served on the island the longest was automatically the President of the group. At his discretion, he could call a meeting and all the Majors in the regiment where "required" to show up at the Officer's Club wearing their YMCA shirts. Almost as soon as you arrived on the island, someone would collect $10 from you and your tailor-made shirt would be made up by one of the many tailoring shops on the island.

It was kind of a fun thing, and offered another pleasant diversion from the monotony of living away from your family.

A couple months after I had arrived on Okinawa our whole regiment was moved from Camp Hague to a Camp Sukiran. The buildings at Sukiran were permanent brick structures. There was a large field house and a theatre. It had been built for the Army and part of the camp was still occupied by an Army Airborne unit. What a difference in living conditions. The field grade officers in the Regiment occupied rooms on the second deck above the officer's mess and the officer's club. I had a very large room at one end of the building, with two large windows looking over the parking lot below. There was a stairwell at that end of the building which made it convenient to enter and leave the building. I was able to purchase a used window air conditioner and had it installed in one of my windows. It did a wonderful job in cooling the room and sleeping was much more enjoyable than it had been in the Quonset hut at Camp Hague. However, some things did not change. I was usually wearing nothing more than skivvies, and I still had my desk and my Akai tape recorder!

When basketball season arrived, the 12th Marines entered a league composed of teams from other Marine regiments as well as Navy and Army units. A good friend of mine, Major Harry Woods was assigned to coach the team and he invited me to assist him. Harry was a graduate of the Naval Academy and had played basketball on the Academy team. He also played on the Quantico base team which had many college teams on its schedule. I told Harry I knew nothing about coaching basketball, but he said it would be OK; he could still use my help. I really didn't learn much about coaching the game, however I enjoyed the season sitting on the bench, keeping score and being certain the official scorekeeper was assigning the fouls and points correctly and not messing with the time clock!

After we returned to the States I only got to see Harry one time as he passed through Quantico on his way to his duty station, Camp Lejeune. Harry Woods died about 1995.

Serving with me on the Regimental staff was an old friend, Lieutenant Colonel James Leon. Jim and I were Battery commanders in the 3rd Battalion, 12th Marines when we were both Captains. Jim was of Lebanese ancestry and really fine individual. However, what I remember most about Jim, having lived with him in the same quarters, was that he was very hairy. Jim wore a hair suit! He used to have to shave his hands up to his wrists so the hair on his arms would not protrude below his shirtsleeve cuffs. He shaved around his neck, front and back, so the hair would not be visible above the neckline of his T-shirts. Jim and I would later serve together again at the Marine Corps Development Center at Quantico. Jim Leon retired as a full Colonel and died in 2009.

Our Regimental Executive Officer, the 2nd in command to Colonel Drake, was Lieutenant Colonel Morris R. Snead. "Mo" Snead was one of the nicest fellows but he had a reputation of not being able to "hold his liquor". "Mo" asked me to go to dinner with him at the officer's club at Fort Buckner, one of the Army's finest clubs. Knowing of his reputation of getting into trouble after a few drinks, I was concerned, but I said, "Yes, I'd like to do that". It was the first of several times that "Mo" and I went "clubbing" and I never found him to be out of line, to the contrary he was a very calm person, even after several drinks! I learned a lot about "Mo" Snead during our time together which gave me a better insight into what made this fellow tick. On one occasion, he told me of the day while living in quarters at Camp Lejeune when he and his wife found their son had accidentally hanged himself in his closet. Perhaps it was after this tragedy that "Mo" acquired the reputation of not being able to control his liquor? "Mo" retired as a Lieutenant Colonel in the 1970s and died in 2003.

I could write little paragraphs about a number of my associates and friends who served with me in Okinawa at that time, however I will only mention one unusual fellow because I have told stories about him for years and I would be remiss if I left him out of these written memoirs. The fellow to whom I refer was Major Gene Kessler. Kessler was a very intelligent fellow who you would see almost every evening in the Officer's club reading some very thick book with a very erudite title. Sometime previously, Gene and I had crossed paths, however, I just can't recall where or when. He was in the Guided Missile business too, so we may have shared some common experience which I just can't remember. In any case, Gene and I were close during this tour in Okinawa. Neither Gene nor I were much of a drinker, so we would often sit with one or two drinks and talk for hours, while others were sloshing more drinks at the bar.

Invariably, Gene and I would have our evening meal together where we would have several glasses of some of the best wines. Gene seemed to be very knowledgeable about wines. In fact, Gene seemed to be very knowledgeable about almost any subject. His manner of speaking and the calculated and measured way he explained some complicated (or uncomplicated) subject instilled a confidence in the veracity of his explanation. However, after a while, I started to have some doubts about the accuracy of some of his explanations. On a couple of rare occasions, I happened to know more about what he was talking about then he did! I began to think he was having fun with some of our colleagues who were dining with us.

As an example, if someone at our table would be using the bottle of ketchup and would remark something like, "I wonder how they ever came up with the name ketchup"? Gene would have likely responded, "Oh, ketchup was named after the notorious Baron Von Strudel Ketchup of Bavaria in the late 1700s" and then go on to fill in the details of the Baron's life and discoveries. He was very intelligent but also one "helluva B. S.'er". Gene resigned from the Marines while still a Major and returned to his Alma Mater, Georgetown to pursue a career in Astronomy. I lost track of him a long time ago. He was different and a pleasure to know and observe!

In 1962, several units of the 3rd Division went to Japan to conduct maneuvers. We found ourselves at the same Camp Fuji where I had been, along with Jim Leon, in 1953. There was an assortment of Marine units from the Division in the camp: infantry, tanks and artillery.

We did have some liberty days, which provided an opportunity to "see Japan". On one weekend, I took a train into Yokosuka to visit with our old friends and neighbors, Frank and Joan Carter, from USNPGS days. Frank was assigned as a representative of Naval Aviation to a Japanese aircraft company, which had a contract to overhaul Navy aircraft.

We had been in Japan just a few of weeks, when suddenly we received orders to break camp, move to the beaches and embark on some Navy ships that were at that moment being moved from their base at Yokosuka to the beaches at Gotemba. It seems some Pathet Lao troops had crossed the Laotian border and entered northern Thailand. We were responding to this communist threat to our ally, Thailand.

The senior officer among all these Marine units at the camp was Colonel Drake, so the responsibility to carry out these orders was his. As his S-4, I was the staff officer responsible for the embarkation of the regiment, and now, all Marine units at Camp Fuji.

Upon receiving my orders, I set up a tent to house the embarkation command central. We augmented my section personnel with representatives from all the units concerned and set up radio and wire communications with these units. We also established a command post on the beach at Gotemba and established communications with them. Once we received information from the Navy on the types of ships available to load and the time of their arrival off shore at Gotemba, we began moving units to the beach area.

The next three days were very exciting, exhausting and at sometime, quite hectic. I set up a cot in the command tent and on occasion, I would catch an hour of sleep. Late on the 3rd day, the last elements were about to be embarked. We struck our command center and moved to the beach command post.

As the trucks had lined up waiting their turn to load aboard the LSTs the troops riding in the trucks would eat their emergency rations. There was a problem with trash that was solved very early when a group of Japanese "scavengers" approached the people on the beach and asked for permission to haul away all of our "trash". Approval was immediately granted. What a relief, one more thing we didn't need to worry about.

As the end was in sight, the leaders of the "scavenger" group appeared in the tent carrying several packages and offered them to the Marines present as a gift for having had the opportunity to pick up our trash. The packages were blocks of shrimp fried rice wrapped neatly in newspaper. The rice was steaming hot and looked very good, especially to those of us there at the time who had been eating canned rations for three days. So, we all ate the shrimp fried rice with gusto! It wasn't until later that night while aboard ship that we suffered the consequences of our action. All of the fellows I knew, including myself, had a case of diarrhea which continued for a day or so. However, I can't remember ever having such good tasting shrimp fried rice ever again!

The emergency situation in northern Thailand subsided and only a few of our ships with the Marines aboard continued on to Thailand.

Most of us went back to our camps in Okinawa and resumed our normal routine.

As a result of my performance during this emergency, the Commanding General of the 3rd Division, General Robert Cushman, presented me with a letter of commendation. Only three officers were so cited. My motor transport officer, Captain Jack Fox and my embarkation officer, First Lieutenant Jerry Lathrop and I were called before the General and presented the commendations. As I said before, I couldn't have planned a better career-enhancing move than leaving Sullivan's S-3 job to work as the Regimental S-4.

While I was still in Okinawa, Jack Sullivan went with a group of officers from our Division on a visit to the South Vietnam to observe the training facilities of the South Vietnam Marines. While there, he volunteered to go off a "jump tower" and tore up one of his knees quite badly. I felt sorry for him, but he should have known better to volunteer to make this "jump", but that was the way he was, always trying to look better than he was in actuality. I noticed a report of his death in an issue of the *Retired Officer* magazine about 1995. He retired as a Lieutenant Colonel.

After experiencing a couple Typhoons and spending hours killing time on the weekends, my tour in Okinawa finally came to an end and I returned to the "real" world. I was assigned to the Marine Corps Equipment Board in Quantico, Virginia.

The Commanding General of the Marine Corps Development Center was then Brigadier General Lewis Walt, who several years later commanded the Marines in Vietnam for several years.

General Walt was a tough infantry officer, renowned as an outstanding troop leader. It was probably unfair, but he was not noted for his intellect. When my sophisticated friend, Gene Kessler, learned of my new assignment and the fact General Walt had been assigned to command the Development Center he remarked. "Putting Lou Walt in charge of the Development Center is like putting Bronco Nagurski in charge of the Ballet Russe".

I looked forward to returning to Quantico for the first time since completing the Artillery School in 1945. But, that's another story!

Chapter 30   Quantico, Annandale And   Out !

I finally made it to "Cinder City!" When I completed PLC in 1945, our Platoon Leader, Lieutenant Scotcher arranged for those of us going on to the Artillery School to be billeted in the BOQ known as "Cinder City". Since I was married, I didn't require accommodations at the BOQ at that time. Now, having just returned from a tour of duty in Okinawa, and with my family remaining in Fenton until Bob graduated from High School, I welcomed the opportunity to have a room in the Cinder City BOQ. It was directly across the street from the Headquarters building of the Marine Corps Development Center. Even though my new office was not in that building Cinder City was a convenient location on the base.

The office building for the Marine Corps Equipment Board was along the Potomac River and you needed to pass through the town of Quantico in order to reach the facility. Quantico was a strange town. It was completely surrounded by the Marine Base. I don't know if there were any businesses in the town not directly or indirectly associated with the Marine Corps. The uniform shops, the restaurants and most other stores were there to serve the Marines stationed at Quantico. It had been that way for decades, so no one thought of it being an unusual situation.

Coming back to Quantico after so many years was like a homecoming in a way. In fact, I found a number of my old and closest friends had preceded me and it was enjoyable renewing our friendships. Sam Dressin was also with the Development Center and he was officed in the Headquarters building. I remember another Major was in the same office as Sam's; it was P.X. Kelly, who many years later became our 28th Commandant. My favorite mathematics teacher at the Guided Missile school in Fort Bliss back in 1948, "Corky" Sheffer was also on board. Jim Leon had left Okinawa a few months before me and we were rejoined at the Equipment Board.

Not long after I arrived, Captain Harold Hatch showed up to attend the Amphibious Warfare School. Harold and I went back all the way to Boot Camp where we stood next to each other in the formations and bunked "up and down" in the barracks. At the end of WW II, Harold was one of the reserve officers who opted for a permanent warrant as a Master Sergeant in lieu of applying for a regular commission. While I was a 2nd Lieutenant with the 10th Marines in 1947, Harold was a Master Sergeant in the 8th Marines, an infantry regiment. On several occasions, I visited and shared a couple beers with him in his quarters at Camp Lejeune. When the Korean War began, Harold, as it was with many other former officers, was given the opportunity to be re-commissioned. Consequently, Harold was now a Captain and I was a Major. However, Harold passed me by after I retired in 1965. The last time I saw Harold Hatch was when I visited him in his office at HQMC, Washington, D.C. where he was a Lieutenant General and the Assistant Commandant for Logistics.

One of my new friends was a Lieutenant Colonel Frank Harte. Frank was a native of Muskegon, Michigan and on several occasions, he would travel to Michigan with me. I would drop off at Fenton and let Frank take my car, an old VW "Beetle" to his home in Muskegon. Frank rekindled my interest in stamp collecting with which I was involved for many years to come.

While "batching it" in Cinder City, the most exciting thing any of us "bachelors" seemed to do was to go to the officer's club on occasion and have a steak dinner. Most of the time, we made the usual trek to one of the mess halls, which were set up to accommodate transient officers. Again, it was to work every day, go out to eat and write letters or go to a movie every night. However, on those weekends when I traveled to Michigan it was more interesting. I would drive the VW "Beetle" at top speed through Maryland and over the Pennsylvania Turnpike: across the Ohio turnpike and finally into Michigan. On a couple occasions I tried desperately to make it home in time to watch Bob play basketball, but I never made it in time.

With the spring came high school graduation and Marie and Patty were free to travel to join me in Quantico. Pat had completed her 9th grade, the first year of high school, at Fenton High School and would attend the base high school at Quantico for her sophomore year.

We were assigned quarters on the base, which marked only the second time in twenty years when officers' quarters were available.

Our home was a three-bedroom apartment in a building with four identical apartments. The floor plan was very unusual, especially for government quarters. All the apartment entrances were at the rear of the building facing the parking lot. The buildings lacked "curb appeal". Upon entering the apartment, you would either move down into the front room or up the stairs to the bedrooms. The lower level also contained the kitchen and a small dining area. The three bedrooms and two baths were on the second level. The entire wall of the front room was glass windows. The view through the windows was of a wild wooded area. The "backyard" was not very deep and beyond the grassy area the terrain fell off precipitously. It wasn't much but it was our "home" for about a year.

Our son, Bob, opted to stay in Michigan for the summer following graduation, find a job and save some money for college. When the school year began, he moved into Wonders Hall on the MSU campus.

It was while we were living in Quantico that President Kennedy was assassinated. I was in a conference room near the main entrance to the Development Center, when I heard the news of his shooting. Marie was at home when Pat returned from school crying. None of us will forget where we were and what we were doing that day.

When we lived in Quantico, we made frequent trips to Washington, D. C. and visited Capitol Hill and many of the points of interest. On those occasions when we had visitors, our practice was to take our guests on an evening tour of Washington. The Capitol building, as well as the monuments such as the Lincoln Memorial, was especially attractive when lit up at night.

I worked as the artillery officer in a section of the MCEB headed by Lieutenant Colonel Hugh Irish. When I first arrived, my first Battery C.O., now Colonel Pete Hahn was in charge, but Hugh Irish relieved him shortly thereafter.

For a period of time during the Kennedy administration the whole Federal government, especially the military services went "gaga" over hiking. The papers were full of some organization or group out hiking some 50 miles or more. It wasn't long before the craze hit Quantico. General Walt was a real "grunt" and it was in his nature to think highly of hiking. So, it came to pass the day arrived when General Walt announced all the officers in the MCDC were to muster on that coming Friday in front of the Headquarters building. The uniform was utilities with a light pack and canteen. We were going on a 25-mile hike and the General was going to lead us. The plan was to hike out to the Officers Basic School (OBS) located in the outer regions of the Quantico base. We were to have lunch there and after lunch hike back into the Main base. The only officers who were excused from making this "conditioning" hike were those who would be away from Quantico on temporary duty. It so happened; that I was traveling to Fort Sill, Oklahoma that week and I would not be in Quantico for the hike. Damn it! I was going to miss the hike!

One of the officers in my section, a new Major David Barker was also scheduled to be away on a trip and he would also miss the hike. On the following Monday, both Dave and I were back in the office having returned from our temporary duty over the weekend. As was our custom at the beginning of the workday, the officers in the section would stand around drinking coffee and conversing about the topics of the day. On this Monday, "the" topic was the hike the past Friday. They were all saying how lucky I was to have not made the trek, when in bounces young Major Barker. Without warning he announced he was going to do a "make-up" hike on his own since he had missed the group session. Then he turns to me, in front of all the others, and asks, "Bob, you missed the hike, do you want to join me on the make-up? I was not very quick that morning and before I realized what I was doing I replied, "Sure, OK".

The next Friday was the day for our make-up hike. When it arrived Dave and I took off from the same place as the others did the week before (Dave wouldn't want to do it any other way!) and we moved out smartly. Before long we had left the main part of the base behind us and were moving along out in the country. It was a lovely day, and I began to think, "This isn't such a bad thing after all". We arrived at the OBS, had lunch and prepared to hike back into the main base.

It turned out that stopping for lunch was not such a good idea. I seemed to have developed a bit of stiffness and soreness. I could feel a couple blisters starting to form on the heel of my right foot! However, we moved along at a good pace and we soon were in sight of some of the outlying buildings of the main base. The black top road on which we were traveling crossed over the highway, US 1, just before getting into the built-up area of the base. I was struggling along about this time, I had blisters on both heels and I imagined that I could feel the blood oozing out into my field shoes. When we arrived at the bridge, I appealed to the young Major to stop for a short rest before we made the last few miles into the main base. The bridge provided an excellent sitting area, so we both sat down for a short breather.

The longer I sat the more tired and sore I became. Finally, it was time to move on; I had great difficulty getting to my feet. My legs and my whole body had stiffened up and I not only had trouble getting up, but I just couldn't walk without pain. I told Dave "I've had it" and he flagged down a jeep that was headed into the base. I boarded the vehicle and the driver drove me to my quarters.

Marie was there when we drove up in the jeep and she watched me struggle to get out of the passenger's seat. As the driver and his jeep left, Marie assisted me into the house. She drew me a very hot bath and I sat in the hot water and soaked for about an hour. But this is not the end of this tale. I was on duty that night! I was to report to the Headquarters building at 1800 (6:00 PM for civilians) to begin my overnight duty as Staff Officer of the Day.

After I had soaked as long as possible, I had to put on my uniform and drive to the Headquarters and assume the duty. After I parked the car, I moved up the walk stiff legged to the entrance of the building. As I took each painful step, I couldn't help but think if anyone was watching they may have thought the "thing" walking toward the building was Frankenstein's monster, minus the neck bolts, donned in Marine greens!

On the next Monday, we were conversing and sipping coffee as usual, and to his credit, Dave Barker didn't comment on my failure to complete the hike. A few days later each of us received a letter of appreciation from General Walt. He had learned of our "make-up" hike and he wanted to express his appreciation and recognition of our commitment and attention to duty.

I was pleased to read, years after I had retired, that Major General David Barker had assumed the command of the 4th Marine Division. I couldn't help but wonder if he had them out hiking.

HQMC had directed the MCDC to conduct a study to determine the ammunition requirements for a Marine force engaging in combat in several different environments. A study group was formed and I was assigned as its artillery representative. It is interesting that a couple of the areas, which we war-gamed, was with a Marine Division landing in the Gaza Strip and engaging Egyptian forces. A second was landing two Marine Divisions abreast in the vicinity of Haiphong and moving to seize Hanoi. In the study, each of the various elements of the force was represented. On the day President Kennedy was shot, I was in a conference room, which had been assigned to the study group, with Major George Annas, an engineer and Major Lou Baeriswyl, an air defense officer

Not long after we had completed the study, the Army convened a study group at nearby Fort Belvoir under a General Jonathon Seaman. General Seaman later relieved General Westmoreland in Vietnam. The Army was also interested in the ammunition requirements for any future combat. I was assigned as the Marine Corps representative to this study group. So, for several weeks, I would commute to Fort Belvoir and work with a group of Army officers. I enjoyed the collegiality but it wasn't very interesting. I got the idea they didn't really care what the Marine Corps thought about the problem.

During the summer of 1964, I was promoted to Lieutenant Colonel and transferred to the Pentagon. I relieved a Marine Colonel Benton H. Elliott, who was retiring, as one of two staff assistants to Major General Robert H. Weinecke, USA. General Weinecke was the Director of ARPA's Remote Area Conflict section. It was more commonly known as Project AGILE. ARPA was the Advanced Research Projects Agency of the Department of Defense.

Essentially, I was the only Marine Officer in this group of about thirty persons. At least one-half of the personnel were Civil Service employees. The others were from the other U.S. uniformed services. I did meet with the "other" Marine officer, a Major William Corson on a couple brief occasions. He seemed to have a privileged position in the organization. It was hinted that he was "CIA" and that he set his own agenda. When he left AGILE he was assigned to the U.S. Naval Academy as an instructor. He wrote a controversial book entitled "The Betrayal" about the war in Vietnam.*

I shared an office on the fifth floor in the "E" ring of the Pentagon. My office mate was Warren Stark, a GS-13 Civil servant. In general, Stark and I maintained liaison for AGILE with other military commands, Congress and the Executive branch of the government. Each of us had other projects to oversee as well. My main project

---

* http://www.arlingtoncemetery.net/wrcorson.htm

QUANTICO, ANNANDALE AND OUT! 247

was a $30 million contract with Battelle Memorial Institute in Columbus, Ohio. Battelle was developing a database for remote area conflict. I didn't have too much activity in my area, while Stark was overloaded. Consequently, I helped him on many occasions.

Early one morning, when Warren came into the office he was visibility excited. I soon learned he had just been told he was to brief the Attorney General Robert Kennedy at 10 o'clock the next morning. Bobby Kennedy wanted to know all about the program AGILE had devised to protect the villages in South Viet Nam from the marauding bands of the Viet Cong. The program was dubbed the "Strategic Hamlet" program.

One might ask, as we did then, what does the Attorney General of the United States need to know about this program in South Vietnam? Even though Lyndon Johnson had succeeded his brother in the Presidency, Bobby Kennedy remained as the Attorney General. Prior to the assassination of John Kennedy, it was general knowledge that Bobby Kennedy had injected himself into many military situations. During the Cuban Missile Crisis, it was reported that Bobby Kennedy was in the war room, deep in the bowels of the Pentagon giving direct orders to Captains of Navy ships, much to the chagrin of the Navy Commanders. He was often referred to as the "Crown Prince" when his brother was President. While it was also common knowledge that neither Lyndon Johnson nor Bobby Kennedy had much respect for each other, it was a surprise when President Johnson asked Bobby to stay on as the Attorney General.

Warren needed to have a first-class presentation, including charts, ready to go early the next day. He enlisted those of us in our small office to help him put the presentation together. I called Battelle and asked them to send a fellow who had worked with us on previous occasions. He was an excellent graphics artist and was outstanding on developing presentations. He hopped the next flight out of Columbus and arrived later that afternoon. Suffice is to say, we all worked late into the night and finally Warren was ready to present!

The next morning, Warren Stark left with his chart case in hand in time to arrive at the Justice Department office of the Attorney General about fifteen minutes before the appointed time. We all anxiously awaited his return to find out how everything went with the briefing.

Shortly after 11 o'clock we were all surprised to see Warren coming into the office. We could tell by his face that something had gone very wrong. After he settled down, he told us what had happened. This is the story he told us about his visit:

... I arrived in his outer office about fifteen minutes before 10 o'clock as I had planned. The receptionist showed me to a waiting room where I sat waiting for the time to meet with the Attorney General. At about 10 o'clock the Attorney General's door opened and a large fellow came out and moving towards me asked if I was the one to do the briefing. As I indicated I was the one, he took me by my elbow and moved me through the open door...

...The room was dimly lighted and I could see Bobby Kennedy sitting behind his desk in his shirtsleeves with a foot on the top of his desk. There were about five or six men in suits standing around the periphery of the office and they didn't move or say anything. As I approached Kennedy's desk, he said something like. "OK, what have you got?" I then set up my stand, placed my charts on the stand and began my presentation. I was about half way through the briefing, when Kennedy says, "OK, that's enough...get him out of here". With that a couple of the men came to me, took me by the arms and hustled me out of the office. Moments later another fellow came out of the office with my charts and other paraphernalia, which he literally threw at my feet. I had just received the "bums rush" ...

Warren Stark's experience fit in perfectly with the other stories of Bobby Kennedy's behavior I had heard since coming to the Pentagon. Although the assassination of Bobby Kennedy was tragic, I was not disappointed with the fact he was not going to be President.

I particularly enjoyed making trips to the Congress, because our Representative from Michigan was an SAE Fraternity brother from Michigan State, John Mackie. John had been the Highway Commissioner for the State of Michigan for years before he was elected to Congress. I would use his office as my home base. His administrative assistant was particularly helpful, especially when I decided to retire from the Marine Corps in order to accept a fellowship at Michigan State University.

Along with the transfer to the Pentagon came a move to a new home. It also meant that Pat would be attending her third high school

QUANTICO, ANNANDALE AND OUT! 249

in as many years. We were fortunate to find a nice three-bedroom house for rent in the city of Annandale in Fairfax County, Virginia. It was a short commute in miles from Annandale on the Shirley Highway to the Pentagon. However, unless you avoided the rush hours, it was bumper-to-bumper traffic all he way. I was assigned to a parking lot at the Pentagon which was very close to the entrance I preferred to use as an entry and an exit to the building. There were about 500 parking spaces in this particular lot. The problem was that they assigned something like 700 people to the lot. It was first come, first served! In order to ensure having a parking place in the lot, I had to arrive a good hour before I was expected to be in my office.

Many times, we would have to work late hours, so arriving early and leaving late, made for long working days. Once I had decided to apply for retirement and accept a fellowship to pursue a doctorate in community college education, I decided to take a sequence of education courses offered by the University of Maryland at the Pentagon during the evening hours. This definitely made for some long days.

The Graduate Record Examination was administered at George Washington University on a Saturday morning and afternoon in the spring of 1965. I was required to take the General exam, given to all prospective Graduate students, and an exam in my area of specialization. Since I was interested in the Community College, my afternoon exam was in Education. Other than the 6 semester hours of education courses I was in the process of taking with the University of Maryland, I had never had any instruction or experience in public education, other than that as a student. In order to prepare for this examination in Education, I purchased copies of the College Outline Series for Educational Psychology, Educational Philosophy, and perhaps one in some other area of education. I crammed on these outlines and concentrated on learning some of the jargon used by professional educators.

On the day of the exam several hundred people came to sit for the exam. I completed the general exam and left feeling quite confident I had done a reasonably good job. I found it very similar to the aptitude test I had taken in the Marine Corps. I had always scored very high on those tests so I thought I would grade high on the exam.

I went into the afternoon's examination on Education with some trepidation. I didn't know what to expect. However, as I went from one question to another, I felt more and more confident in my answers. I seemed to understand the jargon and the rest seemed to be quite straightforward and reasonable.

Every time I tell someone about my scores on the GRE exams I feel uncomfortable. I don't want to come off as a braggart, but I did very well. I was in the 99th percentile in each of the exams.

When we lived in Annandale, we continued to take our visitors on a nighttime tour of the sights in Washington. Marie's Aunt Lottie and Uncle Charlie King were visiting with us from their home in Toronto. The night we took them on the tour it was after midnight when we were driving up the street to the Capitol. It was then I noticed the flag was still flying on the Senate. This meant the Senate was still in session. So, we parked the car across the street and proceeded up the many steps leading to the Senate. Upon entering we made our way to the visitor's gallery of the Senate. The ever-present ushers were there to direct us to a seating section. Once we settled down, we began identifying the different Senators we recognized. Bobby Kennedy was in the President's chair conducting the session. We identified several other prominent Senators of the day.

The Senate was debating the historic Civil Rights Act which was passed that night and shortly thereafter signed by President Johnson. Nowadays, it is difficult to imagine that happening. First of all you would not be able to drive your automobile anywhere near the Capitol building. And imagine how four people off the street, and two of them foreigners, could walk into the building, up the stairs and reach the gallery before meeting anyone who worked for the Senate.

On another occasion, Marie and I along with a couple other visitors were in the basement of the Senate, where the Senators board their train to take them back to their office buildings. As we were standing there along comes Senator "Scoop" Jackson from the State of Washington. Senator Jackson was a very handsome fellow and greatly admired. Marie could not contain herself and she jumped out in front of him and shook his hand and told him how much she liked him. He was very gracious and seemed to enjoy the encounter. Today, Marie would still be serving time in a Federal Penitentiary even if we were allowed access to that area of the building.

I had often told Marie and the children about being in the crowds along the street in Washington and watching the body of President Roosevelt being moved from the Union Station to the White House.

We didn't expect to be a witness to a similar historic event, but Marie, Pat and I traveled to Washington to watch the caisson move President Kennedy's casket from the Capitol Rotunda to the White House.

Later, we again traveled to Washington and stood in the crowd to see President Lyndon Johnson's inauguration. It was a much smaller crowd then now attends the Inauguration ceremonies for our Presidents. As we were standing there near the edge of the crowd, we suddenly noticed that we were standing right next to Van Kliburn, the noted pianist. We have often wondered why Van Kliburn, a celebrated Texan was not provided a better spot to watch the inauguration of a fellow Texan.

During leave in Michigan, I had dropped by to visit with my friend and mentor at Michigan State, Dr. Paul Dressel. During my previous visits, we had talked about what I was going to do once I retired from the Marines. I had thought about teaching mathematics in High School, and in fact that was one of the reasons I had taken the 15 semester credit hours with the University of Maryland while I was stationed at the Pentagon. I would now be able to qualify for a teacher's certification in Michigan.

On this particular visit, Dr. Dressel told me of a new program of the W.K. Kellogg Foundation. The Kellogg people had recognized the rapid expansion of community colleges throughout the nation demanded persons with leadership capabilities. At the time one new community college per week was being built in the United States.

This program called the "Community College Leadership Program" was being operated at selected universities throughout the nation. Michigan State was one of the institutions selected to participate in the program. Those individuals selected for the program would receive a substantial stipend for three years in the program leading to a doctorate He suggested, if I was interested I should apply for the fellowship. I was interested and I applied. Months later, after going through the procedure, I was offered a fellowship.

In order to accept the fellowship, I would be required to retire from active duty in the Marine Corps. *Herein lies the rub*! In order to retire at my present rank of Lieutenant Colonel, I needed to serve a minimum of two years in that rank. I had been a Lieutenant Colonel just a little over one year. Regardless, I requested retirement and explained my interest in accepting the fellowship and the doctoral program as my reasons for making the request. I don't know what the HQMC response would have been if I had not taken other action to bolster my request. I wanted to be able to accept the Fellowship and begin work on my Doctorate, so I asked others to help.

Major General Weinecke wrote a supporting recommendation and delivered it to HQMC personally. The administrative assistant in my congressman's office contacted Senator McNamara, the senior Senator from Michigan, and the Senator supported my request in his letter to HQMC. Whether or not the General's intervention or the Senator's letter was what turned the trick, my request was approved and my orders for retirement were issued. After I had moved my family to East Lansing I returned to Washington to complete my days as an officer of Marines however, I had a few moments of uncertainty even at that late date, but that's another story!

Chapter 31   What A Way To Go!

As a member of the Remote Area Conflict section of the Advanced Research Projects Agency, better known as ARPA, I had the opportunity to interact with several officers and representatives of the Army of Vietnam (ARVN) and the Royal Thai Army (RTA).

Earlier in my tour at the Pentagon, I had the pleasure of escorting a Major General Singchai Menasuta of the Royal Thai Army on a tour of military facilities in the Washington area. This included a stop at the grave of President John Kennedy in Arlington Cemetery, where the General placed a wreath on his grave near the eternal flame. The day before, I had the General and two other RTA officers in my car and was driving them to a meeting at Fort Belvoir, Virginia. We were running late (as usual) and we hadn't had the opportunity to have lunch. I recall asking the General if he would mind "grabbing" a quick lunch on the way, rather than stopping at some restaurant. He said that would be all right, so I pulled into the McDonalds in Springfield, Virginia and we dined on "Big Macs". I am sure it was a very unusual sight for the others at McDonalds that day. Here was one American, in civilian clothes, along with three Thai officers all decked out in their colorful uniforms, sitting on these tile benches eating hamburgers. I understand that when the civilian head of ARPA, learned of this "lunch" he almost "blew his top". But the important thing was that the General enjoyed it!

Once I had my retirement orders in hand, I arranged to move my family back to Michigan and I procured a room at the BOQ at Bolling AFB, just across the river from the Pentagon. I had about a month of active duty before I left the service. I had essentially tied up all my work at that time and when the need for an officer to escort two senior Thai Army officers on a tour of defense facilities came up, I said, "I'm your man!"

I met the two Colonels in San Francisco in late August 1965. One of the Colonels was Lua Karachanapimai. Colonel Lua was a "senior" Colonel, which was equivalent in rank to our Brigadier General. Colonel Prasart Mokkhaves was a younger man. Both of the officers spoke passable English, so we had no difficulty communicating. The agenda for the trip had been previously arranged and the Thai communities in the areas we visited were alerted to their coming. Consequently, they were warmly greeted at our various stops for the next couple weeks.

My job was to make sure we stayed on schedule, ensure they had a nice place to stay and had good food to eat. Ensuring that they had accommodations and ate well was not a problem, but keeping the tight schedule was difficult. But as time went by, the two officers began to recognize the need to move along, and they were very cooperative. I developed a close relationship with the Colonel Prasart and we did a lot of kidding back and forth during our tour. I used to kid him about the fact he carried a bottle of Tabasco sauce in his briefcase. No matter what he ordered to eat, he doused his food with Tabasco sauce. Colonel Lua was friendly but more reserved.

The very first night in San Francisco, the Colonels were the guests of the Stanford Research Institute for dinner at the Four Seasons Restaurant. There was a rather large gathering of about 20 to 25 people in a private dining room. The menu consisted of many exquisitely prepared items of Chinese food. It was a wonderful evening and an excellent start for our travels. Excellent food and drinks and the people were speaking English, but that was about to change!

Our first stop after leaving San Francisco was in Monterey. This was an old stamping ground for me, after having lived in the area for three years while attending the U. S. Naval Postgraduate School in Monterey. Our reason for going to Monterey was to attend a luncheon with the Thai faculty members of the U. S. Army's Foreign Language School at the Presidio of Monterey.

We met about 30 people of Thai ancestry at a Chinese restaurant in Seaside, a small-town bordering on Monterey. I was the only "round eye" in the place and I didn't understand one iota of the conversation for the next couple of hours. I didn't observe the younger Colonel using his Tabasco sauce during the luncheon.   The Chinese dishes that were served included some that were very highly seasoned.   I began to understand why the Thai people are often likened to the Mexicans of the Far East.   They like their food "Hot and Spicy"!

For the next several days we visited a number of facilities in the Los Angeles area and it seemed as if each of the host organizations elected to serve Chinese food for the meal they hosted.   Other than our breakfasts, which we generally ate at the hotel or a restaurant near our hotel or motel, we were "wined and dined" every noon and evening by our hosts.   Inevitably Chinese food was served.   My only chance to eat "American" was at breakfast and I usually ordered eggs, bacon, toast and coffee.   My friend used to douse his eggs with Tabasco sauce and I would often do the same.   I really like Chinese food, I still like it today, but to eat Chinese food every day for over a week was a bit too much to expect of a fellow from Michigan.   I started to feel sorry for the millions of people in China who have to eat Chinese food every day of their life!

Colonel Prasart and me at the Hoover Dam, September 1965

After a "hard" week of touring one facility after another…Rand Corporation, Douglas Aircraft, Northrop Missile, the rocket facilities in Pasadena, etc, etc…. the weekend finally arrived and we had "free time". Our scheduler had anticipated this "free" weekend, and had arranged for us to spend two days in Las Vegas. Of course, we had to drive out to the Hoover Dam, where Prasart and I were captured holding up the dam wall. We also made the rounds of the casinos and show clubs, but since my Thai friends were not terribly proficient in English, they had difficulty understanding what was being said, unless the speaker was speaking slowly and speaking directly to them. Consequently, they were not interested in attending any of the shows where they would have difficulty understanding the jokes, banter and singing. This eliminated some of the shows I would have preferred to attend, such as Steve Allen's show, and we ended up in the audience of the big extravaganza "girly" shows such as Follies Bergere and Lido d'Paris.

After dinner and a show, I would make certain my charges were safely back in the rooms, and then I would head for one of the lounge shows. I was able to see Mel Torme and Keeley Smith perform in an intimate lounge setting. For me that was the highlight of the trip.

During the weekend, it was either Saturday or Sunday; one of the days was September 6th, my birthday. On that day, as I met them to go to dinner, they said words to this effect. "You have been taking us to dinner for days now, so tonight, since it is your birthday, we want to take you to dinner as our guest". What a nice gesture. They had made dinner reservations and called the taxi and away we went. I had no idea where we were going! Soon we pulled up in front of this very nice restaurant…a CHINESE restaurant! It seemed no matter where we were, we were always eating Chinese food!

Leaving Las Vegas and getting back on schedule on Monday morning was almost disastrous. We were ticketed for a flight out of Las Vegas directly to Chicago, where we were to make connections to Dayton, Ohio. Our next scheduled visit was at the Wright-Patterson Air Force facility in Dayton, later that same day. For some reason, I couldn't get the Colonels moving very fast that morning, and we were late in getting to the airport. I urged the taxi driver to make haste, since we had to catch the American flight leaving at 8:15 AM. As we approached the airport I observed an American Airlines plane leaving the boarding area and taxing away. I knew it was our airplane! We had missed our flight! We would miss our connection in Chicago and all that Air Force Brass in Dayton was going to blame that damn Marine for not getting them there on time!

As we raced into the terminal, I headed straight for the American check-in desk, hoping to get them to call "our" flight back to the terminal. All of my pleadings were to no avail. However, the kind people at American said they could arrange for us to fly United to Chicago via Denver and we could still make our connections to Dayton. Wow! What a relief! So, we flew the "friendly skies" of United and actually arrived in Chicago within a few minutes of the American flight we had missed. We arrived in Dayton as scheduled and no one there was the wiser!

After Dayton, we made a stop in Boston where we visited the Army's Natick facility where equipment and other materials are evaluated. The best part of the Boston visit was the dinner in the harbor area where we dined on lobster! American style lobster with lots of butter! The Thai officers had no complaints, and there was no Tabasco bottle in sight.

Right, Me in front of Thai Exhibit at NY Worlds Fair, 1965

Both of the Colonels were anxious to get to New York City. Colonel Lau's wife was a medical doctor and she was working at a New York hospital as a resident in some medical specialty. The first night in New York began with a large party in a restaurant in New

York's China Town. Again, I was the only non-Asian in the crowd. The group was conversing in the Thai language and occasionally; the younger Colonel Prasart would let me know what was going on. In spite of the feeling of being "out of it" I have happy thoughts about the evening.

During our three-day stay in New York, we made a trip to the New York World's Fair. It so happened that one of Colonel Prasart's old girlfriends was operating the Thai Exhibit at the Fair. The picture is of me in front of the Thai exhibit. Of course, we called on her and had a special reception and a tour of her exhibit; followed by a very scrumptious lunch…you guessed it…of Chinese food!

Our next stop was Washington, D.C. and the Pentagon. I had made the full circle and I wanted to get off. I appealed to General Weinecke, my superior, to let some one else escort the Thai officers for the final days of their tour. I had lots of things to do in the few days before my final day on active duty. My request was granted and I bid farewell to my two traveling partners. I often wondered how it was so easy to find someone to take up the escort duties. I wonder if the fact that the next visit was to be with Miss Universe in Miami, Florida. The new Miss Universe was also Miss Thailand and the Colonels insisted on visiting with her during their time in the USA.

The two Colonels were really fine people. They were always polite, had a sense of humor, and seemed to be genuinely appreciative of the efforts being made to make their stay informative and interesting.

A couple weeks later, after I had retired and was residing in Michigan, we received several gifts from the two Colonels, expressing their appreciation for what I had done for them. They sent a nice Princess ring for our daughter Patricia, a ladies wristwatch with several interchangeable faces and bands for my wife Marie, and a large silver colored men's wristwatch for both son Bob and myself. Previously, during my "birthday" dinner "party' in Las Vegas, they had each given me a gift. One was a metal cigarette case for placing on a table and the other was a carved stone set consisting of a cylindrical shaped container for cigarettes and a matching carved stone ashtray. Very interesting gifts when you consider that none of the three of us were cigarette smokers!

It was a wonderful tour of the United States, personally very inexpensive, and a pleasant way to close out my career as a Marine Officer. What a way to go!

Chapter 32   Almost Frozen Again

Even though I had about a month to serve in my post at the Pentagon before retirement, I had already received my orders for retirement and had moved my family to East Lansing, Michigan. The move was made at that time in order to get settled before the beginning of school for Patricia. Pat would be attending East Lansing High School for her senior year, her fourth high school in four years! Bob would be starting his second year at Michigan State and I would be beginning the three-year doctoral program at MSU once I finished my active duty.

After making the move into a rental house at 620 Snyder Street in East Lansing, I was returning to Washington, to finish out a couple of weeks before my retirement date. It was a Sunday, I recall, and I decided to drop in on our friends, Charlotte and "Suds" Sudhoff, who were then living in Springfield, Virginia. Lt. Colonel Ira Sudhoff, USMC was then stationed in Washington, serving with the Navy's Bureau of Ships. "Suds" opened the door and almost immediately asked me if I had seen the *Washington Post*. Since I had been driving all day, I had not had an opportunity to read any newspaper, let alone the *Washington Post*. What I was about to read was a shock!

A headline on the front page of the Sunday *Washington Post* read… **"Navy and Marine Officer Retirements Frozen"**. The article went on to relate that the Department of the Navy had halted the retirement of all Navy and Marine officers because of the new situation in Viet Nam. In the preceding weeks, the Marines had landed a force at Danang and it appeared that United States forces might become directly engaged in the hostilities in that country. For several years prior to our landing in Danang, the United States had been assisting the South Vietnamese government in their struggle with North Vietnam and the rebellious Viet Cong.

When the Marines landed at Danang, my retirement process was well underway. I had already received my orders and on that basis, I had rented a house and moved my family to East Lansing. While waiting for my retirement date, I lived in the BOQ at Bolling AFB and commuted to the Pentagon across the river by boat. The Air Force ran launches from Bolling to the Pentagon on a regular schedule to accommodate their officers living at Bolling and working in the Pentagon.

Soon after the Marines landed at Danang, I visited the Marine Corps Headquarters, Personnel Division, to determine if this action would have any effect on my scheduled retirement. I recall visiting with a Colonel Peterson, who I had known from previous duty together. I told Colonel Peterson, the head of the division at the time, I wouldn't feel right, if this Danang operation developed into a major conflict and they started bringing in reserves through the "front door" as I retired out the "back door". I remember him telling me not to be concerned and that this will be over "in a few weeks". So, I continued with my planning and moved my family back to Michigan.

After reading the *Washington Post* story, I could hardly wait for Monday to arrive so I could go to the Personnel Division at Headquarters, Marine Corps and find out what was going to happen to me. Here I was, my family in Michigan, living in the BOQ, just doing the time before my scheduled retirement date. What if I was "frozen"? What was I to do about my family in Michigan? What was Michigan State going to do with the Kellogg Fellowship I had accepted to work on my doctorate? Who was going to pay for the shipment of all my household goods to Michigan if my retirement orders were cancelled? I had a lot of questions to ask.

As I walked into the offices of the Personnel Section, one of the first persons I saw was a Warrant Officer I had known at a previous duty station. He saw the look on my face and said, "Take your pack off, Harris". (Marine talk for "take it easy"). Then he told me my retirement was not frozen. It seems my retirement orders had already been signed by the Secretary of the Navy and I would be retiring as scheduled. All of those officers whose retirement orders were still in the Secretary's "IN" box would be "frozen". That is why I have the distinction of being the only Marine officer to retire as of October 1, 1965.

Chapter 33 From the Halls Of Montezuma To The Halls Of Ivy

The transition from being a Marine officer to a college student and then a President of a Community College was not as difficult as I was told to expect! What many people fail to realize is both the Marines and Education are "people' businesses.

I have had otherwise intelligent people tell me they thought the military life did not allow for independent thinking. They were of the opinion the military person, when faced with a certain problem, would turn to the "book" for the solution. "Everything by the book" … of course, nothing could be further from the truth.

These people had bought the military "stereotype' hook, line and sinker. They didn't realize that good officers value the input of others. Good officers challenge their subordinates to present and defend alternate proposals on how to proceed.

The big difference between civilians and military persons is that in the military, once the "boss" makes the decision, everyone accepts the decision and takes the necessary actions to achieve success. From what I observed that doesn't always happen in civilian life.

While serving as a Marine officer and as the President of a college, I found the basic situation to be the same. In each instance you are working with the same assets: people, materiel and money:

Your success depends on how well you select, instruct and supervise the people you have working for you. And it depends on how efficiently and effectively you use the materiel and money you have available to accomplish your task.

Graduation Day, June 1968. Son-In-Law To Be Daniel J. Badaluco, B.S., Civil Engineering and Robert G. Harris, PhD, Higher Education. Location: Spartan Stadium, Michigan State University, East Lansing, Michigan.

Marie receives a well-deserved kiss for her support during the three-year quest for the PhD!

My "second" career in Education was different but in its own way as interesting and exciting as my Marine Corps experience. But, that's another story!

Chapter 34   Once A Marine
Always A Marine

Even those who are not a member of "the Brotherhood", seem to understand the significance of the saying "Once A Marine...Always A Marine". It seems that Marines go out of their way to identify with other Marines. Most of us have some kind of sticker on our automobile window that indicates our interest in the Marine Corps. Consequently, it is not unusual that a passing Marine, who served in the past, will stop and ask about the sticker, and once they learn you are a Marine, the "so you're a Jarhead too!' kind of talk begins. Occasionally you discover you were on duty at the same place at the same time, perhaps in the same unit, or you find you have a mutual friend. The meeting is a "happy" occasion and you part as old friends and with a smile on your face and a warm glow in your heart.

Early in my Marine experience, I was told of this fellow who arose each morning and immediately after his feet hit the deck he would stand tall, stretch out his arms to the sky and proclaim in a loud voice... "Another grand and glorious day to serve the Corps". That is what most Marines would term as being "Gung Ho" ...and perhaps a bit too much. However, there are those times when you are so proud to be wearing the Globe and Anchor you are just "full of it" and you look forward to: "stepping out smartly" and "looking sharp".

In the days and months following my retirement in the fall of 1965, I was so busy with getting the family settled, beginning a second career...as a graduate student at Michigan State...that I didn't have much time to do anything else, but I did find time for the Marine Corps. You may recall that 1965 was a year of unrest on most college campuses, and the campus at Michigan State University was no exception. The University had its radical faculty members who seemed to be the Alpha and Omega to the student leaders protesting our presence in Vietnam. The administrators at Michigan State, not unlike those at most of the major universities in our country, were either spineless or completely incompetent of managing the frequent student protests on campus and seemed inclined to go along with every radical far out demand of the anti-war protestors on campus. Student sit-ins in various administrative offices generally ended when the administration submitted to the demands of the law-breaking strikers.

My son had already joined the Marine officer program, known as the Platoon Leaders Class, while a student at Michigan State and the Marine PLC students had formed a social organization and called it the Semper Fidelis Society. They were an official recognized student organization on campus. By the end of my first year in my program, I had been offered and accepted a faculty position with the University's Office of Institutional Research. It was at the lowest faculty rank, that of Instructor, but it did allow me to become the "Faculty Advisor" to the "Semper Fidelis Society" a student organization.

In the past, before the student unrest, the Marine Corps Officer Procurement officers would meet with PLC candidates in the counseling offices of the university, just as the corporations would meet with prospective employees. However, the "wimpy" administrators had "banned" their use of the Counseling Center for recruitment purposes.

When it seemed as if there was "no room in the inn" for our USMC Officer Procurement officers, someone suggested that the Semper Fidelis Society set up a booth in the Student Union and meet with PLC candidates there. It made perfectly good sense. As a student organization, we had a right to use the Union Building for our club purposes. So that was the way it was done. The PLC students set up the booth and manned it along with the Procurement officers. And it was "Mission Accomplished".

In the winter of 1967, the MSU Student Union was the scene of the commissioning ceremony for two PLC graduates, one of which was our son Robert J. Harris. It was my honor to deliver the oath to the two new Second Lieutenants on that occasion. The ceremony was attended by the Marine Corps League's Past National Commandant, Burt Daugherty of Lansing, Michigan and Captain Frank A. Huey Officer Procurement Officer. Lt. Harris had his new gold bars pinned on his undress blue uniform that evening by his mother Marie and his bride-to-be Jean "Duffy" Boyko.

2nd Lt. Gary N. Vanhoverloop and 2nd Lt. Robert J. Harris
receive oath from Lt. Colonel Robert G. Harris, USMC Retired.

Following the ceremony, the group of the young people went on the town to celebrate. They partied into the wee hours of the next day. About 8:00 AM the next morning the Lansing Journal newspaper phoned to inquire about coming to our house for a reenactment of the delivering of the oath to my son. It seems they didn't get a good picture at the event the previous evening. My answer was in the affirmative and they said their cameraman would be there in about 30 minutes. With some effort, we were able to get the new Lieutenant out of his bed and into his blue uniform in time for the posed photo. The newspaper photo was one of a very "hung over" Marine, hand held high, apparently taking an oath, but not really being there!

Bob and Jean were married on January 13, 1968 and they both left for Quantico, where Bob began his three-year tour on active duty. Bob left the Marine Corps in 1971 to begin a new career as a Special Agent of the Federal Bureau of Investigation

Bride-to-Be Jean Boyko and Mother Marie Harris pin Gold Bars
on new 2nd Lieutenant Robert J. Harris, USMCR

Following my graduation from Michigan State University with a PhD in Higher Education, I accepted the position of President of a new community college in Johnson County, Kansas. In the last two years of my seven-year tenure at this new college, I was successful in my efforts to have the U. S. Marine Corps select our college as one of those to provide a two-year educational program for the staff non-commissioned officers selected for the Marine Corps' Warrant Officer Program. The Education Officer at USMC Headquarters was a Colonel Hazel Benn. The Colonel knew the Marines attending our College would receive the very best in education and a truly friendly Marine Corps environment. As one would expect, the Marines at JCCC were outstanding both in and out of the classroom.

One day, Lt Colonel Richard Randolph, USMC Retired came to me with his Masters in Business Administration in hand and asked about a teaching position at our new Community College. I had known Dick since our days in the Michigan V-12 and I knew him well enough to invite him to join my fraternity. We were in the same officer class for commissioning and we had both served as Artillery Officers in the Marine Corps. I hired him! As it turned out Dick was one of the best instructors in the Business area and a very loyal supporter of the plans I had for the College. Dick Randolph retired from JCCC and he and his family continued to reside in his home at Lake Quivera in the State of Kansas.

After leaving Johnson County Community College, I became President of Middlesex County College in Edison, New Jersey. There I found an active veterans organization on campus who were extremely pleased to have their new College President both a veteran and a retired Marine officer. It was during my tenure at MCC that the Marine Corps celebrated their 200th Anniversary. The local Marines, Recruiters primarily, organized the traditional Birthday Ball and I was invited to be the Co- Guest of Honor. My fellow Guest of Honor was a local resident of Edison, NJ, and a well-known artist, then Major Charles Waterhouse. Charles Waterhouse had served as an enlisted Marine in the Pacific during World War II. But now he had been commissioned a Major and was appointed the Artist in Residence for the Marine Corps and placed on active duty. His duty station was his studio in Edison My wife Marie and I visited with Charles Waterhouse and his wife on several occasions and visited his studio which was part of his home in Edison. It was interesting to have him explain the technique he used in his paintings of Marines in action. A year or so later, he invited my son and I to attend the dedication of a "new" Tun Tavern in Philadelphia, in which the now Colonel Waterhouse was a part of the program. At the time, my son was an agent attached to the FBI office in Philadelphia.

In the early months of 2008, I received a telephone call from our son Robert, now living in South Carolina, not far from the Marine Corps Recruit Depot (which Bob reported had a very fine golf course, which he plays quite often!). Bob told me of his intention to attend the fortieth reunion of his Officer's Basic School class at Quantico the following June, and he asked me if I would like to go with him as his guest. I jumped at the chance and flew to South Carolina in time to join him as we traveled to Quantico in his automobile. When we arrived at the designated meeting place, we found the men of 1968 happily renewing old acquaintances.

Many of the old warriors had brought their wives with them, so I found an interesting group with whom to join and converse. We had a lot in common, they didn't know their husbands "buddies" or each other, so we had a great time together.

The program for the reunion was packed solid each day…and evening. For an old retired fellow like me, it was more activity than I had experienced for several years. We visited and were briefed on most of the activities at the Marine Corps Base. One of the highlights was visiting the helicopter squadron that services the needs of the President. Following a briefing, we toured the various helicopters in the squadron. I asked several of the pilots about President George W. Bush and they all responded positively telling of how the President was genuinely a fine fellow. One told of riding dirt bikes with the President when they stayed with him at Camp David. One of the pilots had flown "Marine One" for both President Bush and President Clinton. When I asked him about Clinton, he responded with "I would rather not talk about that".

One of the officers, who had flown President Bush on many occasions, told of the President's habit upon entering the helicopter. He would usually return the salute of the officer standing to his right at the foot of the stairs and as he stepped onto the stairs he would greet the officer standing to his left with a slap on the shoulder. On this particular occasion, a new Captain…a woman Marine…was on her first mission flying the President. She happened to be the one standing to the left of the President as he boarded the helicopter. She was standing at a rigid attention, unusually tense since this was the first time she was this close to the President of the United States. She did not expect a "blow" to her shoulder and when the President greeted her with his customary slap, she lost her balance and almost toppled over. Once the President noticed that he had almost knocked the Captain over, he returned to her and apologized for his action. They parted with big smiles and the President boarded the aircraft without further incident.

In HMX-1 Briefing Room: Author, Robert G. Harris in first row, far left. Son, Robert J. Harris, two seats to his right in this picture. .

In the two photos above the briefing officer is Major Decoteau who is the son of the Reunion Class leader, Colonel Sam Decoteau, USMC Retired.

The group went by bus to the Sunset Parade at the Marine Barracks at Eighth and "I" in Washington following a day of activity. The Parade features the Marine Corps Band and the troops of the Marine Barracks and their "Silent Drill" team. It was a performance that made one proud to be a Marine.

The Marines moving to formation at the beginning of the parade.

The "President's Own" ...the U.S. Marine Corps Band

The group visited the National Museum of the Marine Corps at Quantico and everyone was fascinated with the many realistic exhibits of Marines in combat in past wars. The Museum building is visible from the highway approaching Quantico, as it represents the famous flag raising on Mount Surabachi during the battle for Iwo Jima in World War II.

The awesome main hall of the Museum at the entry*

Prior to leaving Michigan, I phoned the Commanding Officer of the 1st Battalion, 10th Marines at Camp Lejeune, North Carolina. My first duty with an FMF unit was in 1946 when I joined the 1st Battalion at Camp Lejeune. I was a bit surprised on how easy it was to make the call when LtColonel Michael McCarthy answered the phone. I told the Colonel that I was a retired officer and had served in his Battalion many years ago. I also told him my son had served in the 10th Marines during the Vietnam War period and had not been back to Lejeune since his separation in 1969. I asked if he would consider allowing us to visit the Battalion and "catch up" on the things that had changed since we left them years ago. He seemed to be overjoyed with the proposal and he said he would be waiting for our arrival with a hot cup of coffee on hand.

Consequently, on our return trip to South Carolina, Son Bob and I stopped at Camp Lejeune and drove to the area where the 1st Battalion,

---

* The pictures from the reunion of the USMC TBS Class 8-68 are by Charles M. Gerhold, a member of that class.

10th Marines were barracked. I was not surprised to find them in the same area as they were in 1948, but now everything seemed to be more crowded. As he promised, Colonel "Mac" was waiting and we soon had a mug of hot coffee in our hands. He introduced his Executive Officer, Major George Robinson and after a bit of small talk, the Colonel told us that the Battalion had only recently returned from a tour in Iraq and he then told us of the condition of the troops and about the new howitzers that Marine artillery was receiving.

The Colonel told of a recent survey that had made of the men in the Battalion concerning their intention to reenlist. The response from his men was consistent with the response received throughout the whole 2nd Division. There was an overwhelming number of Marines who indicated they intended to reenlist, which presented a problem. You cannot accept the reenlistment of everyone…or in time you would end up with 50- year old Privates. A number of Marines must leave to allow new, younger troopers to enlist. What a problem to have during the conduct of two wars!

The Executive Officer loaded us into a jeep and we visited the Gun Park, where one-gun crew had laid out all their equipment by their howitzer and were standing by for inspection. An exceptionally well-informed Corporal briefed us on the new Howitzer as his crew stood by the weapon. As I looked over the equipment laid out for inspection, I noticed a survey instrument that we were using in 1948, an Aiming Circle. I was surprised to find this relatively primitive instrument in the crew's gear since we now can find one's position with Geographic Positioning Systems.

The new howitzer made substantial use of the GPS, but the Marines were prepared to carry on when and if the GPS failed. While the Coast Guard's motto is Semper Paratus, the Marines are real believers in being ready too!

We had the opportunity to see the "new" officers and their training regimen while at Quantico and then visit with the men they will lead while at Camp Lejeune. I am proud to say there is "Nothing like the Ol' Corps" …I can say with pride and confidence. I believe the "New Corps" is as good as or better than the "Ol' Corps". The citizens of the United States can have confidence the Marines are ready and able.

As I previously reported, my contact with the development and employment of the radar bombing system our small group of Marines had built at Point Mugu and had combat tested in the Korean War was essentially non-existent after I left Korea. I had essentially lost contact with the Air Support organization and only heard comments from old associates that the "factory made" version of our equipment had been deployed in Vietnam during the conflict. Then again, I read in Lieutenant General Krulak's book* about the use of the system in the siege at Khe San.

I was not aware of any current interest in our work in developing the system until I was contacted by Major Phil Woodward of MACG 38 in the late summer of 2010. I knew with the advanced technology of the present day; our old system was quite antiquated. However, I didn't know that the Marines of Marine Air Control Group 38 had been researching the history of Marine Air Support and Control, and had found our development and deployment of the AN/MPQ-14 …with a unit then designated the Marine Air Support Radar Team (MASRT) in the Korean War…was an important step in the history of Marine Air Support.

Major Woodward extended an invitation to be the Guest Speaker at the dedication of an exhibit area …one celebrating the Heritage and Legacy of combat air support in the Marine Corps. I was privileged to accept the invitation and even though at age 87, I didn't travel as well as in the past, Major Woodward convinced me that the trip was important to him and the Marines of Marine Air Control Group 38. Consequently, I attended the "ribbon cutting" and was warmly received by the Group Commanding Officer, Colonel Jeff P Davis, who introduced me to those assembled. Following my unremarkable and forgettable remarks, the Colonel presented me with a fine plague and a Charles Waterhouse painting to commemorate the occasion.

At the gathering I was pleased to meet two retired officers, LtColonel John Wetter and Captain Tim Allen., who were with the radar bombing teams during the Vietnam War. To learn how remarkably well the system performed in that conflict filled me with pride…not only for how well those Marines conducted themselves, but to learn how our efforts in 1949-52, contributed to their success.

---

* *First to Fight by* Lieutenant General Victor H. Krulak USMC Ret.

On the following Monday, the two "Vietnam" officers and myself were the guests of the Marine Air Support Squadron 3 at their compound at Camp Pendleton. Our group was given a briefing and a demonstration of the unit's equipment including a visit to the operations center.

As one might expect, the operations center was very "high tech", with each operator equipped with the best in video and communications gear. However, as the procedures used in the center were being presented, I was attracted by a large battle chart (map) on the bulkhead in the center of the grouping. The chart was covered with a plastic sheet and there was a grease pencil hanging on a string to the upper right-hand corner of the chart.

At the end of the briefing, during the "question" period, I asked about this plastic covered chart and the grease pencil. What was this relic of the past operations doing among all this "hi tech" equipment? I was surprised to learn ... "if all this high tech fails...We can still operate as they used to do..." I was a bit overcome by a "rosy glow" as I thought about our operations in Korea.

LtCol Dan Logan, R.G. Harris, John Wetter. Tim Allen, SgtMaj
David Maddux and a TPQ-10

The briefings continued as we retired to the "ready room" where we learned of the present-day operations in Afghanistan, which was presented by a woman Marine Captain in a very professional manner. Probably because I had left the active service some forty-five years earlier, I did note there were many more women Marines in the organization than would have been in the "ol' Corps" ...officers, NCOs and troopers...and all appeared to be excellent Marines.   Kudos to the "new Corps"!

Following the meeting in the "ready room", we visited the entrance to the Squadron's compound. At the entrance, we found one of the old TPQ-2 radars, much like the one we used in Korea, and a large sign attached to the fence. The sign's background was Marine red with white lettering. The title was **"AN/TPQ-10 RADAR SYSTEM"** and the text presented the story of the development of the original equipment under the leadership of then Captain Marion Cranford Dalby at the Naval Air Missile Test Center, Point Mugu, California. The story told of the deployment of the system to Korea and concluded with its successful employment in Vietnam.

With the new generation of the system, the Air Support Radar Teams in Vietnam controlled more than 38,000 missions, placed more than 121,000 tons of ordnance on 56,753 targets.   The commander of the

Khe San defense, Colonel David Lownds said "Anything but the highest praise could not have been enough".

The sub-title on the sign tells the real story…

A CENTERPIECE OF MARINE AVIATION /GROUND INGENUITY

: Soon after returning from my visit to Miramar, I wrote this email to Elizabeth Baldwin, the widow of Colonel M.C. Dalby USMC Ret. Perhaps this email tells the story better than all the preceding pages?

My dear Elizabeth…a couple months ago, I received a telephone call from a Marine Major Woodward at Miramar. I learned that he and others had been working on an exhibition and a research project tracing the development of Control of Marine Aircraft in support of Marines….as part of this they came upon the work that our group at Point Mugu under the direction of then Captain Dalby…It seems that the system we built and took to Korea for a combat evaluation is considered to be a very significant development and has led to what is being used today….we all knew it was an important step but I personally had lost touch of what happened after Korea….I was the last of the original officers to return from Korea…we went for a four month combat evaluation….and we did so well that both the 1st Marine Division and the 1st Marine Air Wing insisted that we stay….In the meantime the Marine Corps brought in General Electric or some big company like them to build a more sophisticated and commercial version of our "handmade" equipment….I had heard that they had several of these units deployed during the Vietnam War…but I only learned of the significant role they played in that conflict last week.

This Major Woodward and I communicated by phone and email for several weeks and I sent him my book which contained our story of the development and the deployment of our radar bombing system. I apprised him of the fact that only two of the original officers and eight enlisted were alive. That being me and then TSGT Seissiger (now LtCol retired). He wanted both of us to come to Miramar as honored guests for the dedication of the "museum" and for recognition of our contribution.   John could not make it even though he lives in Escondido CA not far from the MCAS...his wife is in poor condition and he couldn't leave her, .so I decided to make the trip to represent all the fellows who had passed on.

On November 13th, they had the ceremony and the ribbon cutting for the exhibit...The Wing Commander a MGEN Conant spoke, then the Group Cmdr, Colonel Davis introduced me.... following my remarks there was a reception...but this is what I want you to know....and I will attempt to be as humble as possible...since I was often referred to in heroic terms. All those I spoke with considered our development as the MOST significant thing that happened in the control of Marine air support....as hard as I tried to say "we were only doing out job"...and "we new it was never done before...but..."...they insisted on heaping the praise on our group.
.

A couple other guests who were in charge of the new MASRTs in Vietnam (one was in the siege of Khe San) ...were lavish in their praise...according to them if we hadn't pioneered and built the system...they would have suffered many casualties and perhaps have lost at Khe San...What I am attempting to do is to have you know how much credit they gave to our endeavor.... In my remarks, I told of the positive strong leadership of Captain Dalby...and how that made it all possible.... I truly believe without Dalby "it" would never have happened.

On the following Monday, they took me to Camp Pendleton to visit the Squadron that now performs the role of controlling the aircraft ....bombing, med evacs, etc many more missions....we were briefed on all of the equipment and systems now employed ...also employed in Afghanistan....it was very high tech...but in the middle of it all was a plastic coated map (chart) and a grease pencil....I asked why that was there surrounded by all kinds of "TV" screens....and the answer was if all the new technology would fail they could still carry on using the our "old" system.

At the entrance to the Squadron compound stood old TPQ 10 radar...like the one we had in Korea (without the 40 mm gun carriage on which we mounted our radar.)...But behind it on the fence was a large sign....red background with white lettering....the text told the story of the work at Pt. Mugu under the leadership of Captain Marion Cranford Dalby....(I told them that Dalby would probably have preferred that they either dropped the Marion or used the initial M.)....It is comforting to note that the sign will be there for years...and Dalby will be recognized for the job he did....and all of us will be pleased to know we really did something very significant... As you can tell from my report...I was very happy I made the trip and very happy to learn of how our effort back in 1949---1952 was appreciated by the "New Corps" I wish my friend had been there ...but maybe he was? Best to all.... Semper Fi   Bob Harris

A transcript of the text on the sign outside the entrance to HQ, MASS 3 is to be found on page 286.

Closing Thoughts

"Regrets, I have a few…too few to mention…"

Paul Anka

From moment to moment, hour-to-hour, day-to-day we are confronted with choices and we are required to make a decision, consciously or not. You may recall my analogy of this never-ending process is as if we are entering a room from which we are required to exit in short order. We choose one of the exit doors and leave, never to return to that room again. We have to live with the choices we make. Living requires us to make choices. We are continually moving through life making one decision after another.

On occasion, some external force moves us through one of the doors. We don't make a conscious choice. We really don't have a choice. Conditions beyond our control make the decision for us. However, in most instances, we make our own choices on how we conduct our life.

It would be the rare person who would go through life and never make a bad choice. So undoubtedly each of us, as we look back on our life, would like to have done things differently in some instances and would welcome a second chance. However, I don't believe it is healthy to ponder on these "second" choices, for life is what you make it and, in my opinion, it is best for you to live with your choices and make the best of your situation.

Consequently, I have few regrets for the choices I have made throughout my life. I often wonder what my life would have been like if I had made other choices, especially as to my choice of occupation. If I had known then what I know now, I might well have begun a career in the financial services. However, that was not an option when I decided to become a career Marine.

My decision to retire from the Marine Corps to pursue a second career in community college education was another important turning point in my life. At the time, the probability of being promoted to Colonel in a reasonable time was not very great. However, with the onset of the Vietnam War, others very junior to me in rank were promoted to Colonel within a year following my retirement. Now, I am certain I would have been promoted to Colonel and I would have served in Vietnam. While the probability of becoming a casualty of that war was small, it was still a possibility. However, this risk would not have influenced my decision to retire. No one in the military really believes he will become a casualty. To think otherwise would be very inhibiting in doing what is necessary in combat.

Therefore, having survived Vietnam, my chances of making General in the next ten years before retirement would have been highly problematical, even though several of my contemporaries attained General rank before they retired. I would have liked to have known if I could have made it. However, I don't regret leaving the Marines at the time of my choice and for the purpose of pursuing the doctorate.

Another major turning point in my life was when my tenure as President of Johnson County Community College was abruptly terminated. I decided at that time to continue in the Community College business and subsequently, I served as President of two other colleges. However, being President of these other colleges, after serving as the founding President of JCCC did not yield any real satisfaction. They were "just a job" and they were not rewarding experiences. If I had it to do all over again, I would have entered another field of endeavor upon leaving JCCC. So, I may have one regret!

One thing is certain. I have absolutely no regrets for having married Marie Durant. Marie has been a wonderful companion and a loving wife. Marie is the mother of our two children and a better mother would be difficult to find. She provided the comfort and maintained the home for our children and me even though I was away for days, months and even a year at a time. Her career has been as a loyal wife, mother and homemaker. If I had it to do all over again, I would ask Marie to marry me. You will have had to ask Marie if she would have said "Yes", if she had known how much stress and strain I would cause for her in making the decisions I made over the years.

As you can tell from reading of my life's experiences, I am a very patriotic person. I am not a "super patriot" by a long way. You won't find me standing along the parade route with my VFW or

Marine Corps League cap, adorned by all kinds of medals or badges. I actually resent the actions and I am a bit contemptuous of those I refer to a "professional veterans". It disgusts me to see these "professionals" in their camouflage gear with their medals attached touching the "wall" and bubbling in tears. I may be wrong, but I suspect many of them are "phonies" who misrepresent their military service. I suspect many of them never left the States or if they did go overseas, served in some rear echelon command. During a recent Presidential election, I detested the fact that Al Gore attempted to make capital of the fact he was a "Vietnam War Veteran". When the truth was he served as an Army journalist in a rear echelon organization and then left after about four months "in country" while others served a thirteen-month tour in Vietnam.

From my experience, the ones who fought the "real" war were the ones who were the most silent. While in Korea, I lived in the same tent with a Marine aviator, Bob Klingman for thirteen months. I had known Klingman for many months before I learned he was a recipient of the Navy Cross, one level below the Medal of Honor. Bob received the medal for his downing of Japanese "Betty" during the battle for Okinawa. At maximum altitude, with his guns frozen, he chopped the tail off the Japanese plane with his propeller while making several runs on the aircraft whose rear seat gunner was firing. His own plane was barely flying as the vibration caused by the damaged propeller was literally tearing his plane apart. After he put the enemy plane down, he turned toward Okinawa, but ran out of fuel as he approached the island landing strip. With great skill, he was able to make a successful dead stick landing. I had to hear this from others, Bob Klingman never mentioned it!

When it comes to "words to live by", I have a few expressions, which I sincerely recommend for your consideration.

First, listen to the beautiful music and the lyrics of the song, "Life Is What You Make It" by Johnny Mercer and Henry Mancini. The melody is charming and stays in your memory long after the music stops. The words tell it like it is*…" Life is what you make it…and you can make it, if you try".* In most instances, it's up to you alone. You make your decisions and "life is what you make it"!

Next, consider an expression so common in the Marine Corps it has become a military principle. "Make the best of the situation". It's true! Consider where you are and what the circumstances are and

282 MANY COME FEW ARE CHOSEN

"make the best of your situation". No wishful thinking, no "what ifs", face reality and do the right thing!

Undoubtedly you have heard the expression, "If they give you lemons, make lemonade". It's just another way of saying, "Make the best of your situation".

While at JCCC, I also framed and displayed a couple of items of writings that express my convictions. They were the excerpts of the pronouncements of Thomas Wolfe and Oliver Wendell Holmes. They read as follows:

"..to every man his chance
...to every man, regardless of his birth, his shining, golden opportunity
...to every man the right to live, to work, to be himself, and to become whatever his manhood and his vision can combine to make him
...this, seeker, is the promise of America
                                                            Thomas Wolfe

I find the great thing in this world is not so much where we stand, as in what direction we are moving...

We must sail sometimes with the wind and sometimes against it...But we must sail and not drift, nor lie at anchor.

                                                    Oliver Wendell Holmes

However, my motto for years, the one that I had posted on my office door while President of JCCC, is still my favorite and a very valid observation. The saying to remember is

"Fortune Favors the Stout Of Heart".

Hold steady, don't waver, persist in your beliefs, have faith because "fortune" will reward your efforts.

Semper Fidelis!

About the Author

Dr. Robert G. Harris - graduated from Fenton (MI) High School in 1941. He married his high school sweetheart, Marie Durant in 1944 and together they have two children, Robert and Patricia. At the time of her death, they had been married 69 years. He received his B.A. (Mathematics) and PhD. from Michigan State University and a M.S. in Electrical Engineering from the U.S. Naval Postgraduate School.

He retired as a Lieutenant Colonel from the United States Marine Corps after twenty-four years of service, during which he distinguished himself in several areas. Most notably he was one of a small group who conceived, developed and combat tested an All Weather Close Air Support Radar Bombing system which became an integral part of Marine aviation.

The combat evaluation of the new bombing system (the first Ground Directed Bombing (GDB) system) was conducted with the 1st Marine Division in Korea.

During the Korean conflict, he was cited on two occasions for his outstanding performance of duty. He served with distinction with the Marine Corps Development Center and the Advanced Research Project Agency in the Department of Defense.

Following retirement from military service, he was the founding President of Johnson County Community College in the Kansas City area. He later served as President of Middlesex County College, the largest community college in the State of New Jersey and President of McHenry County Community College in Illinois.

Returning to his hometown in 1980, he established the Harris Financial Corporation which provides financial services. Harris, who first joined Rotary in 1968, was one of the two men who founded the Fenton Rotary Club, serving as its President in 1999. He was inducted into the Fenton High School Hall of Fame in 2003 and was selected as the Grand Marshall for Fenton's Freedom Festival in 2013.

He has previously authored *"The Village Players"*, *"The Village Players At War"* *"The Village Players During The Post War Years"*, *"The Village-Korea and the Cold War"*, and *"The Village Players in the Late 1950's"*. All are narrative histories of the Village of Fenton for the Years 1937-1941, 1942-1945, 1946-1950, 1951-1955 and 1956-1959 respectively. This book, *"Many Come, Few Are Chosen"*, is available as an "e-book" at Amazon.com.

Glossary of Terms…

Most Americans are quite used to using acronyms in their daily speech and writings. Everyone seems in a hurry to save time, letters, voice or whatever by using an acronym. The U.S. government, and especially the military, is notorious for the use of acronyms. In order for you, the reader, to be able to read these stories and not be confused with my use of acronyms, the following glossary is presented:

AFB	Air Force Base
Air-Evac	Air Evacuation of the wounded
AKA	Troop Ship Cargo
APA	Troop Ship Personnel
ARPA	Advanced Research Projects Agency, DOD
ARVN	Army of Viet Nam
AN/MPQ	Army-Navy Radar System
AN/TPQ	Army-Navy Radar Designation
AO	Aerial Observer
B.A.R.	Browning automatic rifle
BUAIR	U.S. Navy Bureau of Aeronautics
CO	Commanding Officer
CG	Commanding General
CMC	Commandant of the Marine Corps
Cover	Hat or Cap
CSMO	Close Station March Order
CWO	Chief Warrant Officer
DOD	Department of Defense
EMC	Educational Media Center
FAS	Field Artillery School
FDC	Fire Direction Center
FMAW	First Marine Air Wing
FMF	Fleet Marine Force
GRE	Graduate Record Examination
HQMC	Headquarters, U S Marine Corps

JCCC	Johnson County Community College
KMC	Korean Marine Corps
LST	Landing Ship Tank
MASRT	Marine Air Support Radar Team
MB	Marine Barracks
MCAS	Marine Corps Air Station
MCDC	Marine Corps Development Center
MCEB	Marine Corps Equipment Board
MCRD	Marine Corps Recruit Depot
MOS	Military Occupational Specialty
MPQ	Mobile, Special, Radar
MSC	Michigan State College
MSU	Michigan State University
MTACS	Marine Tactical Air Control Squadron
NAD	Naval Ammunition Depot
NAMTC	Naval Air Missile Test Center
NAS	Naval Air Station
NK	North Korean
NOTS	Naval Ordnance Test Station
NTC	Naval Training Center
OBS	Officers Basic School
O-in-C	Officer in Charge
PLC	Platoon Leaders Class
PR	Public Relations
RO	Reconnaissance Officer
ROKA	Republic of Korea Army
RTA	Royal Thai Army
SCR	Signal Corps Radio (Radar)
SNAFU	Situation Normal All Fouled Up
UM (U of M)	University of Michigan
USAADS	United States Army Air Defense School
USNPGS	U.S. Naval Postgraduate School
USNS	United States Naval Ship
USNTC	United States Naval Training Center
VMF	Marine Fighter Squadron
WO	Warrant Officer

AN/TPQ-10 RADAR SYSTEM
A centerpiece of Marine Aviation/Ground Ingenuity

The AN/TPQ-10 Is a radar system developed to provide Marines with all-weather day/night, accurate bomb delivering capabilities. The concept of Ground Directed Bombing (GDB) began in the closing days of World War II and can be accredited to Captain Marian Cranford Dalby and his team of three officers and eight enlisted Marines. Through innovation, drive and "out of the box" thinking, Captain Dalby's team leveraged the Navy's attempt to develop an accurate submarine-launched ballistic missile. Captain Dalby's team simulated the Navy's process using conventional bombs delivered by Marine aircraft modified to receive flight commands from a ground computer. The tests were a complete success, bringing the accuracy of conventional aircraft-delivered bombs to within 50 yards of the intended target.

The GDB concept was first employed during the Korean War. Positioned with the 1st Marine Division just south of the 38th Parallel, Captain Dalby's team quickly validated GDB's effectiveness in combat. Utilizing the AN/MPQ-14 GDB system, the predecessor of the AN/TPQ-10, Marine aviators from 1st Marine Aircraft Wing wary from low-level flying and heavy casualties, were able to deliver accurate aviation fires on North Korean forces from higher altitudes and beyond the range of enemy surface to air fires. The morale of the Marine aviators and ground forces significantly improved as a result. It was clear that a new era in close air support had dawned.

During the Vietnam conflict, Marine Air Support Squadrons (MASS) employed the new generation AN/TPQ-10 GDB system with its Air Support Radar Teams (ASRT). From 1966-1971 MASS-3 ASRTs controlled more than 38,010 TPQ-10 missions, directing more than 121,000 tons of ordnance on 56,753 targets. During the siege of Khe Sahn, the AN/TPQ-10 was a major factor in providing accurate round-the-clock fire support for Marines defending the base. The commander of the Khe Sahn defense, Colonel David M. Lounds said "Anything but the highest praise would not have been enough".

Retired from military service in the early 1980's, the AN/TPQ-10 represents a shining example of Marine vision, ingenuity and an innate ability to adapt, improvise and overcome obstacles.

Roster of MASRT Deployed to Korea

Dalby. Marion Cranford. Major*
Harper, Edwin A. Major
Johnston, Oscar B. Major*
Bezbezbian, George Captain
Doyle, Ernest R. Captain
Klingman, Robert R. Captain
Dinwiddie, Stanley G. Captain
Dressin, Sam A. Captain*
Harris, Robert G. 1st Lt.*
Hayden, Clark D. 2nd Lt. *
Dickover, Floyd D. MSgt*
Holtz, William L. MSgt*
Leber, Hal T. TSgt*
Pringle,, Richard H. GySgt
Seissiger, John E. TSgt*
Beyer, Huston H. SSgt
Brown, George W. SSgt
Darrow, Marvin L. SSgt*
Garrett, Leonard M. SSgt
Hartline, Jimmy H. SSgt
Hauffe, Gerald S. SSgt
Johnson, Warren T. SSgt
Maxwell, Richard D. SSgt
Parent, Amos L. SSgt
Waggener, Robert F. SSgt*
Ash, Edwin G. Sgt
Cameron, James G. Sgt
Graf, Allen D. Sgt
Haag, Raymond R. Sgt
Johnson, James R. Jr. Sgt
Kenyon, William C. Sgt
Lesselyong, Thomas W. Sgt
Roberts, John C. Sgt
Wilson, James H. Sgt
Cooper, Richard G. Jr. Cpl
Mondo, Louis V. Cpl
Hershberger, Everett S. Cpl
LeLouis, Edward C. Cpl
Tadlock, Ronald F. Cpl
Steed, Charles E. Cpl
Schmieg, George T. Cpl
Wilkinson, Elwyn G. Cpl
* Members of original group

Index of Selected Names & Places